MW00637223

WITHDRAWN

WITHDRAWN

WITHDRAWN

THE JOURNEY OF FRAY MARCOS

The Journey of Fray Marcos de Niza

by

Cleve Hallenbeck

Introduction by David J. Weber

Illustrated by José Cisneros

SOUTHERN METHODIST UNIVERSITY PRESS

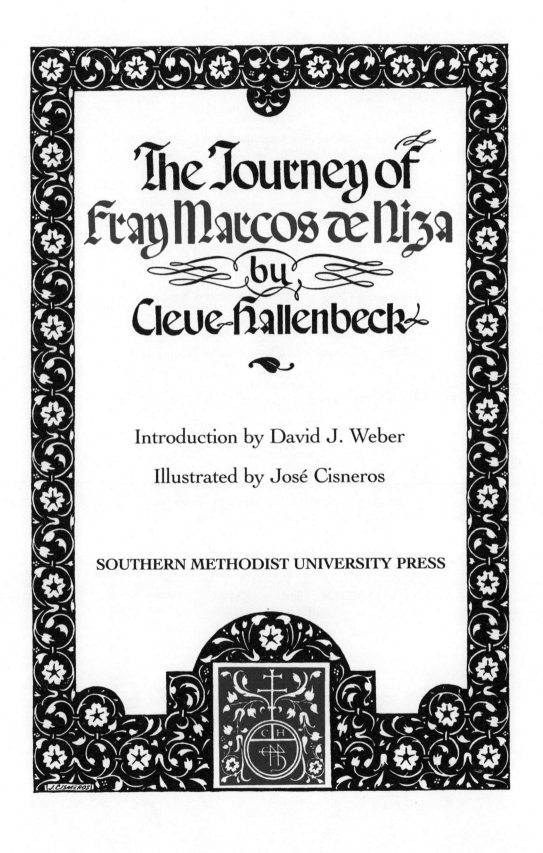

Copyright © 1987 by Southern Methodist University Press
All rights reserved
Printed in the United States of America

First edition, 1987

Requests for permission to reproduce material from this work
should be sent to:
Permissions
Southern Methodist University Press
Box 415
Dallas, Texas 75275

Library of Congress Cataloging-in-Publication Data

Hallenbeck, Cleve.
The journey of Fray Marcos de Niza.

"Fray Marcos' Relación": p.
Bibliography: p.
Includes index.
1. Marco, da Nizza, ca. 1495–1558 — Journeys —
Southwest, New.   2. Explorers — America — Biography.
3. Explorers — Spain — Biography.   4. Franciscans —
Southwest, New — Biography.   5. America — Discovery
and exploration — Spanish.   6. Southwest, New — History —
To 1848.   7. Cibola, Seven Cities of.   I. Marco,
da Nizza, ca. 1495–1558. Relación. English and
Spanish. 1987.   II. Title.
E125.M3H34   1987   973.1'6   87-9702
ISBN 0-87074-215-9

···Contents···

ILLUSTRATIONS

··· Introduction ···

First published in December 1949 by the University Press in Dallas, as Southern Methodist University Press was then called, *The Journey of Fray Marcos de Niza* won plaudits for three extraordinary Southwesterners: author Cleve Hallenbeck, for his careful and spirited reconstruction of the route of Fray Marcos' epochal 1539 journey to the American Southwest; artist José Cisneros, for his handsome maps and line drawings of the principal figures in the story; and printer Carl Hertzog for an exquisite design. For his work on *Fray Marcos,* José Cisneros received the Texas Institute of Letters 1949 award for "Best Illustrations by a Texas Artist"—the first of many such prizes for the talented artist. That same year, the Texas Institute of Letters award for the best Texas-designed book went to Carl Hertzog for *Fray Marcos.* In addition, Hertzog's design earned *Fray Marcos* a place on the American Institute of Graphic Arts' 1949 list of Fifty Books of the Year, the most prestigious award in American bookmaking. As a result, the handsome volume went on exhibition in Boston, New York, Philadelphia, Washington, Chicago, and San Francisco, bringing national recognition to a youthful regional press.[1]

Cleve Hallenbeck's *Journey of Fray Marcos de Niza* appears in this handsome new edition for reasons that transcend the American university press tradition of keeping significant titles in print. SMU Press chose to publish this new edition of *Fray Marcos* to commemorate the 75th anniversary of Southern Methodist University and the 50th anniversary of its press. The choice of *Fray Marcos* as a commemorative volume seems especially appropriate, for this book represents a triumph of the Southwestern printing arts and stands as a monument to the region's most celebrated printer.

CARL HERTZOG
Drawn in pen-and-ink by José Cisneros for Al Lowman's *Printer at the Pass* (1972). *From the collection of Al Lowman, Institute of Texan Cultures.*

CARL HERTZOG AND THE BOOK

While outsiders saw *Fray Marcos* as an extraordinary example of the bookmaker's art, only insiders knew the hard work and anguish that had brought it into being. By 1949 Carl Hertzog had come to enjoy a reputation as one of the nation's leading printers and designers of fine books. He had operated a small press in El Paso since 1934, but he had a special relationship with clients in Dallas.[2] As he would later recall: "Although I lived in El Paso, as I began to do more limited editions my greatest encouragement continued to come from friends in Dallas. Especially Allen Maxwell who contracted for *The Journey of Fray Marcos de Niza*, our prize-winning achievement."[3]

In the spring of 1948, Allen Maxwell, then director of the press at Southern Methodist University, asked Hertzog if he would be interested in printing Cleve Hallenbeck's manuscript on Fray Marcos. Hertzog proposed printing a deluxe, oversize book, limited to one thousand copies, at a cost of $3,500. The figure caused Maxwell considerable concern, but there seemed to be no way to lower cost without diminishing quality. In mid-October, the Board of Publications at Southern Methodist University authorized Hertzog to proceed. Hertzog's timetable was clear: he would have galley proofs by the first of the year and would deliver the finished books early in the spring of 1949. But a combination of happenstance and Hertzog's admitted perfectionism delayed the project. By the first of the year, Hertzog had not begun to set type. When he did, he was destined to change it.[4]

By February 1949 Hertzog had a page of *Fray Marcos* set in Baskerville type. Baskerville had pleased Hertzog until he saw a study of four hundred years of printing in Mexico in a special issue of *Mexican Art & Life*, brought to him by José Cisneros. In late February he abandoned Baskerville because it looked too "English" and decided to replace it with Centaur, a typeface similar to those he believed to have been used in Mexico in the sixteenth century. "Centaur sure has the flavor and character of those early books," Hertzog explained to Maxwell. The switch to Centaur would, of course, delay the book and raise its cost, but "if the cost goes up it will be mostly my sweat," Hertzog told Maxwell. Centaur was an expensive monotype, available only in San Francisco. Although machines would set the type, Hertzog noted that it would have to be "reworked by hand — my hands."[5]

Because Centaur lacked accents, Hertzog's work included the delicate tasks of cutting accents by hand, and of putting the hand-cut accents in place. As Hertzog explained to Maxwell, in order to render the word *relación,* he had to cut off the top of the *o* and the *n* and fasten the accent in place with chewing gum. "But in the case of *Cíbola,*" Hertzog lamented, "I am in trouble because there are high letters on both sides of the *i.*" It was difficult to squeeze the accent in between the high letters, and to make matters worse, "the word *Cíbola* occurs many times in the translation."[6]

The change to Centaur and the placement of accents took time, but these were minor matters compared to the shocking news that Hertzog received from Maxwell in early March. The author of the book had died. Cleve Hallenbeck's death apparently prompted Hertzog to go to even greater lengths to make *Fray Marcos* a fitting memorial to the author. "Since Mr. Hallenbeck did not get to see it, I will have to make it better," Hertzog wrote to Maxwell.[7]

Without the author to read galleys and prepare the final index, work on the book would be delayed still further. Happily, Cleve Hallenbeck's widow, Juanita Williams Hallenbeck, had collaborated with her husband and knew his work. She located her husband's typescript of topics to be included in the index to *Fray Marcos* and sent it on to Maxwell with apologies. Although the index was not "polished," she noted that given the condition of her late husband's health, "it is remarkable that he wrote it at all."[8] Cleve Hallenbeck's index contained no page numbers and a considerable number of inconsistencies, leading Maxwell to entertain the idea of publishing the book without an index. Following Hertzog's advice, Maxwell consulted the distinguished SMU historian Herbert Gambrell, who was "quite positive" that the book needed an index. So it was done, with the burden of the work taking place in Maxwell's office.[9] Mrs. Hallenbeck became involved in other aspects of the book's production, too. She read the galley proofs, sent to her directly by Hertzog, and gave her approval to the reworking, by editor Margaret Hartley, of a short biography that Mrs. Hallenbeck had written of her husband.[10] That the biography of Cleve Hallenbeck appeared in the book — at the end just before the index — was due largely to Hertzog's urging.[11]

In June of 1949 Hertzog predicted that copies of *The Journey of Fray Marcos* would be delivered to Dallas by October or November at the latest, in time for Christmas sales, but perfectionism struck again. He could not locate paper that seemed "just right." Then he came across a book printed in Spain in 1537 on off-white, laid paper — paper with evenly spaced parallel lines watermarked in it — and Hertzog went in search of similar paper.[12] In New Jersey he located a creamy-colored, deckle-edged, 70-pound Enfield Text with watermarked laid lines similar to those of the sixteenth-century paper that he sought to emulate.

A problem with the binding cloth also threatened to delay production. Hertzog had ordered dark brown "Winco 977" from Interlaken Mills in Fiskeville, Rhode Island, but the cloth did not suggest the rough texture of a Franciscan habit. He neatly solved the problem by reversing the cloth and covering the boards inside out. This produced a coarser effect, although it would have required a much different fabric to simulate woolen sackcloth. Hertzog had selected brown cloth because he believed that it resembled the color of the habits of Franciscans of Fray Marcos' generation. In this he had made the common error of projecting the present into the past. Franciscans of Hertzog's day wore brown, but sixteenth-century Franciscans wore gray robes, made of a blend of undyed wool shorn from black and white sheep. Luckily for Hertzog, his mistake went unnoticed by book reviewers and by those who gave awards to *Fray Marcos* for its distinctive design.[13]

A number of mishaps delayed the publication of *The Journey of Fray Marcos* project still further: excessive ink on one press run, paper stretching during a spell of uncharacteristically damp weather in El Paso, a broken die that stopped printing, and glue squirting onto the map pages of two hundred books because of a binder's error.[14] Not all of the delays came from Hertzog's side of the operation. In mid-summer, when Maxwell failed to get corrected proofs back on time, Hertzog wrote to him, "Since no proof I am going to the mountains for the week." Maxwell's delays in getting the proofs, the index, and the biography of Hallenbeck to Hertzog continued to slow the project into September.[15] Even after the first books were printed and bound, production problems continued. The dust jackets began to split and needed to be rerun on what Hertzog called "tougher paper." The perfectionist printer took advantage of the need for a reprinting to modify the dust covers by lightening their tan and white tones and adding his own name, printed in light silver ink, on the back cover beneath the printer's ornamental mark.[16]

The number of "bugs" and difficulties encountered in printing *Fray Marcos* had been so extraordinary that Maxwell playfully wondered if he and the printer had offended the "Deity" by publishing a book that said a Franciscan was a liar. Hertzog considered writing an article about the experience. In one fit of frustration, he announced to Maxwell, "I wouldn't print a second edition for $10,000."[17] *Fray Marcos*, Hertzog complained, had "caused the printer to lose his shirt, just as Coronado did lose his."[18] After all of the accounts were settled, however, Hertzog reported to Maxwell, "I didn't lose my shirt after all." Hertzog reckoned that he had made some $1,000 on the project, but he lamented, "I think I did about $2000 worth of work and $5000 worth of worrying."[19] Years later, Hertzog would recall that he had printed the book with "sweat & blood."[20]

Despite the mishaps and the worry, or perhaps because of them, Hertzog had produced an extraordinary book. Never one to lavish praise on his own work, Hertzog laconically told Maxwell, "You will have nothing to be ashamed of." And he incorrectly predicted that *Fray Marcos* would not make the American Institute of Graphic Arts list of the Fifty Books of the Year. "I demand *No Superlatives* in your publicity," the crusty printer wrote to Maxwell when he delivered the first sample pages of the book in September.[21] Nonetheless, when Maxwell received the first two bound copies in early November, he sent Hertzog a telegram, "Book is magnificent if you will pardon superlative."[22]

Protestations aside, Hertzog must have been pleased that the book achieved the effect that he had sought. "The book was designed," he wrote,

> to reflect the period of the story: special laid paper and hand lettering of the Spanish Medieval style; and the Centaur type has the flavor of the first Roman types used in Spain. The brown cloth is similar to the color worn by the Franciscan friars. . . . Gold stamping is appropriate for the "Seven Cities of Gold" which are the basis of the "Lying Monk's" report.[23]

Reviewers immediately praised Hertzog's design — even before all copies of *Fray Marcos* were bound and before the book's official regional release date of December 5 (the book also had a national release date of December 12). Maxwell, frustrated by delays at the bindery and "desperate" to have the book reviewed before Christmas, had prevailed upon Hertzog to send him some unbound review copies, and those had gone out to the two Dallas newspapers.[24] On Sunday, December 4, before local bookstores had copies for sale and before SMU Press had enough copies of the book to meet advance sale orders, *Fray Marcos* received front-page, illustrated reviews in the book review sections of both Dallas dailies.[25] Everette Lee DeGolyer, Dallas petroleum geologist and Chairman of the Board of Editors of *Saturday Review,* reviewed the book for the *Dallas Morning News* (accompanied by a specially colored reproduction of José Cisneros' drawing of Esteban, the black slave sent by the viceroy to guide Fray Marcos). DeGolyer wrote a laudatory and lengthy review, performing the task very quickly because he was already familiar with the work. A year before he had evaluated the manuscript for SMU Press and had recommended it for publication.[26] Himself the editor of a sixteenth-century North American travel narrative designed and printed by Carl Hertzog, DeGolyer concluded his review by noting that *Fray Marcos* "is another piece of fine printing by Carl Hertzog, Master Printer of the Pass of the North." That same day, Kenneth Rockwell noted in the *Dallas Times Herald* that Carl Hertzog "has been responsible for some of the most beautiful books of our time, and this volume . . . is one of the finest examples of typography to come from the Hertzog press."

But praise does not always bring unmitigated pleasure to a perfectionist. When Carl Hertzog learned from Allen Maxwell in January 1950 that the American Institute of Graphic Arts had awarded *The Journey of Fray Marcos* a place on its prestigious list of the fifty best-designed books of the year, he fretted:

> The news is a shock. I would not have submitted Niza to AIGA because I thought it was hopeless. . . . Of course I am very happy about the whole thing but also worried. Collectors will be after the book with a "Fifty" award and I know there are many copies with imperfections. Unless we both have our fingers crossed, those are the ones which will fall into the hands of the experts.[27]

A month later Hertzog told Maxwell: "Since the AIGA news I am afraid to ship the balance of the books to you. I want to look at them one by one — but it will take all summer." It did not take all summer, but it did take Hertzog until early June to examine each book before shipping the balance to Maxwell. Some "had stains on the paper which I cleaned off with clorox — good trick. I also touched up some red letters."[28]

Hertzog hid the "imperfections" well, for they apparently went unnoticed by others. Reviewers in scholarly journals and in the national press invariably praised Hertzog's design, describing the book in terms such as "handsomely designed and printed," "sumptuous and lavish," and "a masterpiece of the printer's art."[29] Critics have sustained those initial laudatory judgments. In his *Guide to Life and Literature of the Southwest,* J. Frank Dobie, then Texas' premier literary figure, termed *Fray Marcos* "one of the most beautiful books in format published in America."[30] Walter Campbell (alias Stanley Vestal), the popular Western writer and professor of English at the University of Oklahoma, went even further. In *The Book Lover's Southwest,* Campbell praised *Fray Marcos* immoderately as "one of the handsomest volumes produced in the Americas"![31] Subsequent evaluation has been more restrained, but generous. At the very least, *Fray Marcos* has been regarded as one of the finest of some two hundred books designed by the Southwest's premier printer.[32]

Notwithstanding its award-winning artwork and design, and the interest of its subject, *The Journey of Fray Marcos* sold slowly. It brought no significant income to SMU Press or to Hallenbeck's widow, Juanita, who struggled after the death of her husband to support herself and her teen-age daughter, Pomona, to whom *Fray Marcos* is dedicated.

The limited edition of 1,065 copies had received a substantial number of advance orders, and sales numbered over 250 within a couple of weeks after the publication of the book. After that, sales dropped off, but picked up again in April with the public announcement that the book had won an award from the American Institute of Graphic Arts.[33] A year later, by June 30, 1950, 415 copies of *Fray Marcos* had sold, either to individuals or to dealers who had the right to return them. Mrs. Hallenbeck received a welcome check for $207.50, representing 5 percent of the $10.00 list price of the book. She had protested the book's high price, and she complained that a bookstore in her hometown would not carry it because it was so expensive. Allen Maxwell acknowledged that pricing *Fray Marcos* at ten dollars a copy had hurt its sales — regular trade and university press books sold for half as much — but he explained to Mrs. Hallenbeck that "it's just a case of not being able to have your cake and eat it too — if the book could have been produced and sold more cheaply, then it would not have received all the acclaim that it has garnered for its superiority in design and production."[34]

Distribution fell off sharply in the early 1950s, with the book selling eighteen copies in 1951–52, twenty-three copies in 1952–53, fifteen copies in 1953–54, nine copies in 1954–55, and five copies in 1955–56.[35] In 1958, Carl Hertzog asked Allen Maxwell how many copies of *Fray Marcos* remained, and he offered, perhaps with tongue in cheek, to buy the remainder. "Could I make it O.P. and corner the market? I never could understand why it didn't sell out sooner."[36] SMU Press sold the last copies in 1964, and the title remained out of print until the Press signed a contract in 1973 allow-

ing Greenwood Press to manufacture and distribute a facsimile.[37]
The Greenwood Press facsimile is now also out of print. Meanwhile, demand for the original edition has driven the price above
two hundred dollars on the rare book market.

Our "Nameographs"

CLEVE, JUANITA, AND POMONA HALLENBECK

The author's self-portrait and his drawings of his wife and daughter, all
done as pen-and-ink "nameographs," with each sketch containing the
letters of the subject's name. *From the collection of Pomona Hallenbeck.*

CLEVE HALLENBECK, FRAY MARCOS, AND THE HISTORIANS

In some circles *The Journey of Fray Marcos* has been admired more for its appearance than for its contents. Carl Hertzog succeeded too well in making a book that would serve as a monument to its author, and Allen Maxwell's concern "that the format of the book might overwhelm its content in the minds of reviewers" proved to be well founded.[38] Cleve Hallenbeck was not then as well-known an author as he is today: "Who is Hallenbeck?" asked writer-artist Tom Lea, when he learned that Hertzog was printing the book. Moreover, Hallenbeck had examined a technical subject unlikely to be appreciated by the general reader.[39] Nonetheless, Hallenbeck was a master of the meticulous, cross-disciplinary research required to probe secrets from the fragmentary texts of sixteenth-century explorers.

A meteorologist by profession, for some thirty years Hallenbeck had spent much of his non-working hours tracing the trails of Spanish-Mexican explorers in Texas, New Mexico, Arizona, and northern Mexico — "by auto, motorcycle, horse, mule and afoot," as he told Maxwell.[40] Working out of Roswell, New Mexico, where he had been in charge of a regional office of the U.S. Weather Bureau from 1915 until illness forced his retirement at the end of 1941, Hallenbeck had published a number of works on meteorology and three earlier books on Southwestern history. It was a remarkable achievement for a man who worked without the aid of a large research library and in isolation from other scholars. His first books examined popular topics — *Spanish Missions of the Old Southwest* (1926) and *Legends of the Spanish Southwest* (1938). He wrote the latter with Juanita Williams who, like himself, suffered from tuberculosis and who in 1929 became his second wife.[41]

By the late 1930s, Hallenbeck's interests had turned to a narrower, more technical subject: *The Journey and Route of Alvar Núñez, Cabeza de Vaca* (1940). The question of where Cabeza de Vaca went on his incredible journey, from the Texas coast across the unexplored interior of North America to northwestern Mexico, had intrigued generations of scholars. Like geographer Carl Sauer, whose work he complemented, Hallenbeck went over the terrain himself, sometimes going to great lengths to understand conditions of travel in the sixteenth century. For example, to test the viability of his thesis that Cabeza de Vaca had traveled at a latitude somewhat higher than other authors had suggested, Hallenbeck tried to duplicate Cabeza de Vaca's experience. For three consecutive nights in mid-October, with the temperature falling below fifty degrees each night, Hallenbeck slept outdoors naked, covered with grass in a trench he had dug himself.[42] Little wonder, then, that his work on Cabeza de Vaca was praised for its meticulous research. Twenty years after Hallenbeck's study of Cabeza de Vaca's route first appeared, it could still be said that it "incorporates and supersedes all previous scholarship on the subject."[43] Hallenbeck's interpretation has been challenged by some scholars, but it remains the standard work.[44]

With the completion of his study of Cabeza de Vaca, Hallenbeck began a book-length manuscript called "Southwestern Trails," in which he intended to tell the stories of a number of famous roads, including the routes between New Mexico and California and the Santa Fe Trail. In the course of studying those trails he became diverted by Fray Marcos. "That old boy really took my husband on a wild goose chase," Juanita Hallenbeck recalled. "It took a book to settle [Fray Marcos]."[45] That book, she remembered, was written three times, "from start to finish."[46]

Hallenbeck apparently finished his study of Fray Marcos in 1945 and sent the manuscript to the University of New Mexico Press. He believed that "such material should be first offered to one's own state university press." The manuscript remained under consideration in Albuquerque for two years before Hallenbeck withdrew it. The University of New Mexico Press apparently gave Hallenbeck some encouragement, but failed to make a decision. This hesitancy, Hallenbeck believed, occurred because he had criticized the work on Fray Marcos by Lansing Bloom, a professor at the University of New Mexico. In September 1947, Hallenbeck offered the manuscript to Southern Methodist University Press, replacing a paraphrase of Fray Marcos' firsthand report of his journey with a fresh translation.[47]

Allen Maxwell quickly accepted Hallenbeck's offer to examine
the manuscript and by early December had secured an evaluation
from Everette Lee DeGolyer. On March 23, 1948, Maxwell told
Hallenbeck that the evaluation was favorable and that preliminary
discussions with the Press's Board of Publications had gone well.
"While we are not yet able to give you definite and final word . . .
the prospects of our being able to accept the book for publication
are quite good."[48] On May 25, Maxwell sent a definite answer.
SMU would publish the book, and a contract would be forthcoming. By then, Maxwell had begun discussions with Carl Hertzog
and had good reason to assure Hallenbeck that the Press planned
"a very fine job of book making . . . with which you will be very
much pleased."[49]

Cleve Hallenbeck did not live long enough to be pleased. He
died on February 20, 1949, at age sixty-four, after eight years of
poor health. Coincidentally, a letter from Mrs. Hallenbeck convey-
ing the news of her husband's death arrived in Maxwell's office in
the same mail with a package from Carl Hertzog containing a
sample page and illustrations for *Fray Marcos*.[50]

Hallenbeck had followed Fray Marcos de Niza into one of the
knottiest controversies in the annals of the exploration of North
America — a controversy that has not yet been resolved. Did Fray
Marcos' journey of 1539 take him into the heart of the American
Southwest, as he said it did, or is his account of that journey exag-
gerated? If Fray Marcos told the truth, then he deserves to be re-
membered as the first European to explore purposefully what is
today the American Southwest; only the party of Alvar Núñez
Cabeza de Vaca, shipwrecked and lost, appears to have preceded
Fray Marcos' expedition into the region.

A peripatetic Franciscan (apparently born in Nice and hence
"de Niza"), Fray Marcos had served in Central America and in
Peru before making his way to Mexico.[51] Fray Marcos established
himself in Mexico City in 1537, the year after Cabeza de Vaca had
returned from his extraordinary trek. In the wake of Cabeza de
Vaca's return came rumors that he had found magnificent cities,
rich with gold. Viceroy Antonio de Mendoza, eager to establish the

Crown's claim and to stave off rivals such as Hernán Cortés and Hernando de Soto, sought to investigate these reports quietly. In the autumn of 1538 the viceroy entrusted to Fray Marcos, for reasons Hallenbeck explains, the task of reconnoitering the region from which Cabeza de Vaca had returned. To guide Fray Marcos, Mendoza sent Esteban, a black slave who had been with Cabeza de Vaca.

Within a year, Fray Marcos had returned to Mexico City. In a written *Relación,* or report, he claimed to have seen a city "bigger than the city of Mexico."[52] The city, the friar had learned, was called Cíbola[53] and was just the smallest of seven cities in a country that appeared to be "the greatest and best of the discoveries." This was an extravagant recommendation from a man who knew first-hand the wealth of Mexico and Peru. Fray Marcos did not, however, claim to have entered Cíbola. He noted in his report that he had feared he might meet the same fate as Esteban, whom the Cibolans had killed. Thus, he said, he had viewed the rich city from a prudent distance.

On the strength of Fray Marcos' *Relación* (ably translated by Hallenbeck in this volume),[54] and of verbal reports that apparently contained even greater exaggerations,[55] Viceroy Mendoza launched one of the most elaborate and significant of Spain's reconnaissances of the interior of North America, that of Francisco Vázquez de Coronado. With Fray Marcos along as a guide, Coronado reached "Cíbola" in July of 1540. Before him stood one of the modest villages of the Zuni Indians in what is today western New Mexico, near the Arizona border. The gulf between the tiny Indian pueblo, numbering perhaps one hundred families, and the great city of Fray Marcos' description led Coronado to pronounce Fray Marcos a liar. "He has not told the truth in a single thing that he said, but everything is the opposite of what he related, except the name of the cities and the large stone houses."[56] Another of Fray Marcos' contemporaries, Pedro de Castañeda, a soldier who marched with Coronado in 1540, learned that when Fray Marcos had received reports of the death of Esteban he had still been sixty leagues from Cíbola. "Seized with such fear . . . they turned back without seeing more land than what the Indians had told them of. On the contrary, they were traveling by forced marches, with their habits up to their waists."[57]

Since Coronado's day, scholars have been divided as to whether or not Fray Marcos came within sight of Cíbola on his 1539 journey, as he said he did, or whether fear of meeting the same fate as Esteban had led him to fabricate that entire portion of his report to the viceroy. In the 1940s, when Hallenbeck was preparing his manuscript, Fray Marcos' story appeared as fact in the writings of the most eminent historians and anthropologists of the Southwest, including Hubert Howe Bancroft, Adolph Bandelier, Woodbury Lowery, Herbert Eugene Bolton, George P. Hammond, and Hallenbeck himself (in an earlier work).[58] Only a handful of scholars doubted Fray Marcos. Among the skeptics were two nineteenth-century writers, Henri Ternaux-Compans and Henry Haynes;[59] in the twentieth century, bibliophile Henry R. Wagner, historical geographer Carl Sauer, and Coronado's biographer A. Grove Day unequivocally challenged Fray Marcos' veracity and led other writers to take an equivocal stance.[60]

Both Wagner and Sauer wrote extended essays on the subject and both influenced Day and Hallenbeck. Wagner put his doubts in writing at least as early as 1926, arguing that Fray Marcos failed to get north of the Gila River, "all the rest being imagination."[61] Wagner elaborated upon this theme in subsequent writing, by which time he seems to have been influenced by Carl Sauer.[62] Sauer knew the terrain over which Fray Marcos had traveled, and argued that the Franciscan could not have made the journey in the length of time that he said he did. Sauer pointed out serious inconsistencies in Fray Marcos' story, which he labeled "a tissue of fraud, perhaps without equal in the history of New World explorations."[63] Wagner termed Fray Marcos a "liar," but excused his exaggerations because Wagner regarded Fray Marcos as a victim of an "overheated imagination" warped by the "overcharged atmosphere" of early sixteenth-century gold rushes.[64] Sauer took a less charitable view of Fray Marcos' motives. Sauer explained Fray Marcos' *Relación* as a calculated lie — "a political instrument" designed to block the claims of Cortés and others to the north country. Hallenbeck embraced Sauer's conspiratorial view.[65]

Refining and elaborating upon the Wagner-Sauer position, Hallenbeck was the first to devote a book to the question of Fray Marcos. In *The Journey of Fray Marcos*, Hallenbeck termed Fray Marcos a "plain liar."[66] Like Sauer, with whom he had corresponded, Hallenbeck argued that the friar could not have maintained the pace of travel that would have taken him to Zuni and back to Compostela as quickly as his official report suggests. Hallenbeck concluded that Fray Marcos had traveled no farther than the upper Sonora Valley, only two-thirds of the way to Cíbola and *below* the present-day boundary between Arizona and New Mexico. Hallenbeck found no evidence in Fray Marcos' *Relación* that the priest had seen any of the topographic features or peoples of present-day Arizona. Hallenbeck offered additional evidence that Fray Marcos had not seen Arizona, observing that when Fray Marcos returned to the Far North with Coronado, he was unable to provide Coronado with "any idea how far it was to Cíbola," and that on the one occasion when Fray Marcos offered an estimate of distance, he was extraordinarily far from the mark.[67]

In the carefully reasoned but polemical essay that forms the bulk of *The Journey of Fray Marcos*, Hallenbeck called on his own firsthand knowledge of the terrain, weather conditions, flora and fauna, native peoples, travel conditions in the sixteenth century, and the documentary sources themselves. Hallenbeck brought the same kind of meticulous research to the problem of the route of Fray Marcos that he had brought to bear on the problem of Cabeza de Vaca. For example, curious to know how the Zuni Pueblo of Hawikuh, which Fray Marcos claimed to have seen, would have looked in the mid-1500s, Hallenbeck consulted the best archaeological studies, made a scale model of Hawikuh in his backyard, and photographed the model from several angles. From those photographs, Hallenbeck, who was also an accomplished drafts-man, drew a sketch that José Cisneros would use to decorate the map for *Fray Marcos*. Although he went to considerable pains to make an accurate reconstruction, Hallenbeck recognized that "everything above the first story is largely conjectural and based upon the amount of debris remaining *in situ*."[68] When one reviewer of *Fray Marcos* noted that Hallenbeck went at his task as Sherlock Holmes did, Mrs. Hallenbeck noted that her husband did not like fiction, "but the Sherlock Holmes stories were great favorites and were read over and over again."[69]

Taken together, the arguments of Sauer and Hallenbeck seemed to make an overwhelming case against Fray Marcos' assertion that he had seen Cíbola. As Hallenbeck put it, "There can be no question as to what would be the ruling of any civilized court of today on this case."[70] Most reviewers of *Fray Marcos*, with the exception of the Franciscan historian Angélico Chávez, agreed. They expressed sentiments much like those of Hubert Herring, Professor of History at Pomona College, who wrote in the *New York Herald Tribune* that "Hallenbeck disposes of whatever reputation for veracity the monk had." Hallenbeck's conclusions, another reviewer noted, "appear to be inescapable."[71]

Appearances, of course, can be deceiving. A substantial number of writers and Southwestern specialists have found Hallenbeck's conclusions eminently escapable. Nearly forty years after the publication of *Fray Marcos*, the Wagner-Sauer-Hallenbeck school has made some impact on the region's historiography, but most writers have ignored the controversy and continue to take Fray Marcos at his word. Among general overviews of the history of the Southwest written since Hallenbeck's day, only those written by Paul Wellman and David Lavender retell Fray Marcos' story with skepticism.[72] Most of the general histories of the Southwest (including those by Paul Horgan, W. Eugene Hollon, Lynn Perrigo, and Odie Faulk) not only take Fray Marcos all the way to Cíbola, but also fail to give their readers a hint that the Franciscan might have fabricated his account.[73] The same pattern prevails among general works on the spanish era in the Southwest[74] and among histories of the individual Southwestern states of California, Arizona, New Mexico, and Texas.[75] The authors of most of these works take Fray Marcos to the edge of Cíbola; a minority suggest that he might have failed to cross the international boundary into what is today Arizona or New Mexico.

Carl Sauer once suggested a simple reason for the failure of

the Wagner-Sauer-Hallenbeck position to win widespread accept-
ance. Because "we three . . . are not professors of History," he
wrote, "[we] remain voices in the wilderness."[76] Perhaps that argument has some merit, but less conspiratorial explanations also suggest themselves, such as the possibility that the Wagner-Sauer-
Hallenbeck school is not sufficiently convincing. The failure that
Sauer lamented can also be explained, in part, by inadvertence.
Historians do not always read one another's work. As one result,
the historical literature has perpetuated many previously demol-
ished arguments and hoary myths.[77] Then, too, specialists themselves have remained divided. Thus, the contradictory interpretations offered by writers of general histories may reflect the
contradictory conclusions of scholars who specialize in the history
of the sixteenth-century Southwest.[78]

Part of the confusion in the historiography surrounding Fray
Marcos has arisen because the few specialists who represent each
side of the argument have not, in the last few decades, engaged one
another in direct, sustained debate. Since World War II, the most
ambitious effort to refute Fray Marcos' critics was that made by
George Undreiner. His valuable essay appeared in 1947, prior to
the publication of Hallenbeck's work, and so Undreiner could not
challenge Hallenbeck's arguments directly. Conversely, Hallenbeck
did not address Undreiner's arguments because he had apparently
completed the manuscript for *Fray Marcos* by the time Undreiner's
article appeared. Seriously ill and isolated from the scholarly community at his home in Roswell, New Mexico, Hallenbeck probably
did not know of Undreiner's work.[79]

Since the publication of *Fray Marcos* in 1949, scholars have
sniped at Hallenbeck's position, but no serious critique has appeared. Instead, most historians and anthropologists currently interested in Fray Marcos have lightly dismissed the Wagner-Sauer-
Hallenbeck school and have shifted the focus of the debate. Instead
of asking *if* Fray Marcos saw Cíbola, ethnohistorian Madeleine
Rodack has assumed that he did and asks *which* of the six Zuni villages Fray Marcos saw — Hawikuh, as Hallenbeck and others have
argued, or Kiakima, for which Rodack makes a case.[80] Instead of

asking *if* Fray Marcos entered present-day Arizona and New Mexico, scholars such as Albert Schroeder and Charles Di Peso have asked *which* route he took through the present Southwest.[81] Scholars have postulated at least three hypothetical routes that Fray Marcos may have taken to Zuni.[82]

Since Hallenbeck's day, the most detailed effort to reconstruct Fray Marcos' route was that published by Charles Di Peso in 1974. Di Peso took Fray Marcos across the present-day international boundary near the New Mexico–Arizona line, much to the east of the routes suggested by other writers. He dismissed the arguments of Carl Sauer and Cleve Hallenbeck with the offhand remark that they had "maligned" Fray Marcos "primarily because the padre did not travel where the historian would have him travel."[83] Di Peso did not, however, try to refute the Wagner-Sauer-Hallenbeck position; he simply offered an alternative. For example, Di Peso asserted that Fray Marcos returned to Culiacán on July 22, 1539, thus ignoring completely Hallenbeck's evidence that the padre had already made it to Compostela, three hundred miles to the south, a month earlier. The question is important, for it goes to the heart of whether or not Fray Marcos had time to cover the distance that he said he did.[84]

Even if scholars engage one another's work more directly, however, it seems likely that confusion about whether or not Fray Marcos made it to Zuni would still prevail, for the question may not be susceptible to a definitive answer. A study that incorporates recent scholarship and examines divergent viewpoints would be of great use, but no one is likely to write a definitive analysis of Fray Marcos' journey unless fresh documentation appears.[85] For the moment, the only document available to modern scholars is Fray Marcos' own *Relación,* and that is so sketchy that it lends itself to multiple interpretation. Hallenbeck, for example, observed that Fray Marcos' account "does not give us one identifiable point anywhere on or near his route. . . . Nevertheless, I think we can trace his course in some detail with a measure of confidence."[86] Statements of such intellectual bravado notwithstanding, it must be remembered that Fray Marcos' *Relación* is sufficiently vague that even those scholars who agree that he made it to Zuni cannot agree on the route that he took, or on the location of key places, such as Vacapa and Chichilticale, that would help establish his route.

Fray Marcos' narrative carries liabilities much like those that one writer has attributed to Cabeza de Vaca's account: "A reconciliation of all the data is impossible. We must believe that Cabeza de Vaca was, naturally enough, occasionally forgetful, confused, or mistaken."[87] The fact of Cabeza de Vaca's confusion is easily understood—he had been shipwrecked and lost. In contrast, Viceroy Mendoza sent Fray Marcos to explore and to report on what he found, and Mendoza chose Fray Marcos in part because he believed that the friar had sufficient competence and experience to carry out that task. Thus, it is more difficult to explain the errors in Fray Marcos' account—errors that nearly every writer including Hallenbeck must attempt to reconcile if Fray Marcos' *Relación* is to make sense.

Fray Marcos' journey, then, raises more questions than it answers. Among those questions, we should ask if Fray Marcos' spare account has become a kind of Rorschach test, allowing scholars to read into it that which they wish to see. Could it be that Catholic historians who are men of the cloth, such as the Franciscans Bonaventure Oblasser and Angélico Chávez, and Rt. Rev. Msgr. George Undreiner, have found Fray Marcos truthful because they are reluctant to brand a confrère a liar?[88] Or is it that writers who have questioned Fray Marcos' veracity are "anti-friar"? Angélico Chávez leveled this charge against Hallenbeck, whose prose suggested to Chávez "the almost pathological hate which Hallenbeck harbored against a friar four hundred years dead."[89] Could it be that anthropologists, eager for scraps of information about the protohistorical Southwest, have been reluctant to admit that Fray Marcos might not be a useful source? Could it be that historians from the United States find Fray Marcos "the first white man who indisputably set foot on the soil of New Mexico" or "the discoverer of Arizona . . . and *the first European to set foot on Arizona soil*" because they are eager to push the history of their region back in time?[90] Have American historians been guilty of the kind of ethnocentric reading of evidence that one scholar believes has led us to place the route of Cabeza de Vaca erroneously in the United States instead of in Mexico?[91]

In *The Journey of Fray Marcos,* Hallenbeck took one other controversial position. Unlike nearly all other writers, Hallenbeck argued that Fray Marcos' guide, Esteban (also referred to by his contemporaries in the diminutive forms of "Estebanillo" or "Estevanico"), was not a Negro but rather a dark-skinned Arab.[92] Fray Marcos identified Esteban on at least five occasions as "Estévan, the black [*Estéban, negro*],"[93] but Hallenbeck dismissed this by noting that "the Spanish called all Hamitic races, as well as the Negroes, 'blacks.'" Citing Cabeza de Vaca, "who was associated with Estévan for nine years, [and who] says he was an Arab from Azamor [a town on the Atlantic Coast of what is today Morocco]," Hallenbeck concluded that Esteban was an Arab and not a Negro. Hallenbeck apparently failed, however, to note that Cabeza de Vaca referred to Esteban as a "*black* Arab, native of Azamor."[94] That statement, together with the references of Fray Marcos and other contemporaries to Esteban as a "black," has convinced most historians that Esteban was a Negro. In this case, Hallenbeck seems to have failed to win a significant number of adherents to his position.[95]

Esteban's race might be of little consequence except that he was, as one writer has put it, "the first man from the Old World who pioneered a path deep into what is the United States." Those in search of black heroes in American history have wished to claim him, and have tended to dismiss writers such as Hallenbeck as racists who possess "attitudes which cannot grant heroic qualities to a black man and slave."[96] As one result, the question of Esteban's race has generated considerable heat in some circles. In 1972 the issue divided the New Mexico State Bicentennial Commission. State Historian Dr. Myra Ellen Jenkins, who paraphrased Hallenbeck, insisted that Esteban "was actually an African Caucasian Moor or Arab." On the other side of the argument, Charles Becknell, Director of Afro-American Studies at the University of New Mexico, leveled charges of racism at those who took Jenkins' position. Becknell insisted that "the man was from Africa and he was Black."[97]

Scholars who have written about Esteban have agreed with Becknell's position, if not with his reason for adopting it. Esteban's precise racial or genetic makeup will never be known, and he may have been of a racially mixed background. It seems clear, however, that he was, as one anthropologist has written, "sub-Saharan enough, phenotypically, for the Spaniards to feel comfortable in giving him a black ethnic classification."[98] The question of Esteban's race, it would appear, is no longer a matter of contention among contemporary scholars.[99]

JOSE CISNEROS AND THE ILLUSTRATIONS

Even with its handsome design, *Fray Marcos* would not be as striking without the illustrations of José Cisneros. Soon after accepting the *Fray Marcos* assignment from Allen Maxwell, Hertzog urged the publisher to employ Cisneros, a Mexican-born El Paso artist with whom the printer had worked on two previous books.[100] Initially, Hertzog asked that Cisneros be commissioned to redraw Hallenbeck's maps. "One of the maps is a very topographical drawing," Hertzog explained to Maxwell, "but in colors not practical for reproduction, and all of Hallenbeck's lettering is amateurish."[101] Subsequently it was decided that Cisneros would also do an ornamental title page, chapter initials, and pen-and-ink portraits of the book's three main characters — Fray Marcos, Esteban, and the viceroy of Mexico, Antonio de Mendoza. Enthusiastic about the subject, Cisneros agreed to do all of the work for two hundred dollars.[102] "When Carl handed me the manuscript I was elated with its topic," Cisneros would later recall.[103] Even as the typesetting and book production fell behind, Cisneros completed the artwork on schedule.[104]

Cisneros drew the costumes and accoutrements of the principal characters with his customary attention to historical fidelity. In addition, he sought to depict Esteban and Fray Marcos as Hallenbeck had described them, although he later recalled becoming "disappointed at the way Hallenbeck, in his effort and eager-

JOSE CISNEROS

Pen-and-ink self-portrait, drawn in 1986 at age seventy-five for the new edition of *The Journey of Fray Marcos. From the collection of David J. and Carol Bryant Weber.*

ness to prove his scholarly point of view, relentlessly attacked the good old friar."[105] Nonetheless, Cisneros tried to evoke Hallenbeck's characterization of Fray Marcos, giving him the face of "a sensual brigand," in the judgment of one reviewer.[106] Reaction to the drawing of Fray Marcos apparently depended on one's opinion of him. Juanita Hallenbeck, who shared her husband's low regard for Fray Marcos, was "pleased with all the illustrations, particularly the friar's face." As she told Maxwell, "The friar looks the part he played."[107] Since Hallenbeck believed that Esteban was an Arab rather than a black, Cisneros did not give him stereotypically Negro features. Cisneros' drawing of Esteban caused some consternation at the Press, where Maxwell wondered whether the drawing should be faithful to Hallenbeck's interpretation of Esteban's race or to the popular notion that Esteban was a Negro. Maxwell decided to support Cisneros' interpretation, but many readers must have reacted as did Juanita Hallenbeck, who said that the drawing of Esteban "surprised me. Though I know better, I'm inclined to think of him as a Black instead of an Arab."[108]

In 1986, thirty-seven years after drawing Fray Marcos, Esteban, and Viceroy Mendoza for the first edition of *Fray Marcos*, seventy-five-year-old José Cisneros made fresh pen-and-ink drawings of these three men for the introduction to this new printing of *Fray Marcos*.[109] Since 1949 Cisneros has illustrated over one hundred books with his authentically detailed drawings, and he is widely recognized as the premier artist of the Spanish-Mexican Southwest.[110] A comparison of Cisneros' new drawings with the old (see pp. 8, 14, & 38) shows remarkable consistency in his technique, as well as in the evolution and maturity of his understanding of the characters, their clothing, and their accoutrements.

In the new drawing, Antonio de Mendoza retains his pose, while Mexico City and the two volcanos of Popocatépetl and Ixtaccíhautl remain in the background. But the viceroy, one of Mexico's finest, looks more kindly and intelligent than he did in the 1949 drawing. In this new rendition, Cisneros hoped to make Mendoza typify "the glorious, golden era of Spanish power with newly acquired lands, fabulous wealth, and countless new subjects — the Spain of Charles V."[111]

xxx

Similarly, Fray Marcos appears less sensual and sinister in the 1986 drawing than he did in the original. In the new version, Cisneros has placed Fray Marcos in a different setting, with a giant saguaro in the background. "Despite the author's opinion about Fray Marcos, I intended to portray him as more dignified, more dynamic and at the core of the environment that he traveled." Fray Marcos wears essentially the same robe, sandals, and accoutrements that he did in the original drawing, but instead of a medal, a cross now hangs from his neck because Cisneros has come to understand that "medals, crosses, and scapulars were extensively used as religious symbols by Spanish lay people, while relicaries and crucifixes were favored by those in the service of the Church."

Esteban's costume has been changed considerably in the new drawing, where he wears a different hat, cape, boots, breeches, and a more elegant doublet, covered by a vest of armor, or a cuirass. The historical record provides no indication of what Esteban wore, and so Cisneros indulged himself.

> I wanted to display my love of costume without deviating too much from reality. Creativity is allowed, sometimes, to take some liberties. I wanted to get away from the stereotyped, conventional depiction of the former slave and give him a glamour and importance that he probably never enjoyed.

Although Fray Marcos' report provides little information about Esteban's appearance, it does indicate that Esteban traveled with "two Castilian greyhounds," and with a gourd decorated with feathers and bells. Cisneros omitted the dogs and the gourd (which Fray Marcos believed to be the source of Esteban's fatal troubles at Zuni) from the original drawing of Esteban, but they appear in the new one. Fray Marcos termed the bells "cascabeles," and Hallenbeck believed them to be rattlesnake rattles. Cisneros disagrees:

> "Cascabeles" were very common in horse equipment, on poles in "autos sacramentales" and "pastorelas," on dancers' costumes, shoes, etc. If those in Estebanico's gourd were rattlesnake rattles it would have been clarified, no doubt, in the report as "cascabeles de víbora."[112]

From the scholar's point of view, Cisneros' decorative map was

The illustration shows the coat of arms with the words GRATIA PLENA and AVE MARIA.

VICEROY ANTONIO DE MENDOZA
From the collection of David J. and Carol Bryant Weber.

FRAY MARCOS
From the collection of David J. and Carol Bryant Weber.

less successful than his other illustrations, for it lacks many of the rivers that the reader needs to visualize in order to follow Hallenbeck's narrative. Although Hallenbeck's original map for *Fray Marcos* is no longer among his private papers, a map with the same title, "The Road to Cíbola," that Hallenbeck prepared for another book, *Land of the Conquistadores*, provides more detail, including some of the major rivers along the route of Fray Marcos, and indicates the sources of some of the visual information that he gave to Cisneros.[113]

Cisneros' small inset map of the six cities of Cíbola came from a reconstruction by Frederick Webb Hodge. Hallenbeck's drawing of Hawikuh came from a ground plan by archaeologist Victor Mindeleff. Cisneros' three-dimensional rendition of Hawikuh appears to be an artist's fanciful reconstruction, but it was based more on archaeological data than on imagination. Cisneros worked from Hallenbeck's drawings of models that he had constructed from Mindeleff's ground plan.[114]

With the original edition of *The Journey of Fray Marcos de Niza* no longer available at a price affordable to most readers and specialists, it seems appropriate for SMU Press to reissue this distinguished volume. This reprint does, of course, contain more than the first edition. In addition to a new introduction, the 1987 edition of *Fray Marcos* contains previously unpublished drawings by José Cisneros and Cleve Hallenbeck, and the Spanish version of Fray Marcos' *Relación* — a document that apparently has never been published in the United States. By reprinting the *Relación*, the Press has made the document more available to scholars and has facilitated a comparison of Hallenbeck's translation with the original. Serious scholars, of course, will want to make comparisons because translation, by its very nature, leaves much interpretation to the discretion of translators, and obdurate sixteenth-century documents pose their own special challenges.[115]

Cleve Hallenbeck's *Fray Marcos* does not represent the last word on the subject, but it may constitute a useful point of departure for the next generation of scholars.

ESTEBAN
From the collection of David J. and Carol Bryant Weber.

The enthusiasm of the former director of SMU Press, Trudy McMurrin, helped to bring this new edition of *Fray Marcos* into being, and the active participation of José Cisneros, Carl Hertzog's widow Vivian Hertzog, and Cleve and Juanita Hallenbeck's daughter Pomona, has helped to give the new edition special charm and significance. I am grateful to them, as well as to a number of people who came to my assistance: Bernard L. Fontana of the University of Arizona, Michael V. Gannon of the University of Florida, William E. Gibbs of New Mexico Military Institute, Al Lowman of the Institute of Texan Cultures, Allen Maxwell and Lee Milazzo of Southern Methodist University, Francisco Morales of the American Academy of Franciscan History, Morgan Nelson of Roswell, New Mexico, Carroll L. Riley of Southern Illinois University at Carbondale, Van Robinson of Dallas, Madeleine T. Rodack of the Arizona State Museum, and John O. West of the University of Texas at El Paso.

David J. Weber
Robert and Nancy Dedman Professor of History
Southern Methodist University
Autumn 1986

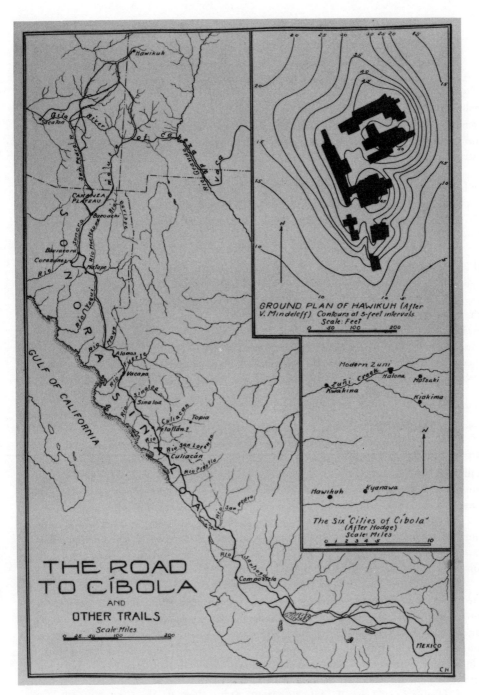

"THE ROAD TO CIBOLA AND OTHER TRAILS"
Drawn by Cleve Hallenbeck for *Land of the Conquistadores*. *From the collection of Pomona Hallenbeck.*

NOTES TO THE INTRODUCTION

1. John O. West, "The Artistic Journey of José Cisneros," in José Cisneros, *Riders Across the Centuries: Horsemen of the Spanish Borderlands* (El Paso: Texas Western Press, 1984), p. xxvii, mentions Cisneros' awards; Allen Maxwell to Juanita Hallenbeck, Dallas, February 9, 1951, Hallenbeck Collection (a private collection in possession of Pomona Hallenbeck, Roswell, New Mexico, hereinafter cited as Hallenbeck Collection), mentions the TIL award to Hertzog. For the American Institute of Graphic Arts award, see the *Dallas Morning News*, April 9, 1950.

2. For brief biographies and appreciations of Hertzog's work, see three works by Al Lowman: *Printer at the Pass: The Work of Carl Hertzog* (San Antonio: Institute of Texan Cultures, 1972); *Printing Arts in Texas* ([Austin]: Roger Beacham, Publisher, 1975); and *Remembering Carl Hertzog: A Texas Printer and His Books* (Dallas: Still Point Press, 1985).

3. Speech of Carl Hertzog, February 27, 1977, quoted in Robert S. Sparkman, ed., *A Day in the Life of Lon Tinkle* (Dallas: Friends of the Dallas Public Library, [1982]), p. 42.

4. Maxwell apparently began to discuss *Fray Marcos* with Hertzog in May 1948, when the Hertzogs visited the Maxwells in Dallas. The earliest extant correspondence on the matter is Hertzog to Maxwell, El Paso, May 24, 1948, in the private collection of Allen Maxwell in a folder entitled "Hertzog; *Journey* (1948–50)" (hereinafter cited as Maxwell Collection, Journey File). See, too, Hertzog to Maxwell, El Paso, September 30 & December 8, 1948, January 7, 1949, and Maxwell to Hertzog, Dallas, October 12, 1948, all in the J. Carl Hertzog Collection, correspondence with Allen Maxwell, ACC. #540, Box 4, ff. 21, Special Collections Department, University of Texas at El Paso Library (hereinafter cited as Hertzog Collection, UTEP).

Copies of some of the correspondence between Hertzog, Maxwell, and Hallenbeck exist in each of their private papers. My citations are often to letters in the Hertzog or Hallenbeck collections, even though a copy might exist in the Maxwell Collection, because Allen Maxwell could not locate his side of the correspondence until after I had consulted the other collections and had completed writing this introduction.

Those who wish to learn even more about Hertzog's printing of *Fray Marcos* should consult Charlotte T. Whaley, "A Particular Guy: Carl Hertzog Designs a Fine Book," *Southwest Review* 64 (Winter 1979): 1–16. Whaley relied upon Allen Maxwell's collection, which was then in the files of SMU Press.

5. Hertzog to Maxwell, El Paso, February 28, 1949, Hertzog Collection, UTEP. The quote about "sweat" is from Hertzog to Maxwell, March 9, 1949, Maxwell Collection, Journey File. See, too, Lowman, *Printer at the Pass*, pp. 31 & 33, who reproduces a page set in the original Baskerville—the page is preserved in Maxwell Collection, Journey File. The story that Cisneros brought an issue of *Mexican Art & Life* to Hertzog is in Whaley, "Particular Guy," p. 3; Hertzog to Maxwell, February 28, simply says "I ran into a book on Mexican Incunabula which upset me."

6. Hertzog to Maxwell, July 25, 1949, Maxwell Collection, Journey File; also quoted in Whaley, "Particular Guy," p. 7. Hertzog elaborated on this in another letter to Maxwell, December 19, 1949, quoted in Lowman, *Printer at the Pass*, p. 34: "Actually

the type was set by Mackenzie & Harris, San Francisco (machine work) but technically the type setting was done by me, because I inserted all the italics, accents, headings, and did the make-up, and actually reset by hand those pages where the spacing was bad. . . . To say that I am a great printer who used type X and paper Y does not show any appreciation for what I was sweating to achieve and does not flatter me."

7. Hertzog to Maxwell, March 7, 1949; Hertzog repeated those sentiments in somewhat different wording in another letter to Maxwell, two days later. Both letters are in Maxwell Collection, Journey File.

8. Juanita Hallenbeck to Maxwell, Roswell, New Mexico, August 13, 1949, Hallenbeck Collection.

9. Maxwell to Hertzog, August 10 & 23, 1949, Maxwell Collection, Journey File. See, too, Hertzog to Maxwell, August 13, 1949, carbon copy, and Maxwell to Juanita Hallenbeck, August 15, 1949, Hallenbeck Collection.

10. Hertzog to Juanita Hallenbeck, August 20, 24, & 29, 1949, Hallenbeck Collection. Maxwell to Hertzog, September 30, 1949, Maxwell Collection, Journey File, identifies Hartley as the "author" of the biography of Hallenbeck, although it would be more accurate to describe her as the editor since she worked from a draft sent to her by Mrs. Hallenbeck.

11. Hertzog to Maxwell, El Paso, August 13, 1949, carbon copy, Hallenbeck Collection. "Although you said to forget about Introduction or Foreword I think you should reconsider. A book published posthumously should have some explanation and something should be said about the author. Since we cannot disrupt the front arrangement with map, here is a solution: A short biography could very well be placed at the end, just before the Index."

12. Hertzog to Maxwell, June 28, 1949, Maxwell Collection, Journey File.

13. Proud of its association with this book whose cloth it had "manufactured, bale to book," Interlaken Mills took out a full-page ad touting *Fray Marcos* in the February 4, 1950, issue of *Publishers' Weekly* and in the February 1950 issue of *Bookbinding and Book Production*. Maxwell to Juanita Hallenbeck, January 18, 1949, Hallenbeck Collection. A copy of the advertisement is in the SMU Press Archives, DeGolyer Library, SMU. For more on Hertzog's confusion about Franciscan robes, see below, n. 23.

14. The Hertzog-Maxwell correspondence is replete with problems of this sort. See, for example, Hertzog to Maxwell, November 26, 1949, in Maxwell Collection, Journey File.

15. The quote about going to the mountains comes from Hertzog to Maxwell, July 18, 1949, and Hertzog complained to Maxwell about delays on subsequent occasions, as in undated letters of ca. September 24, 1949 ("You are holding up presswork — could finish last week"), and September 29, 1949 ("You sure delayed the presswork"). All are in Maxwell Collection, Journey File.

16. "I am ordering a rerun of 250 jackets on tougher paper . . . using white paper instead of grey." Hertzog to Maxwell, January 16, 1950 [*sic*], quoted in Lowman, *Printer at the Pass*, p. 34, original dated January 26, 1950 [*sic*], in Maxwell Collection, Journey File. Lee Milazzo, book collector, connoisseur, and critic, who serves as University Archivist at SMU, has a copy of *Fray Marcos* with both dust jackets. Milazzo's copy bears the following inscription from Hertzog: "Most people don't know that a

University Press is a publisher, not a printer. Then they ask, 'what then does a publisher do? if they don't *produce?*' They don't know about editing and merchandising — [they believe] a book just happens. Some of my friends ask me, 'How come you had this book printed in Dallas?' Of course you know I printed the book in El Paso [with sweat & blood] for the now SMU Press — crazy world we live in! — — ?"

17. Letter of December 3, 1948, quoted in Whaley, "Particular Guy," p. 13, original in Maxwell Collection, Journey File. The idea that Hertzog might write an article about his difficulties appears in various pieces of correspondence, including Maxwell to Juanita Hallenbeck, August 10, 1949, Hallenbeck Collection, and Hertzog to Maxwell, January 14, 1950, Hertzog Collection, UTEP. Maxwell's comment about the "Deity" is in Maxwell to Hertzog, September 2, 1949, Maxwell Collection, Journey File.

18. Hertzog to Maxwell, November 16, 1949, quoted in Lowman, *Printer at the Pass*, p. 34, original letter in Maxwell Collection, Journey File.

19. Hertzog to Maxwell, January 14, 1950, copy in Hertzog Collection, UTEP.

20. The "sweat & blood" quote is from the inscription in Lee Milazzo's copy of *Fray Marcos*, cited above, n. 16.

21. Hertzog to Maxwell, September 7, 1949, quoted in Lowman, *Printer at the Pass*, p. 31, original letter in Maxwell Collection, Journey File.

22. Copy of Western Union telegram, November 1, 1949, and Hertzog to Maxwell, October 31, 1949, both in Maxwell Collection, Journey File.

23. Hertzog to Interlaken Mills, quoted without an indication of the date in Whaley, "Particular Guy," pp. 14–15. A carbon copy, dated November 28, 1949, is in Maxwell Collection, Journey File. Hertzog noted in this same letter: "De Niza actually wore a blue habit. When the clothes of the first priests in the New World wore out, and they had to make new ones, the only dye they could find was Indigo." Here, both of Hertzog's assertions appear to be wrong. Fray Marcos notes that he wore a habit of Saragossa cloth, *paño pardo*, given to him by Coronado. Hallenbeck has cautiously translated that as "dark woolen cloth" (Hallenbeck, *Fray Marcos*, p. 23), but the word *pardo* commonly means gray. Blue habits were worn by some Franciscans in the seventeenth century, but the reason may have had nothing to do with the availability of dye, since the gray robes were not dyed either (see Fray Angélico Chávez, "The Unique Tomb of Fathers Zarate and de la Llana in Santa Fe," *New Mexico Historical Review* 40 [April 1965]: 113 n. 6). For the color of Franciscan habits, see Raphael M. Huber, *A Documented History of the Franciscan Order: From the Birth of St. Francis to the Division of the Order Under Leo X, 1182–1517* (Washington, D.C.: Catholic University, 1944), pp. 670–71, 683–98. For advice on sources regarding the obscure question of the color of sixteenth-century Franciscan robes, I am indebted to John Kessell of the University of New Mexico; Fray Francisco Morales of the Parroquia de San Juan Bautista in Mexico City; and Michael Gannon of the University of Florida, who called the Huber study to my attention and who has special empathy for Hertzog since Gannon made the same error in his book, *The Cross in the Sand: The Early Catholic Church in Florida, 1513–1870* (Gainesville: University of Florida Press, 1965), p. 36.

24. The arrival of three unbound copies on November 19 is noted in Whaley, "Particular Guy," p. 12, and in Maxwell to Hertzog, November 19, 1949, Maxwell Collec-

tion, Journey File. See, too, Maxwell to Hertzog, November 15, 1949: "I am desperate about the review copy situation locally."

25. Maxwell to Kenneth Rockwell of the *Dallas Times Herald*, Dallas, December 6, 1949, in SMU Press Archives, DeGolyer Library, SMU.

26. A copy of DeGolyer's assessment of the book remains in his own copy of *Fray Marcos* in the DeGolyer Library at SMU. DeGolyer found himself convinced by Hallenbeck, but noted, "I feel that the argument would be more convincing if it were more emphatic upon the critical points where it seems to be most definite and not cluttered up so much on minor issues which are largely matters of opinion." He guessed that the market for the book would be "on the order of five or six hundred copies." DeGolyer to Elizabeth Stover, December 4, 1947. Also preserved in DeGolyer's copy of *Fray Marcos* is a letter, dated November 23, from Lon Tinkle, book editor of the *Dallas Morning News*, giving DeGolyer less than a week to do the review and indicating "confidentially" that he wanted to reprint large illustrations from the book.

27. Hertzog to Maxwell, January 22, 1950, copy in Hertzog Collection, UTEP.

28. The two quotes are from Hertzog to Maxwell, February 9 & June 3, 1950, Hertzog Collection, UTEP.

29. These quotes, in order, come from three reviews: Joseph Henry Jackson, *San Francisco Chronicle*, July 9, 1950; John T. Winterich, *Saturday Review*, May 6, 1950; and Fray Angélico Chávez, *New Mexico Historical Review* 25 (July 1950): 255.

30. J. Frank Dobie, *Guide to Life and Literature of the Southwest* (Dallas: Southern Methodist University Press, 1952), p. 39.

31. Walter Campbell [Stanley Vestal], *The Book Lover's Southwest: A Guide to Good Reading* (Norman: University of Oklahoma Press, 1955), p. 54. Emphasis added.

32. William R. Holman, "A Hertzog Dozen," in Lowman, *Printer at the Pass*, p. xvii, ranked *Fray Marcos* among the twelve best of some two hundred books designed by Hertzog: "This volume has one of the most beautiful and well-proportioned page layouts ever achieved by any designer."

33. Although Maxwell learned of the award on January 20, the date for releasing the news to the Press was April 3 (Maxwell to Hertzog, January 20, 1950[2], and February 6, 1950, Hertzog Collection, UTEP).

34. Maxwell to Juanita Hallenbeck, Dallas, April 25, 1950, Hallenbeck Collection. Other information in this paragraph comes from letters from Maxwell to J. Hallenbeck, December 21, 1949, and August 17, 1950; from J. Hallenbeck to Maxwell, August 16, 1949, and May 30, 1950; and from a royalty statement, dated July 15, 1950, Hallenbeck Collection.

35. Annual royalty statements, Hallenbeck Collection. Sales figures of *Fray Marcos* for 1950–51 apparently have not been preserved.

36. Hertzog to Maxwell, January 6, 1958, Hertzog Collection, UTEP.

37. In a telephone interview, September 4, 1985, Allen Maxwell told me that the book went out of print in 1964. The contract with Greenwood Press is in the files of SMU Press.

38. Maxwell to Rockwell, December 6, 1949, SMU Press Archives, DeGolyer Library, SMU.

39. Hertzog to Maxwell, July 18, 1949, Maxwell Collection, Journey File.

40. Hallenbeck to Maxwell, March 26, 1948, Maxwell Collection, Hallenbeck File. See, too, the "Biographical Note" in Hallenbeck, *Fray Marcos*, p. 109.

41. Information concerning Juanita Hallenbeck derives from my interview with Pomona Hallenbeck, the only child of Cleve and Juanita, January 18, 1986, Roswell, New Mexico.

42. Cleve Hallenbeck, *The Journey and Route of Alvar Núñez, Cabeza de Vaca* (Glendale: Arthur H. Clark Co., 1940), pp. 158–59.

43. Cyclone Covey, ed. and trans., *Cabeza de Vaca's Adventures in the Unknown Interior of America* (1961; reprint, Albuquerque: University of New Mexico Press, 1983), p. 8. Among the laudatory reviews of *Cabeza de Vaca* were those by Francis Borgia Steck, in the *Catholic Historical Review* 26 (July 1940): 256–57; Dorothy Woodward, in the *Mississippi Historical Review* 26 (April 1940): 562–63; and Morris Bishop, in the *Hispanic American Historical Review* 20 (February 1940): 141–42.

44. Perhaps the harshest criticism came from Alex D. Krieger, "The Travels of Alvar Núñez Cabeza de Vaca," in *Homenaje a Pablo Martínez del Río en el XXV aniversario de la edición de Los Orígenes Americanos* (Mexico: Instituto Nacional de Antropología e Historia, 1961), p. 465.

45. Juanita Hallenbeck to Maxwell, Roswell, New Mexico, August 13, 1949, Hallenbeck Collection. Mrs. Hallenbeck says, "Last winter, my husband worked frenziedly to finish a book-length [manuscript] that had been hanging fire for several years." She goes on to say that he was "diverted to investigate Alvar Nunez," but I believe that she misspoke. Had Cabeza de Vaca diverted Hallenbeck's attention from the trails manuscript, which had been "hanging fire for several years," then the trails manuscript would have gone back to the 1930s — more than several years — because the Cabeza de Vaca book appeared in 1940. The Hallenbecks' daughter, Pomona, also recalls that Fray Marcos, not Cabeza de Vaca, was the diversion. The "Southwestern Trails" manuscript is in the Hallenbeck Collection.

46. Juanita Hallenbeck to Hertzog, Roswell, New Mexico, August 25, 1949, Hallenbeck Collection.

47. The quote in this paragraph is from Hallenbeck to Maxwell, Roswell, New Mexico, September 26, 1947, Maxwell Collection, Hallenbeck File. Among the evidence that Hallenbeck received encouragement from UNM Press is the statement by his wife that the manuscript was "accepted by one publisher and then withdrawn from him" before it was sent to SMU Press. Juanita Hallenbeck to Hertzog, Roswell, New Mexico, August 25, 1949, Hallenbeck Collection.

48. Maxwell to Hallenbeck, March 23, 1948, Maxwell Collection, Hallenbeck File. This file also contains copies of the following correspondence upon which this paragraph is based: Maxwell's response of September 29, 1947, to Hallenbeck's inquiry; Hallenbeck's covering letter of October 2, accompanying the manuscript; Maxwell to Hallenbeck, October 8 & 24, 1947. The Maxwell Collection, Journey File, contains DeGolyer to Maxwell, December 4, and Maxwell to DeGolyer, December 8, 1947.

49. Maxwell to Hallenbeck, May 25, 1948, Maxwell Collection, Hallenbeck File. Maxwell sent a contract to Hallenbeck on August 5, 1948, reducing the royalties from

10 percent to 5 percent because of the high cost of book production. A copy of the contract is in the SMU Press files.

50. Juanita Hallenbeck to Maxwell, March 1, 1949, Maxwell Collection, Hallenbeck File. Maxwell to Juanita Hallenbeck, March 4, 1949, Hallenbeck Collection.

51. Only scanty information about Fray Marcos exists. The most up-to-date summary of his life is in Madeleine Turrell Rodack, trans. and ed., *Adolph F. Bandelier's The Discovery of New Mexico by the Franciscan Monk, Friar Marcos de Niza in 1539* (Tucson: University of Arizona Press, 1981), pp. 28–30.

52. Hallenbeck, *Fray Marcos*, p. 34.

53. Some contemporaries applied the name to the Zuni province, consisting of six towns, and some applied the name to the single Zuni town that Esteban and Coronado, and perhaps Fray Marcos visited. For a discussion of this question, see Carroll L. Riley, "The Road to Hawikuh: Trade and Trade Routes to Cibola-Zuni During Late Prehistoric and Early Historic Times," *The Kiva* 41 (Winter 1975): 140–44.

54. Hallenbeck's was by no means the first translation of the *Relación* into English, and his work probably benefited from previous translations. No fresh translation has appeared in print since Hallenbeck's. His must be considered the standard work. The *Relación* first became available to the English-reading public in the final and enlarged edition of Richard Hakluyt's *Principall navigations, voiages and discoveries of the English nation*, 3 vols. (London: 1598–1600), 3: 366–73. Although the flawed Hakluyt translation had been rendered from an Italian translation rather than from the original Spanish, and even though Adolph Bandelier characterized the translation as "quite indifferent," it was reprinted in Fanny Bandelier, trans., and Adolph Bandelier, ed., *The Journey of Alvar Nuñez Cabeza de Vaca* (New York: A. S. Barnes, 1905), pp. 195, 203–31. At least three other English language translations appeared prior to Hallenbeck's: Percy M. Baldwin, "Fray Marcos de Niza and His Discovery of the Seven Cities of Cíbola," *New Mexico Historical Review* 1 (April 1926): 193–223; Bonaventure Oblasser, *His Own Personal Narrative of Arizona Discovered by Fray Marcos de Niza who in 1539 First Entered these Parts on His Quest for the Seven Cities of Cíbola* (Topawa, Ariz.: n.p., 1939); and George P. Hammond and Agapito Rey, eds. and trans., *Narratives of the Coronado Expedition, 1540–1542* (Albuquerque: University of New Mexico Press, 1940), pp. 58–82.

Baldwin and Hallenbeck based their translation on the printed version found in *Colección de documentos inéditos relativos al descubrimiento, conquista y organización de las antiguas posesiones españolas de América y Oceanía*, 42 vols. (Madrid: various publishers, 1864–1884), 3: 325–51 (reprinted in the present edition of *The Journey of Fray Marcos*). Oblasser and Hammond and Rey made their translations from identical manuscript copies in the Archivo General de Indias, in Seville. Henry R. Wagner, "Fr. Marcos de Niza," *New Mexico Historical Review* 9 (April 1934): 202, found the differences between the printed and the manuscript versions inconsequential. Carl Sauer, "The Credibility of the Fray Marcos Account," *New Mexico Historical Review* 16 (April 1941): 233, finds the printed version "remarkably exact except for . . . three mistakes," the most important of which had to do with substituting *legua* for *jornada* — an error that Hallenbeck corrected (see Hallenbeck, *Fray Marcos*, p. 103 n. 136).

55. Wagner, "Fr. Marcos de Niza," p. 223, quotes letters of August 23 & Octo-

ber 9, 1539, from Bishop Zumárraga and Fray Gerónimo Ximenez, with whom Fray Marcos apparently spoke. See, too, Carl Ortwin Sauer, *Sixteenth Century North America: The Land and the People as Seen by the Europeans* (Berkeley: University of California Press, 1971), p. 128.

56. Coronado to Viceroy Mendoza, August 3, 1540, in Hammond and Rey, eds. and trans., *Narratives of the Coronado Expedition*, p. 170. For the size of Hawikuh, see Hallenbeck, *Fray Marcos*, p. 40.

57. Hammond and Rey, eds. and trans., *Narratives of the Coronado Expedition*, p. 199. Cortés also believed Fray Marcos to be a liar; see Wagner, "Fr. Marcos de Niza," pp. 218–20.

58. Hubert Howe Bancroft, *History of Arizona and New Mexico, 1530–1888* (San Francisco: History Company, 1889), p. 34; Rodack, trans. and ed., *Adolph F. Bandelier's The Discovery of New Mexico*, cites Bandelier's writings on this subject; Woodbury Lowery, *The Spanish Settlements Within the Present Limits of the United States, 1513–1561* (New York: Putnam, 1901), pp. 260–78, 467–68; Herbert Eugene Bolton, *The Spanish Borderlands: A Chronicle of Old Florida and the Southwest* (New Haven: Yale University Press, 1921), pp. 86–87 (Bolton later modified his views — see below, n. 60); George P. Hammond and Agapito Rey, eds. and trans., *New Mexico in 1602: Juan de Montoya's Relation of the Discovery of New Mexico* (Albuquerque: Quivira Society, 1938), p. 16; and Hammond and Rey, eds. and trans., *Narratives of the Coronado Expedition*, p. 5. For Hallenbeck's own earlier endorsement of Fray Marcos' story, see his *Legends of the Spanish Southwest*, written with Juanita H. Williams (Glendale: Arthur H. Clark Co., 1938), p. 20: "A careful perusal of his [Fray Marcos'] written report convinces us that Fray Marcos did not intentionally fabricate his evidence."

59. Henri Ternaux-Compans, *Voyages, relations et mémoires originaux, pour servir a l'histoire de la découverte de l'Amérique*, 21 vols. (Paris: Arthus Bertran, 1837–41), 9: vi; Henry Haynes, "Early Exploration of New Mexico," in Justin Winsor, ed., *Narrative and Critical History of America*, 8 vols. (Boston: Houghton Mifflin & Co., 1884–1889), 2: 473–504. Vol. 2 was copyrighted in 1886; Hallenbeck's 1889 date is incorrect.

60. Wagner and Sauer are discussed below. For A. Grove Day, see his *Coronado's Quest: The Discovery of the Southwestern States* (Berkeley: University of California Press, 1940), p. 59 and note 22, pp. 331–33, which provides a fine summary of the arguments against Fray Marcos. Wagner and Sauer apparently also influenced Frederick Webb Hodge, *History of Hawikuh, New Mexico: One of the So-Called Cities of Cíbola* (Los Angeles: Ward Ritchie Press, 1937), pp. 26–27, and Herbert Eugene Bolton, *Coronado: Knight of Pueblos and Plains* (Albuquerque: University of New Mexico Press, 1949), pp. 35–36, both of whom judiciously provide their readers with both interpretations (Bolton's biography appeared in the same year as Hallenbeck's *Fray Marcos*, and could not have influenced Hallenbeck or been influenced by him).

61. Henry Wagner, letter to the editor of the *New Mexico Historical Review* 1 (July 1926): 371, taking issue with Baldwin, "Fray Marcos de Niza," p. 193, who credited Fray Marcos with being the first European to "indisputably set foot on the soil of New Mexico."

62. Wagner, "Fr. Marcos de Niza," pp. 184–227, and Henry R. Wagner, *The Spanish Southwest, 1542–1794: An Annotated Bibliography*, 2 vols. (1937; reprint, New York: Arno Press, 1967), 1: 89–103.

63. Between 1932 and 1940, Sauer advanced his arguments in at least three publications, all noted in Hallenbeck's bibliography, and summarized those arguments in *Sixteenth Century North America*, pp. 127–29. The quote is from Sauer, "The Credibility of the Fray Marcos Account," p. 243. (This article was published in 1941; Hallenbeck incorrectly cites 1940 in his bibliography.)

64. Wagner, "Fr. Marcos de Niza," pp. 216, 226–27.

65. Hallenbeck summarizes the views of a number of historians on this question of motivation, in *Fray Marcos*, pp. 70–73.

66. Hallenbeck, *Fray Marcos*, p. 73. Hallenbeck also summarized his views on Fray Marcos in another book published after his death: *Land of the Conquistadores* (Caldwell, Idaho: Caxton Printers, 1950), pp. 21–27.

67. "At the Gila River, Marcos told Coronado that the coast was only five leagues (fifteen miles) away, and that he had seen it; but Coronado learned from the Indians that it was ten *jornadas* (about three hundred miles) distant, as in fact it was." Hallenbeck, *Fray Marcos*, p. 76. Following Hallenbeck's death, Hertzog and Maxwell discussed the possibility of getting Carl Sauer to write an introduction to *Fray Marcos*, an idea that Mrs. Hallenbeck endorsed, indicating that "the two men conducted a lively correspondence . . . and there seemed to be a good deal of mutual admiration." Maxwell to Hertzog, August 15, 1949, quoting Juanita Hallenbeck, Maxwell Collection, Journey File.

68. Hallenbeck, on a page headed "illustrations," accompanying a letter to Maxwell, March 26, 1948, Maxwell Collection, Journey File. Juanita Hallenbeck to Hertzog, August 26, 1949, Hallenbeck Collection. Interview with Pomona Hallenbeck, Roswell, New Mexico, January 18, 1986.

69. Juanita Hallenbeck to Maxwell, January 21, 1950, Hallenbeck Collection, referring to the review by Joseph Henry Jackson in the *San Francisco Chronicle*.

70. Hallenbeck, *Fray Marcos*, p. 76.

71. Herring's review appeared in the *New York Herald Tribune Book Review*, October 29, 1950. The second quote is from John T. Winterich, *Saturday Review*, May 6, 1950. See, too, Jackson, *San Francisco Chronicle*, July 9, 1950; Gerald Ashford, "'Journey of Fray Marcos' Explodes Historic Lie," *San Antonio Express*, March 26, 1950; and E. DeGolyer, *Dallas Morning News Book Supplement*, December 4, 1949, who also find Hallenbeck convincing. Exceptions include Chávez in the *New Mexico Historical Review* 25 (July 1950): 255–59, and perhaps Arthur Aiton, whose confused statement appeared in the *American Historical Review* 55 (July 1950): 1006.

72. Paul I. Wellman, *Glory, God and Gold: A Narrative History* (Garden City, N.Y.: Doubleday & Co., Inc., 1954), pp. 16–17, and David Lavender, *The Southwest* (New York: Harper & Row, 1980), p. 39.

73. Paul Horgan, *Great River: The Rio Grande In North American History*, 2 vols. (New York: Rinehart & Co., 1954), 1: 106–7; Lynn Perrigo, *Texas and Our Spanish Southwest* (Dallas: Banks Upshaw & Co., 1960), pp. 18–20; W. Eugene Hollon, *The Southwest: Old and New* (New York: Alfred A. Knopf, 1967), pp. 54–55; Odie B. Faulk, *Land of Many Frontiers: A History of the American Southwest* (New York: Oxford University Press, 1968), p. 10; Lynn Perrigo, *The American Southwest: Its People and Cultures* (New York: Holt, Rinehart & Winston, 1971), p. 22.

74. Olga Hall-Quest, *Conquistadores and Pueblos: The Story of the American Southwest*,

1540–1848 (New York: E. P. Dutton, 1969), p. 37, and Elizabeth A. H. John, *Storms Brewed in Other Men's Worlds: The Confrontation of Indians, Spanish, and French in the Southwest, 1540–1795* (College Station: Texas A&M University Press, 1975), p. 14, accept Fray Marcos' story without a hint to their readers that a controversy exists. John Francis Bannon, *The Spanish Borderlands Frontier, 1513–1821* (New York: Holt, Rinehart & Winston, 1970), p. 16, mentions the controversy, cites the sources, and concludes that Fray Marcos "probably" saw Cíbola. David B. Quinn, *North America from Earliest Discovery to First Settlements: The Norse Voyages to 1612* (New York: Harper & Row, 1977), p. 195, questions whether Fray Marcos "saw the pueblo of Háwikuh," but does not take a position in the controversy. Mexican scholars also take Fray Marcos at his word. See, for example, Alfonso Trueba, *Las 7 Ciudades: Expedición de Francisco Vázquez de Coronado* (Mexico: Editorial Campeador, 1955), pp. 16–17.

75. This discussion of sources is not meant to be exhaustive, but merely indicative of the pattern. Among contemporary histories of individual states that suggest Fray Marcos reached Cíbola are John Caughey, *California*, 2nd ed. (Englewood Cliffs, N.J.: Prentice-Hall, 1963), pp. 46–47; Walton Bean, *California: An Interpretive History* (New York: McGraw-Hill, 1968), pp. 14–15; Robert Glass Cleland, *From Wilderness to Empire: A History of California*, ed. Glenn S. Dumke (New York: Alfred A. Knopf, 1969), p. 5; Warren A. Beck and David A. Williams, *California: A History of the Golden State* (Garden City, N.Y.: Doubleday & Co., 1972), p. 34; Jay J. Wagoner, *Early Arizona: Prehistory to Civil War* (Tucson: University of Arizona Press, 1975), p. 50 (who takes Fray Marcos all the way to Zuni, giving his readers only a hint of the controversy when he writes that Fray Marcos' account "is yet to be verified"); Marc Simmons, *New Mexico: A History* (New York: W. W. Norton & Co., 1977), p. 18; and T. R. Fehrenbach, *Lone Star: A History of Texas and the Texans* (New York: Macmillan, 1968), pp. 23–25.

Some writers of state histories tell the story of Fray Marcos without taking a clear position on how far he got. A good example is Seymour V. Connor, *Texas: A History* (New York: Thomas Y. Crowell, 1971), p. 14, who says that the friar "crossed into the present United States somewhere in eastern Arizona. Estevanico was murdered by Indians, and the padre scampered back to the safety of Mexico." It is the exceptional state history that states explicitly the Hallenbeck position that "the imaginative clergyman never got beyond the present international boundary," as does Warren Beck in his *New Mexico: A History of Four Centuries* (Norman: University of Oklahoma Press, 1962), p. 44. More venturesome than most writers of state histories, historical novelist James A. Michener, *Texas* (New York: Random House, 1985), pp. 34–35, accuses Fray Marcos of concocting a "massive" lie.

Some state histories do not, of course, mention Fray Marcos at all. For example: Andrew F. Rolle, *California: A History* (New York: Thomas Y. Crowell, 1963), and Lawrence Clark Powell, *Arizona* (New York: W. W. Norton & Co., 1976).

76. Sauer, "The Credibility of the Fray Marcos Account," p. 233. Writing prior to the appearance of *Fray Marcos*, Sauer included Hallenbeck in his triumvirate because of Hallenbeck's book on the route of Cabeza de Vaca, but the same charge certainly applied to the work of these three on Fray Marcos.

77. For examples, see Thomas A. Bailey, "The Mythmakers of American History," *Journal of American History* 55 (June 1968): 5–21.

78. See, for example, Fr. Angélico Chávez, *Coronado's Friars* (Washington, D.C.: Academy of American Franciscan History, 1968), pp. 11 and 76 n. 4, who accepts Fray Marcos' story at face value and who does not cite the work of Sauer or Hallenbeck. On the other hand, Jack D. Forbes, *Apache, Navaho, and Spaniard* (Norman: University of Oklahoma Press, 1960), p. 6, expresses skepticism and cites the work of Sauer.

79. George J. Undreiner, "Fray Marcos de Niza and His Journey to Cíbola," *The Americas* 3 (April 1947): 415–86. Assuming that the April issue of *The Americas* appeared on schedule, there would have been little time for Hallenbeck to see it. His manuscript was at SMU Press by the autumn of 1947, if not before (Everette DeGolyer had completed his reader's report of the manuscript by December 4 — letter, DeGolyer to Mrs. Elizabeth M. Stover, Dallas, December 4, 1947, preserved in E. DeGolyer's copy of *Fray Marcos* in the DeGolyer Library, SMU). Carl Sauer did have the opportunity to address Undreiner's argument in his *Sixteenth Century North America*, pp. 127–29, but apparently declined to do so.

80. Madeleine Turrell Rodack, "Cíbola Revisited," in Charles H. Lange, ed., *Southwestern Culture History: Papers in Honor of Albert H. Schroeder. Papers of the Archaeological Society of New Mexico, no. 10* (Santa Fe: Ancient City Press, 1985), pp. 163–85. In making a case for Kiakima, Rodack revives an argument made by Adolph Bandelier. See her introduction to *Adolph F. Bandelier's The Discovery of New Mexico*, p. 35 (where *Kiakima* is rendered *Qaquima*), and ibid., p. 38, in which she dismisses Wagner and Hallenbeck thus: "They have written detailed analyses of his travels in order to show that the timing could not have allowed him to reach Cíbola and return when he did. It is true that there are several inconsistencies in the schedule of his journey, but, since his exact route is still unknown, it seems presumptuous to say that he could not have done it without being certain of just what he did."

81. Ethnohistorian Albert Schroeder, "Fray Marcos de Niza, Coronado, and the Yavapai," *New Mexico Historical Review* 30 & 31 (October 1955 & January 1956): 265–96 & 24–37, did not cite Hallenbeck. Rather, he accepted uncritically Undreiner's projection of Fray Marcos' route up to the international boundary. From that point, Schroeder attempted his own reconstruction of Fray Marcos' route through Arizona. Schroeder trivialized the arguments of Fray Marcos' critics with the statement that they "have ignored the fact that he [Fray Marcos] guided Coronado to Cíbola" (p. 266). Schroeder fails, however, to provide evidence that Fray Marcos knew the way or guided Coronado well (see Hallenbeck, *Fray Marcos*, p. 76). Certainly Coronado did not think Fray Marcos had done well. Charles Di Peso, *Casas Grandes: A Fallen Trading Center of the Gran Chichimeca*, 8 vols. (Flagstaff, Ariz.: Northland Press, 1974), 3: 806–8; 4: 75–89. Franciscan historian Kieran McCarty, in supporting the Di Peso route, has used an ingenious textual argument to defend Fray Marcos. See his "Franciscans North from Mexico, 1527–1580," in Francisco Morales, ed., *Franciscan Presence in the Americas: Essays on the Activities of the Franciscan Friars in the Americas, 1492–1900* (Potomac, Md.: Academy of American Franciscan History, 1983), p. 243.

82. For brief summaries of the literature on what might be termed the western, central, and eastern routes to Cíbola, see Rodack, trans. and ed., *Adolph F. Bandelier's The Discovery of New Mexico*, pp. 35–37, and Riley, "The Road to Hawikuh," pp. 137–59. Riley has been careful not to take a stand on the Fray Marcos question. See ibid.,

p. 140; Carroll L. Riley, *The Frontier People: The Greater Southwest in the Protohistoric Period*, Center for Archaeological Investigations Occasional Paper: No. 1 (Carbondale, Ill.: Southern Illinois University, 1982), p. 9; and Carroll L. Riley, "The Location of Chichilticale," in Lange, ed., *Southwestern Culture History*, p. 157, in which he says, "I am . . . uncertain as to whether Marcos actually made the final leg of the journey to Cíbola."

83. Di Peso, *Casas Grandes*, 3: 981 n. 58.

84. Di Peso, *Casas Grandes*, 4: 88; Hallenbeck, *Fray Marcos*, pp. 63–64. If Di Peso accepted Hallenbeck's date of June 25 for return to Compostela, he would have to subtract thirty-seven days from the round trip from Culiacán to Cíbola and back, thereby having Fray Marcos average 18.8 miles per day, without resting (and Fray Marcos himself tells us of many days of rest). By ignoring Hallenbeck, Di Peso provides Fray Marcos with enough time to average 13.6 miles per day, again without resting. I am using Di Peso's own mileage estimates in making these calculations. For comparison, it is worth noting that Hallenbeck estimates that if Fray Marcos made the round trip journey from Culiacán to Compostela by way of Cíbola, he would have traveled 2,350 miles, or 21.9 miles per day, without resting a single day. (I am using the mileages in Hallenbeck, *Fray Marcos*, p. 46, and the dates March 7 to June 25.)

85. At least one study of the route of Fray Marcos is presently in progress, that of Donald Juneau of Hammond, Louisiana. Juneau to Weber, March 10, 1986.

86. Hallenbeck, *Fray Marcos*, p. 45.

87. Morris Bishop, reviewing Hallenbeck's *Cabeza de Vaca* in the *Hispanic American Historical Review* 20 (February 1940): 141. See, too, Riley, "The Location of Chichilticale," pp. 153–62.

88. In addition to translating Fray Marcos' account, without reference to other authorities, Bonaventure Oblasser summarized Fray Marcos' journey, with references to other scholars, in "The Franciscans in the Spanish Southwest," *Franciscan Educational Conference Report* 18 (1936): 99–101.

89. Chávez, review of *The Journey of Fray Marcos* in the *New Mexico Historical Review* 25 (July 1950): 258.

90. Quotes are, respectively, from Baldwin, "Fray Marcos de Niza," p. 193, and Oblasser, "Franciscans in the Spanish Southwest," p. 101.

91. Krieger, "Travels of Alvar Nuñez Cabeza de Vaca," pp. 460, 465.

92. Hallenbeck, *Fray Marcos*, p. 98 n. 29. Hallenbeck first advanced this argument in 1940, in his book *The Journey and Route of Alvar Núñez, Cabeza de Vaca*, p. 101 n. 183.

93. Hallenbeck, *Fray Marcos*, pp. 15, 18, 28, 29, and *Colección de documentos*, 3: 330, 332, 333, 342, 343.

94. This quote ("es negro alárabe, natural de Azamor") appears as the last sentence of the *Naufragios* of Alvar Núñez Cabeza de Vaca, which exists in many editions. I have used *Naufragios y Comentarios*, 2nd ed. (Buenos Aires: Espasa-Calpe Argentina, 1946), p. 109. Elsewhere in the *Naufragios*, Cabeza de Vaca refers to "Estebanico el Negro" (ibid., p. 51). The earliest extant editions of Cabeza de Vaca's account, *La relación que dio Aluar nuñez cabeça de vaca. . . .* (Zamora, 1542), and *La relación y comentarios del gouernador Aluar nuñez cabeça de vaca. . . .* (Valladolid, 1555), also contain the same wording ("es negro Alárabe natural de Azamor"), with only slight changes in capitaliza-

tion and punctuation. The important point is that the word *negro* appears in both editions, although Hallenbeck, who translated the 1542 edition into English (a copy of his manuscript is in the Hallenbeck Collection), omitted the word *negro* from his translation. In a fifteenth-century Portuguese chronicle, Moors are mentioned frequently with no color ascribed to them, but certain Moors are singled out as "Black Moors," who have been enslaved by the others. See Gomes Eannes De Azurara, *The Chronicle of the Discovery and Conquest of Guinea*, trans. Charles R. Beazley and Edgar Prestage, 2 vols. (London: Hakluyt Society, Series I, Nos. 95 & 100, 1896–1899), 1: 43, 49–50, 54, 56–57, called to my attention by Albert J. Raboteau, *Slave Religion: The "Invisible Institution" in the Antebellum South* (New York: Oxford, 1978), p. 5.

95. A notable exception was Covey, ed. and trans., *Cabeza de Vaca's Adventures*, pp. 65, 141.

96. Both quotes in this paragraph are from Jeannette Mirsky: "Zeroing in on a Fugitive Figure: The First Negro in America," *Midway* 8 (June 1967): 2, and *The Gentle Conquistadores* (1969: reprint, London: Kaye & Ward, 1972), p. 214.

97. Both the Jenkins and Becknell quotes appeared in the *Albuquerque Journal*, October 26, 1972—references courtesy of Marc Simmons. The newspapers did not, of course, provide the scholarly source of Jenkins' information, but she appeared to have been influenced by Hallenbeck when she said "the Spanish often called all Hamitic races negro as well as the Black," *Albuquerque Journal*, October 23, 1972.

98. Carroll L. Riley, Professor of Anthropology, Southern Illinois University, to David J. Weber, February 10, 1986; I am grateful to Professor Riley for good advice on this question.

99. See, for example, Carroll L. Riley, "Blacks in the Early Southwest," *Ethnohistory* 19 (Summer 1972): 247–60; Tendai Mutunhu, "Estevanico: Africa's Greatest Explorer of the Southwest of the United States and 'Discoverer' of Arizona and New Mexico," *Kenya Historical Review* 3 (1975): 217–33; Roberto Nodal, "Estebanillo: Pionero Negro en la conquista de America," *Revista de Historia de America*, no. 89 (enero-junio, 1980): 49–55; Rayford W. Logan, "Esteban [Estevanico, Estebanillo, Esteban de Dorantes]," in Rayford W. Logan and Michael R. Winston, eds., *Dictionary of American Negro Biography* (New York: W. W. Norton & Co., 1982), p. 213; and John Francis Bannon's introduction to *The Narrative of Alvar Nuñez Cabeza de Vaca*, trans. Fanny Bandelier (Barre, Mass.: The Imprint Society, 1972), pp. xii, xxix.

100. West, "Artistic Journey," pp. xxii–xxvii. Hertzog apparently first suggested employing Cisneros to redraw the maps in a letter to Maxwell, May 24, 1948, Maxwell Collection, Journey File.

101. Hertzog to Maxwell, July 9, 1948, copy in Hertzog Collection, UTEP.

102. Ibid.

103. Cisneros to Weber, El Paso, October 16, 1985. The caption on illustration no. 13 in Lowman, *Remembering Carl Hertzog*, incorrectly attributes the chapter initials in *Fray Marcos* to artist Tom Lea.

104. Cisneros had completed preliminary drawings in February 1949, Hertzog to Maxwell, February 28, 1949, copy in Hertzog Collection, UTEP. In April he completed the three main drawings, and was at work on the rest of the work, Hertzog to Maxwell, April 8 & 20, 1949, Maxwell Collection, Journey File.

105. Cisneros to Weber, October 16, 1985.

106. Chávez, *New Mexico Historical Review* 25 (July 1950): 259.

107. These quotes are, respectively, from Juanita Hallenbeck to Maxwell, August 13 & November 15, 1949, Hallenbeck Collection.

108. Juanita Hallenbeck to Maxwell, Roswell, New Mexico, August 13, 1949, Hallenbeck Collection. Everette DeGolyer criticized the drawing before the book was published. See Hertzog to Maxwell, March 7, 1949, and Maxwell to Hertzog, March 14 & May 5, 1949, Maxwell Collection, Journey File.

109. Cisneros sent the completed drawings to Weber on January 19, 1986: "My idea is to have a prize-winning book again."

110. Jeff Dykes, *Fifty Great Western Illustrators* (Flagstaff, Ariz.: Northland Press, 1975), pp. 53–63, provides references to biographies of Cisneros, catalogues of exhibitions of his work, and the titles of 110 books that he has illustrated. For a more recent interpretation, see West, "Artistic Journey."

111. This and subsequent quotes from Cisneros describing the 1986 drawings come from Cisneros to Weber, El Paso, January 29, 1986.

112. Fray Marcos mentions the greyhounds on p. 24; he says that the gourd "carried some rows of cascabels and two feathers, one white and the other red" (Hallenbeck, *Fray Marcos*, p. 29). Cisneros has drawn more feathers and fewer bells than the report mentions. For Hallenbeck's identification of the cascabels as rattlesnake rattles see ibid., p. 101 n. 83.

113. Hallenbeck, *Land of the Conquistadores*, p. 20. Hallenbeck's original drawing of this map is in the Hallenbeck Collection. Hallenbeck's original map for *Fray Marcos* (two versions of which he sent to Maxwell and which he mentions by title on a page headed "illustrations," accompanying a letter to Maxwell, March 26, 1948, Maxwell Collection, Journey File) almost certainly indicated more rivers, for such detail was important to him. Hertzog and Cisneros probably decided to keep the map uncluttered. Hertzog offered a dubious explanation for the lack of rivers: "Note: No rivers on map as Hallenbeck used Modern names not in the story anyway." Hertzog to Maxwell, July 2, 1949, Maxwell Collection, Journey File.

114. Victor Mindeleff, "A Study of Pueblo Architecture: Tusayan and Cibola," *Eighth Annual Report of the Bureau of Ethnology* (Washington, D.C.: Government Printing Office, 1891), pp. 13–227. Hallenbeck's original drawings (there were two: restorations of Hawikuh "looking west" and "looking east") are no longer among his papers, but his daughter Pomona recalls seeing them, along with the mud model of Hawikuh that he constructed in his backyard. Interview with Pomona Hallenbeck, Roswell, New Mexico, January 18, 1986. See above, n. 68. Hallenbeck also sent Maxwell a pantographic drawing of Mindeleff's ground plan, but that illustration was not used in the book (Hallenbeck to Maxwell, July 16, 1948, Maxwell Collection, Hallenbeck File).

115. For the source of the *Relación* and a brief discussion of its similarity to the original manuscript, see above, n. 54. Hallenbeck criticized portions of earlier translations (see, for example, *Fray Marcos*, notes 43, 128, and 184), and other writers such as Angélico Chávez and Donald Juneau have found inadequacies in parts of Hallenbeck's translation.

l

···Fray Marcos' Relación···

Spanish versions of Fray Marcos' instructions from Viceroy Mendoza and of Fray Marcos' *Relación* to the viceroy follow. These pages are reprinted from *Colección de documentos inéditos relativos al descubrimiento, conquista y organización de las antiguas posesiones españolas de América y Oceanía*, 42 vols. (Madrid: various publishers, 1864–1884), 3: 325–51, through the courtesy of the DeGolyer Library, SMU. Hallenbeck based his translation on this source (see note 54 of the new Introduction to this edition of *The Journey of Fray Marcos*). — David J. Weber

INSTRUCCION DE DON ANTONIO DE MENDOZA, VISOREY DE NUEVA ESPAÑA.

Descubrimiento de las siete ciudades, por el P. Fr. Márcos de Niza.[1]

Primeramente: luego como llegáredes á la provincia de Culuacan, exhortareis y animareis á los españoles, que residen en la villa de San Miguel, que traten bien los indios que están de paz y no se sirvan dellos en cosas ecesivas, certificándoles que haciéndolo así, que les serán hechas mercedes y remunerados por S. M. los trabajos que allá han padescido, y en mí ternán buen ayudador para ello; y si hicieren al contrario, que serán castigados y desfavorecidos.

Dareis á entender á los indios que yo os envio, en nombre de S. M., para que digais que los traten bien y que sepan que le ha pesado de los agravios y males que han rescibido; y que de aquí adelante serán bien tratados, y los que mal les hicieren serán castigados.

Asimismo les certificareis que no se harán mas esclavos dellos, ni los sacarán de sus tierras; sino que los dejarán libres en ellas, sin hacelles mal ni daño; que pierdan el temor y conozcan á Dios Nuestro Señor, que está en el cielo, y al Emperador, que está puesto de su mano en la tierra para regilla y gobernalla.

Y porque Francisco Vazquez de Coronado, á quien S. M. tiene proveido por gobernador de esa provincia, irá con vos hasta la villa de San Miguel de Culuacan, avisarme heis como provee las cosas de aquella villa, en lo que toca al servicio de Dios Nuestro Señor y conversion y buen tratamiento de los naturales de aquella provincia.

Y si con el ayuda de Dios Nuestro Señor y gracia del Espíritu Santo, halláredes camino para pasar adelante y entrar por la tierra adentro, llevareis con vos á Estéban de Dorantes por guia, al cual mando que os obedezca en todo y por todo lo que vos le mandáredes, como á mi misma persona; y no haciéndolo así, que incurra en mal caso y en las penas que caen los que no obedescen á las personas que tienen poder de S. M. para poderles mandar.

Asimismo lleva el dicho gobernador, Francisco Vazquez, los indios que vinieron con Dorantes y otros que se han podido recoger de aquellas partes, para que, si á él y á vos os paresciere que lleveis en vuestra compañia algunos, lo hagais y useis dellos, como viéredes que conviene al servicio de Nuestro Señor.

Siempre procurareis de ir lo mas seguramente que fuere posible, é informándoos primero si están de paz ó de guerra los unos indios con los otros, por que no deis ocasion á que hagan algun desconcierto contra vuestra persona, el cual será causa para que contra ellos se haya de proceder y hacer castigo; porque desta manera en lugar de ir á hacelles bien y dalles lumbre, seria al contrario.

Llevareis mucho aviso de mirar la gente que hay, si es mucha ó poca, y si están derramados ó viven juntos.

La calidad y fertilidad della, la templanza de la tierra, los árboles y plantas y animales domésticos y salvajes, que hubiere, la manera de la tierra, si es áspera ó llana, los rios, si son grandes ó pequeños, y las piedras y metales que hay en ella; y de las cosas que se pudieren enviar ó traer muestra, traellas ó enviallas, para que de todo pueda S. M. ser avisado.

Saber siempre si hay noticia de la costa de la mar, así de la parte del Norte como de la del Sur, porque podria ser estrecharse la tierra y entrar algun brazo de mar la tierra adentro. Y si llegáredes á la costa de la mar del Sur, en las puntas que entran, al pié de algund árbol señalado de grande, dejar enterradas cartas de lo que os paresciere que conviene avisar, y al tal árbol donde quedare la carta hacelle alguna cruz porque sea conocido; asímismo en las bocas de los rios y en las dispusiciones de puertos, en los árboles mas señalados, junto al agua, hacer la misma señal de la cruz y dexar las cartas, porque, si enviare navíos, irán advertidos de buscar esta señal.

Siempre procurareis de enviar aviso con indios de como os va y sois recibido, y lo que halláredes, muy particularmente.

Y si Dios Nuestro Señor fuese servido que halleis alguna poblacion grande, donde os paresciese que habrá buen aparejo para hacer monesterio y enviar religiosos que entendiesen en la conversion, avisareis con indios ó volvereis vos á Culuacan. Con todo secreto dareis aviso para que se provea lo que convenga sin alteracion, porque en la pacificacion de lo que se hallare, se mire el servicio de Nuestro Señor y bien de la gente de la tierra.

Y aunque toda la tierra es del Emperador Nuestro Señor, vos en mi nombre tomareis posesion della por S. M., y hareis las señales y autos, que os pareciesen que se requieren para tal caso; y dareis á entender á los naturales de la tierra que hay un Dios en el cielo y el Emperador en la tierra, que está para mandalla y gobernalla, á quien todos han de ser subjetos y servir. — *D. Antonio de Mendoza.*

CERTIFICACIONES.

Digo yo Fra. Márcos de Niza, de los Observantes de San Francisco, que rescibí un treslado desta instruccion firmada del Ilustrísimo Sr. D. Antonio de Mendoza, visorey y gobernador de la Nueva España, la cual me entregó, por mandado se S. S., y en su nombre, Francisco Vazquez de Coronado, gobernador desta nueva Galicia; el cual treslado es sacado desta instruccion de *verbo ad verbum*, y con ella corregida y concertada, la cual dicha instruccion prometo de la cumplir fielmente y de no ir ni pasar contra ella ni contra cosa de lo en ella contenido, agora ni en ningun tiempo. Y por que así lo guardaré y cumpliré, firmé aqui mi nombre, en Tonala, á veinte dias del mes de Noviembre, de mill y quinientos é treinta é ocho años, á donde me dió y entregó en el dicho nombre la dicha instruccion, ques en la provincia desta Nueva Galicia. — Fra. Márcos de Niza.

Digo yo Fray Antonio de Cibdad-Rodrigo, fraile de la órden

de los Menores y ministro provincial que á la sazon soy de la provincia del Santo Evangelio desta Nueva España, ques verdad que yo envié á Fra. Márcos de Niza, sacerdote, fraile, presbítero y religioso y en toda virtud y religion tal, que de mi y de mis hermanos los definidores diputados para dellos tomaron consejo en las cosas árduas y dificultosas, fué aprobado y habido por idoneo y suficiente para hacer esta jornada y descubrimiento, así por la suficiencia arriba dicha de su persona, como por ser docto, no solamente en la teología, pero aun en la cosmografía, en el arte de la mar; y ansi consultado y difinido que fuese él, fué con otro compañero, fraile lego, que se llama Fra. Onorato, por mandado del Señor Don Antonio de Mendoza, visorey desta dicha Nueva España; y S. S. le dió todo el aparejo y recabdo que fué menester para el dicho camino y jornada; y esta instruccion que aquí está escrita, la cual yo ví y S. S. lo comuco conmigo, preguntándome lo que de ella me parecia y paresciéndome bien, se dió al dicho Fra. Márcos, por mano de Francisco Vazquez de Coronado; la cual el rescibió sin falta y executó fielmente, como en efeto ha parecido. Y por que lo sobre dicho es ansí verdad y en ello no há falencia ninguna, he escrito esta fée y testimonio y lo firmé de mi nombre. — Fecha en México, á veinte y seis dias de agosto, año de mill é quinientos é treinta é nueve. — *Fra. Antonio de Cibdad-Rodrigo,* ministro provincial.

RELACION.

Con el ayuda y favor de la Sacratísima Vírgen Maria, Nuestra Señora y del Seráfico nuestro padre San Francisco, yo Fra. Marcos de Niza, fraile profeso de la órden de San Francisco, en cumplimiento de la instruccion, arriba contenida, del Ilustrísimo Sr. D. Antonio de Mendoza, visorey y gobernador por S. M. de la Nueva España, partí de la villa de San Miguel de la provincia de Culuacan, viernes siete dias del mes de marzo de mill é quinientos é treinta é nueve años, llevando por compañero al padre Fra. Onorato y llevando conmigo á Estéban de Dorantes, negro, y á ciertos indios, de los quel dicho Sr. Visorey libertó y compró para este efecto, los cuales me entregó Francisco Vazquez de Coronado, gobernador de la Nueva Galicia, y con otra mucha cantidad de indios de Petatean, y del pueblo que llaman del Cuchillo, que serán cincuenta leguas de la dicha villa. Los cuales vinieron al valle de Culuacan, significando gran alegria, por habelles certificado los indios libertados, quel dicho Gobernador envió delante á hacelles saber su libertad y que no se habian de hacer esclavos dellos ni hacelles guerra ni mal tratamiento, diciéndoles que asi lo quiere y manda S. M. Y con esta compañia que digo, tomé mi camino hasta allegar al pueblo de Petatean, hallando en el camino muchos rescibimientos y presentes de comida, rosas y otras cosas desta calidad, y casas que me hacian de petates y ramas, en todas las partes donde no habia poblado. En este pueblo de Petatean holgué tres dias, porque mi compañero Fra. Onorato adoleció de enfermedad, que me convino dexallo allí; y conforme á la dicha instruccion, seguí mi viaje por donde me guió el Espíritu Santo, sin merescello yo. E yendo conmigo el dicho Estéban de Dorantes, negro, y algunos de los libertados y mucha gente de la tierra, haciéndome en todas partes que llegaba muchos rescibimientos y regocijos y arcos triunfales y dándome de la comida que tenian, aunque poca, porque dicen haber tres años que no llovia, y porque los indios de aquella comarca mas entendian en esconderse que en sembrar, por temor de los christianos de la villa de San Miguel, que hasta allí solian llegar á les hacer guerra y esclavos. En todo este camino, que serian 25 ó 30 leguas de aquella parte de Petatean, no ví cosa digna de poner aquí, ecebto que vinieron á mí indios de la isla en que estuvo el Marqués del Valle, de los cuales me certifiqué ser isla, y no como algunos quieren decir, tierra firme; y ví que della pasaban á la tierra firme en balsas, y de la tierra firme á ella, y el espacio, que hay de la isla á la tierra firme, puede ser de media legua de mar, poco mas ó menos. Asimismo me vinieron á ver indios de otra isla mayor quella, questá mas adelantre, de los cuales tuve razon[2] haber otras treinta islas pequeñas, pobladas de gente y pobres de comida, ecebto dos, que dicen que tienen maiz. Estos indios traian colgadas de la garganta muchas conchas, en las cuales suele haber perlas; é yo les mostré una perla que llevaba para muestra, y me dixeron que de aquellas habia en las islas, pero yo no les ví ninguna. Seguí mi camino por un despoblado de cuatro dias, yendo conmigo indios, así de las islas que digo como de los pueblos que dejaba atrás; y al cabo del despoblado, hallé otros indios, que se admiraron de me ver, porque ninguna noticia tienen de christianos, á causa de no contratarse con los de atrás por el despoblado. Estos me hicieron muchos rescibimientos, y me dieron mucha comida, y procuraban de tocarme en la ropa, y me llamaban *Sayota,* que quiere decir en su lengua "hombre del cielo", á los cuales, lo mejor que yo pude, hice entender por las lenguas lo contenido en la instruccion, que es el conoscimiento de Nuestro Señor en el cielo y de S. M. en la tierra. Y siempre, por todas las vias que podia, procuraba de saber tierra de muchas poblaciones y de gente de mas policía y razon que con los que topaba; y no tuve nueva mas de que me dixeron que la tierra adentro, cuatro ó cinco jornadas do se rematan las cordilleras de las sierras, se hace una abra llana y de mucha tierra, en la cual me dixeron haber muchas y muy grandes poblaciones, en que hay gente vestida de algodon. Y mostrándoles yo algunos metales que llevaba, para tomar razon de los metales de la tierra, tomaron el metal de oro y me dixeron que de aquel hay vasijas entre aquella gente de la abra, y que traen colgadas de las narices y orejas ciertas cosas redondas de aquel oro, y que tienen unas paletillas dél, con que raen y se quitan el sudor. Y como esta abra se desvia de la costa, y mi intencion era no apartarme della, determiné de dejalla para la vuelta, porque entonces se podria ver mejor. Y ansí anduve tres dias, poblados de aquella misma gente, de los cuales fuí rescibido como de los de atrás. Llegué á una razonable poblacion que se llama Vacapa, donde me hicieron grande rescibimiento y me dieron mucha comida, de la cual tenian en abundancia, por ser toda tierra que se riega. Hay, desta poblacion á la mar cuarenta leguas; y por hallarme tan apartado de la mar y por ser dos dias antes de la Dominica de Pasion, determiné de me estar allí hasta la Páscua, por certificarme de las islas que arriba digo que tuve noticia. Y así envié mensajeros indios á la mar, por tres vias, á los cuales encargué que me trujesen gente de la costa y de algunas de aquellas islas, para informarme dellos; y por otra parte envié á Estéban de Dorantes, negro, al cual dixe que fuese por la derrota del Norte, cincuenta ó sesenta leguas, para ver si por aquella via se podria tener razon[3] de

alguna cosa grande de las que buscábamos; y concerté con él que
si tuviese alguna noticia de tierra poblada y rica que fuese cosa
grande, que no pasase adelante, sino que volviese en persona ó me
enviase indios con esta señal que concertamos: que si la cosa fuese
razonable, me enviase una cruz blanca de un palmo; y si fuese cosa
grande, la enviase de dos palmos; y si fuese cosa mayor y mejor que
la Nueva España, me enviase una gran cruz. Y así se partió el dicho
Estéban, negro, de mi, Dominica de Pasion despues de comer, que-
dando yo en esta poblacion, que digo que se dice Vacapa. Y de ahí á
cuatro dias, vinieron sus mensajeros de Estéban con una cruz muy
grande, de estatura de un hombre, y me dixeron, de parte de Estéban, que á la hora me partiese en su seguimiento, porque habia
topado gente que le daba razon de la mayor cosa del mundo; y que
tenia indios que habian estado en ella, de los cuales me envió uno.
Y este me dixo tantas grandezas de la tierra, que dexé de creellas
para despues de habellas visto ó de tener más certificacion de la
cosa; y me dixo que habia treinta jornadas, desde donde quedaba
Estéban, hasta la primera ciudad de la tierra, que se dice Cibola. Y
por que me pareció digno de poner en este papel lo queste indio,
que Estéban me envió, dice la tierra, lo quiero hacer, el cual afirma
y dice: que en esta primer provincia hay siete ciudades muy grandes, todas debajo de un señor, y de casas de piedra y de cal, grandes; las mas pequeñas de un sobrado y una azutea encima, y otras
de dos y de tres sobrados, y la del señor de cuatro, juntas todas por
su órden; y en las portadas de las casas principales muchas labores
de piedras turquesas, de las cuales, dijo, que hay en gran abundancia. Y que las gentes destas cibdades anda muy bien vestida. Y
otras muchas particularidades me dixo, así destas siete cibdades
como de otras provincias mas adelante, cada una de las cuales dice
ser mucho mas cosa questas siete ciudades; y para saber dél como
lo sabia, tuvimos muchas demandas y respuestas; y halléle de muy
buena razon. Dí gracias á Nuestro Señor, diferi mi partida en
seguimiento de Estéban de Dorantes, creyendo que me aguardaria,
como concerté con él, y tambien porque prometí á los mensajeros
que envié á la mar que los aguardaria, porque siempre propuse de
tratar, con la gente que tratase, mucha verdad. Los mensajeros vi-

nieron dia de Páscua Florida, y con ellos gente de la costa y de dos islas, de los cuales supe ser las islas, que arriba digo, pobres de comida, como lo habia sabido antes, y que son pobladas de gente; traian conchas en la frente y dicen que tienen perlas. Certificáronme de treinta y cuatro islas, cerca las unas de las otras, cuyos nombres pongo en otro papel, donde asiento el nombre de las islas y poblaciones. La gente de las costa dicen que tiene poca comida, asi ellos como los de las islas, y que se contratan los unos con los otros por balsas; aquí la costa se va al Norte cuanto mas puede. Estos indios de la costa me truxeron rodelas de cuero de vacas, muy bien labrados, grandes, que les cubren de pies á cabeza, con unos agujeros encima de la empuñadura para poder ver detras dellas; son tan récias, que creo que no las pasára una ballesta. Este dia me vinieron tres indios de los que llaman pintados, labrados los rostros y pechos y brazos; estos estan en cerco á la parte del E. y llegan á confinar gente dellos cerca de las siete ciudades. Los cuales dixeron: que me venian á ver, porque tuvieron noticia de mi; y entre otras cosas, me dieron mucha noticia de las siete ciudades y provincias quel indio de Estéban me dixo, casi por las misma manera que Estéban me le envió á decir; y así despedí la gente de la costa; y dos indios de las islas dixeron que se querian andar conmigo siete ó ocho dias. Y con ellos y con los tres pintados que digo, me partí de Vacapa, segundo dia de Páscua Florida, por el camino y derrota que llevaba Estéban, del cual habia recibido otros mensageros, con otra cruz del tamaño de la primera que envió, dándome priesa y afirmando ser la tierra, en cuya demanda iba, la mejor y mayor cosa que jamas se oyó. Los cuales mensajeros, particulamente, me dijeron sin faltar en cosa punto de lo que dixo el primero: antes dixeron mucho mas y me dieron mas clara razon. Y así caminé aquel dia, segundo dia de Pascua, y otrros dos dias por las mismas jornadas que llevó Estéban; al cabo de los cuales, topé con la gente que le dió la noticia de las siete ciudades y de la tierra de adelantre. Los cuales me dixeron que, de allí, iban en treinta jornadas á la ciudad de Cibola, que es la primera de las siete; y no me lo dijo solo uno, sino muchos; y muy particularmente me dixeron la grandeza de las casas y la manera dellas, como me lo dixeron los primeros. Y de-

cíanme que, demas destas siete ciudades, hay otros reinos que se
llaman Marata y Acus y Totonteac; quise tres saber á qué iban tan
lejos de sus casas, y dixéronme que iban por turquesas y por cueros
de vacas y otras cosas; y de lo uno y de lo otro tienen en aqueste
pueblo cantidad; asímismo quise saber el rescate con que lo habian,
y dixéronme que con el sudor y servicio de sus personas, que iban á
la primera cibdad, que se dice Cibola, y que sirven allí en cabar las
tierras y en otros servicios, y que les dan cueros de vacas, de aquellos que allí tienen, y turquesas, por su servicio. Y estos deste
pueblo traen todos turquesas colgadas de las orejas y de las narices,
finas y buenas, y dicen que dellas están hechas labores en las puer-
tas principales de Cibola. Dixéronme que la manera del vestido de
los de Cibola es: unas camisas de algodon, largas hasta el empeine
del pié, con un boton á la garganta y un torzal largo que cuelga dél,
y las mangas destas camisas, anchas tanto de arriba como de abajo;
á mi parescer es como vestido bohemio. Dicen que andan ceñidos
con cintas de turquesas, y que encima destas camisas, los unos
traen muy buenas mantas y los otros cueros de vacas, muy bien
labrados, que tienen por mejor vestido, de que en aquella tierra
dicen que hay mucha cantidad, y asimismo las mujeres andan ves-
tidas y cubiertas hasta los piés, de la misma manera. Rescibiéronme
estos indios muy bien y tuvieron mucho cuidado de saber el dia que
partí de Vacapa, para tenerme en el camino comida y aposentos; y
traíanme enfermos que los curase, y procuraban de tocarme en la
ropa, sobre los cuales yo decia el Evangelio. Diéronme algunos
cueros de vaca, tan bien adobados y labrados, que en ellos parecia
ser hechos de hombres de mucha pulicia, y todos decian que venian
de Cibola. Otro dia seguí mi camino, llevando conmigo los pintados
que no me querian dexar. Llegué á otra poblacion, donde fuí muy
bien recibido de la gente della, los cuales asimismo procuraban de
tocarme la ropa, y me dieron noticia de la tierra que yo llevaba, tan
particularmente como los de atrás, y me dixeron como de allí habia
ido gente con Estéban Dorantes, cuatro ó cinco jornadas; y aquí
topé una cruz grande, que Estéban me habia dexado, en señal de
que la nueva de la buena tierra siempre crescia, y dexó dicho que
me dixesen que me diese mucha priesa, que él me aguardaria al

cabo del primer despoblado. Aquí puse dos cruces y tomé posesion, conforme á la instruccion, porque me pareció ser aquella mejor tierra que la que quedaba atrás, y que convenia desde allí hacer autos de posesion. Y desta manera anduve cinco dias, hallando siempre poblado y gran hospedaje y rescibimiento y muchas turquesas y cueros de vaca y la misma razon de la tierra; y luego me decian todos de Cibola y de aquella provincia, como gente que sabia que iba en demanda della, y me decian como Estéban iba delante, del cual tuve allí mensajeros de los vecinos de aquel pueblo que habian ido con él, y siempre cargándome la mano en decir la grandeza de la tierra y que me diese priesa. Aquí supe que, desde á dos jornadas, toparia con un despoblado de cuatro jornadas, en que no hay comida, mas que ya estaba prevenido para hacerme casas y llevarme comida; díme priesa, pensando de topar al fin dél con Estéban, porque allí me envió á decir que me aguardaria. Antes de llegar al despoblado, topé con un pueblo fresco, de regadio, á que me salió á rescibir harta gente, hombres y mujeres, vestidos de algodon y algunos cubiertos con cueros de vacas, que en general tienen por mejor vestido quel de algodon. Todos los deste pueblo andan *encaconados* con turquesas que les cuelgan de las narices y orejas, y á esta llaman *cacona*; entre los cuales venia el Señor deste pueblo y dos hermanos suyos, muy bien vestidos de algodon, encaconados, y con sendos collares de turquesas al pescuezo; y me truxeron mucha caza de venados, conejos y codornices, y maiz y piñol, todo en mucha abundancia; y me ofrescieron muchas turquesas y cueros de vaca, y xícaras muy lindas y otras cosas, de lo cual no tomé nada, porque así lo acostumbro á hacer despues que entré en la tierra donde no tenian noticia de nosotros. Y aquí tuve la misma relacion que antes, de las siete cibdades y reinos y provincias, que arriba digo que tuve; é yo llevaba vestido un hábito de paño pardo, que llaman de Saragoza, que me hizo traer Francisco Vazquez de Coronado, gobernador de la Nueva Galicia; y el Señor deste pueblo y otros indios tentaron el hábito con las manos, y me dixeron que de aquello habia mucho en Totonteac, y que lo traian vestido los naturales de allí, de lo cual yo me reí, y dixe que no seria sino de aquellas mantas de algodon quellos traian; y dixéronme: "¿piensas que no sabemos que eso que tú traes y lo que nosotros traemos es diferente? sabe que en Cibola todas las casas están llenas desta ropa que nosotros traemos mas; mas en Totonteac hay unos animales pequeños, de los cuales quitan lo con qué se hace esto que tú traes." Yo me admire, porque no habia oido tal cosa hasta que llegué aquí, y quíseme informar muy particularmente dello, y dixéronme que los animales son del tamaño de dos galgos de Castilla que llevaba Estéban; dicen que hay muchos en Totonteac; no pude atinar que género de animales fuese.

Otro dia entré en el despoblado, y donde habia de ir á comer, hallé ranchos y comida bastante, junto á un arroyo, y á la noche hallé casas y así mismo comida, y así lo tuve cuatro dias que me duró el despoblado. Al cabo dellos, entré en un valle muy bien poblado de gente, donde en el primer pueblo salieron á mi muchos homhombres y mugeres con comida; y todos traian muchas turquesas que les colgaban de las narices ye de las orejas, y algunos train collares de turquesas, de las que digo que traian el Señor y sus hermanos, del pueblo antes del despoblado, eceto que aquellos traian sola una vuelta, y estos traian tres y cuatro, y muy buenas mantas y cueros de vaca; y las mujeres las mismas turquesas en las narices y orejas, y muy buenas naguas y camisas. Aquí habia tanta noticia de Cibola, como en la Nueva España, de México y en el Perú, del Cuzco; y tan particularmente contaban la manera de las casas y de la poblacion y calles y plazas della, como personas que habian estado en ella muchas veces, y que traian de allá las cosas de pulicía, que tenian habidas por su servicio, como los de atrás. Yo les decia que no era posible que las casas fuesen de la manera que me decian, y para dármelo á entender, tomaban tierra y ceniza, y echábanle agua, y señalabanme como ponian la piedra y como subian el edificio arriba, poniendo aquello y piedra hasta ponello en lo alto; preguntábales á los hombres de aquella tierra si tenian alas para subir aquellos sobrados; reíanse y señalábanme el escalera, tambien como la podria yo señalar, y tomaban un palo y poníanlo sobre la cabeza y decian que aquel altura hay de sobrado á sobrado. Tambien tuve aquí relacion del paño de lana de Totonteac, donde dicen que las casas son como las de Cibola y mejores y muchas mas, y que es cosa muy grande y que no tiene cabo. Aquí supe que la costa se vuelve al Poniente, muy de recio, porque hasta la entrada deste primer despoblado que pasé, siempre la costa se venia metiendo al Norte; y como cosa que importa mucho volver la costa, quíselo saber, y así fuí en demanda della y ví claramente que, en los treinta y cinco grados, vuelve al Oeste, de que no menos alegría tuve, que de la buena nueva de la tierra. Y así me volví á proseguir mi camino, y fuí por aquel valle cinco dias, el cual es tan poblado de gente lucida y tan abastado de comida que basta para dar de comer en el á mas de trescientos de caballo; riégase todo y es como un vergel, están los barrios á media legua y á cada cuarto de legua, y en cada pueblo destos hallaba muy larga relacion de Cibola, y tan particularmente me contaban della, como gente que cada año van allí á ganar su vida. Aquí hallé un hombre, natural de Cibola, el cual díxo haberse venido de la persona que el Señor tiene allí en Cibola puesta, por quel Señor destas siete cibdades vive y tiene su asiento en la una dellas, que se llama Ahacus, y en las otras tiene puestas personas que mandan por él. Este vecino de Cibola es hombre de buena dispusicion, algo viejo y de mucha mas razon que los naturales deste valle y que los de atrás; díxome que se queria ir conmigo para que yo le alcanzase perdon. Informéme particularmente dél, y díxome que Cibola es una gran cibdad, en que hay mucha gente y calles y plazas, y que en algunas partes de la cibdad hay unas casas muy grandes, que tienen á diez sobrados, y que en estas se juntan los principales, ciertos dias del año; dicen que las casas son de piedra y de cal, por la manera que lo dixeron los de atrás, y que las portadas y delanteras de las casas principales son de turquesas; díxome que, de la manera desta cibdad, son las otras siete, y algunas mayores, y que la mas principal dellas es Ahacus; dice que á la parte del Sueste, hay un reino, que se llama Marata, en que solia haber muchas y muy grandes poblaciones, y que todas tienen estas casas de piedra y sobrados, y questos han tenido y tienen guerra con el Señor destas siete cibdades, por la cual guerra se ha disminuido en gran cantidad este reino de Marata, aunque todavia está sobre sí y tiene guerra con estotros. Y así mismo dixo que, á la parte del Sueste, está el reino que llaman de Totonteac;

dice que es una cosa, la mayor del mundo y de mas gente y riquezas; y que aquí visten paños de lo que es hecho esto que yo traigo, y otros mas delicados y que se sacan de los animales que atrás me señalaron, y que es gente de mucha pulicía, y diferente de la gente que yo he visto. Tambien dixo que hay otra provincia y reino muy grande, que se dice Acus, porque hay Ahacus: y Ahacus, con aspiracion, es una de las siete cibdades, la mas principal, y sin aspiracion, Acus, es reino y provincia por sí; díxome que los vestidos que traen en Cibola son de la manera que atrás me habian dicho; dice que todos los de aquella cibdad duermen en camas altas del suelo, con ropas y toldos encima, que cubre las camas; díxome que iria conmigo hasta Cibola y adellantre, si lo quisiere llevar. La misma relacion me dieron en este pueblo otras muchas personas, aunque no tan particularmente. Por este valle caminé tres dias, haciéndome los naturales todas las fiestas y regocijos que podian; aquí en este valle ví mas de dos mill cueros de vacas, estremadamente bien adobados, ví mucha mas cantidad de turquesas y collares dellas, en este valle, que en todo lo que habia dejado atrás; y todo dicen que viene de la cibdad de Cibola, de la cual tienen tanta noticia, como yo de lo que traigo entre las manos; y así mismo la tienen del reino de Marata, y de Acus y del de Totonteac. Aquí en este valle, me truxeron un cuero, tanto y medio mayor que de una gran vaca, y me dixeron ques de un animal, que tiene solo un cuerno en la frente y queste cuerno es corbo hácia los pechos, y que de allí sale una punta derecha, en la cual dicen que tiene tanta fuerza, que ninguna cosa, por recia que sea, dexa de romper, si topa con ella; y dicen que hay muchos animales destos en aquella tierra; la color del cuero es á manera de cabron y el pelo tan largo como el dedo. Aquí tuve mensajeros de Estéban, los cuales de su parte me dixeron que iba ya en el postrer despoblado, y muy alegre, por ir mas certificado de las grandezas de la tierra; y me envió á decir que, desde que se aparto de mí, nunca habia tomado á los indios en ninguna mentira, y que hasta allí todo lo habia hallado por la manera que le habian dicho y que ansí pensaba hallar lo demás. Y así lo tengo por cierto, porque es verdad que, desde el primer dia que yo tuve notica de la cibdad de Cibola, los indios me dixeron

todo lo que hasta hoy he visto; diciéndome siempre los pueblos que
habia de hallar en el camino y los nombres dellos; y en las partes
donde no habia poblado, me señalaban donde habia de comer y
dormir, sin haber errado en un punto, con haber andado, desde la
primera nueva que tuve de la tierra hasta hoy, ciento y doce leguas,
que no paresce poco dina de escribir la mucha verda desta gente.
Aquí en este valle, como en los demás pueblos de atrás, puse cruces
é hice los autos y diligencias que convenian, conforme á la instruccion. Los naturales de esta villa me rogaron que descansase aquí
tres ó cuatro dias, porque estaba el despoblado cuatro leguas de
aquí; y desde el principio dél hasta llegar á la ciudad de Cibola, hay
largos quince dias de camino; y que me querian hacer comida y
aderezar lo necesario para él. Y me dixeron que con Estéban,
negro, habian ido de aquí mas de trescientos hombres acompañán-
dole y llevándole comida, y que conmigo tambien querian ir muchos,
por servirme y porque pensaban volver ricos; yo se lo agradescí y
les dixe que adereszasen presto, porque cada dia se me hacia un
año, con deseo de ver á Cibola. Y así me detuve tres dias sin pasar
adelante, en los cuales siempre me informé de Cibola y de todo lo
demás, y no hacia sino tomar indios y preguntalles aparte á cada
uno por sí, y todos se conformaban en una misma cosa, y me decian
la muchedumbre de gente y la órden de las calles y grandeza de las
casas y la manera de las portadas, todo como me lo dixeron los de
atrás. Pasados los tres dias, se juntó mucha gente para ir conmigo,
de los cuales tomé hasta treinta principales, muy bien vestidos con
aquellos collares de turquesas, que algunos dellos tenian á cinco y á
seis vueltas; y con estos tomé la gente necesaria que llevase comida
para ellos y para mí, y me puse en camino. Por mis jornadas, entré
en el despoblado, á nueve dias de Mayo, y así fuimos: el primero
dia, por un camino muy ancho y muy usado: llegamos á comer á
una agua; donde los indios me habian señalado, y á dormir á otra
agua, donde hallé casa que habian acabado de hacer para mí y otra
questaba hecha donde durmió Estéban cuando pasó, y ranchos vie-
jos, y muchas señales de fuego, de la gente que pasaba á Cibola por
este camino. Y por esta órden, caminé doce dias, siempre muy
abastado de comidas de venados, liebres y perdices del mismo color

y sabor de las de España, aunque no tan grandes, pero poco menores. Aquí llegó un indio, hijo de un principal de los que venian
conmigo, el cual habia ido en compañia de Estéban, negro, y venia
aquexado el rostro y cuerpo, cubierto de sudor, el cual mostraba
harta tristeza en su persona, y me dixo que, una jornada antes de
allegar á Cibola, Estéban envió su calabazo, con mensajeros, como
siempre acostmubraba enviallo delantre, para que supiesen como
iba; el calabazo llevaba unas hileras de cascabeles y dos plumas,
una blanca y otra colorada; y como llegaron á Cibola, ante la persona que el Señor tiene allí puesta, y le dieron el calabazo; como le
tomó en las manos y vido los cascabeles, con mucha ira y enojo
arrojó el calabazo en el suelo, y dijo á los mensajeros que luego se
fuesen, quél conoscia que gente era aquella, que les dijesen que no
entrasen en la cibdad, sino que á todos los matarian; los mensajeros
se volvieron y dixeron á Estéban lo que pasaba, el cual les dixo que
aquello no era nada, que los que se mostraban enojados, les rescibian mejor; y así prosiguió su viaje hasta llegar á la cibdad de
Cibola, donde halló gente que no le consintió entrar dentro, y le
metieron en una casa grande, que está fuera de la ciudad, y le
quitaron luego todo lo que llevaba, de rescates y turquesas y otras
cosas que habia habido en el camino de los indios; y que allí estuvo
aquella noche sin darle de comer ni de beber, á él ni á los que con
él iban. Y otro dia de mañana, este indio hubo sed y salió de la casa
á beber, en un rio questaba cerca, y de ahí á poco rato, vido ir
huyendo á Estéban y que iban tras él gente de la cibdad, y que
mataban algunos de los que iban con él; y que como esto vió, este
indio se fué, escondido, el rio arriba y despues atravesó á salir al
camino del despoblado.

Con las cuales nuevas, algunos de los indios que iban comigo
comenzaron é llorar, yo con las ruines nuevas temí perderme, y no
temí tanto perder la vida, como no poder volver á dar aviso de la
grandeza de la tierra, donde Dios Nuestro Señor puede ser tan servido y su santa feé ensalzada y acrescentado el patrimonio Real de
S. M. Y con todo esto, lo mejor que pude los consolé y les dixe que
no se debia de dar entero crédito á aquel indio; y ellos, con muchas
lágrimas, me dixeron quel indio no diria sino lo que habia visto; y

así me aparté de los indios, á encomendarme á Nuestro Señor y á suplicarle guiase esta cosa como mas fuese servido y alumbrase mi corazon; y esto hecho, me volví á los indios y con un cuchillo corté los cordeles de las petacas, que llevaba de ropa y rescates, que hasta entonces no habia llegado á ello ni dado nada á nadie, y repartido lo que llevaba por todos aquellos principales, y les dixe que no temiesen y que se fuesen comigo; y así lo hicieron. Y yendo por nuestro camino, una jornada de Cibola, topamos otros dos indios, de los que habian ido con Estéban, los cuales venian ensangrentados y con muchas heridas; y como llegaron, ellos y los que venian comigo comenzaron tanto llanto, que de lástima y temor, tambien á mí me hicieron llorar; y eran tantas las voces, que no me dexaban preguntalles por Estéban, ni lo que les habia subcedido, y roguelles que callasen y supiésemos lo que pasaba y dixeron: que "¿cómo callarian, pues sabian que de sus padres, hijos y hermanos, eran muertos mas de trescientos hombres, de los que fueron con Estéban?, y que ya no osarian ir á Cibola como solian." Todavia, lo mejor que pude, procuré de amansallos y quitalles el temor, aunque no estaba yo sin nescesidad de quien á mi me lo quitase; pregunte á los indios que venian heridos, por Estéban y lo que habia pasado, y estuvieron un rato sin me hablar palabra, llorando con los de sus pueblos, y al cabo, me dixeron qué como Estéban llegó una jornada de la ciudad de Cibola, envió sus mensajeros con su calabazo á Cibola al Señor, haciéndole saber su ida, y como venia á hacer paces y á curallos; y como le dieron el calabazo y vido que los cascabeles, muy enojado arrojó en el suelo el calabazo y dixo: "yo conozco esta gente, porque estos cascabeles no son de la hechura de los nuestros, decidles que luego se vuelvan, sino que no quedará hombre dellos;" y así se quedó muy enojado. Y los mensajeros volvieron tristes, y no osaban decir á Estéban lo que les acaesció, aunque todavia se lo dixeron, y el les dixo: "que no temiesen, que él queria ir allá, porque, aunque le respondian mal, le rescibian bien"; y así se fué y llegó á la cibdad de Cibola, ya que se queria poner el sol, con toda la gente que llevaba, que serian mas de trescientos hombres, sin otras muchas mugeres; y no los consintieron entrar en la cibdad, sino en una casa grande y de buen aposento, questaba fuera de la cibdad. Y luego tomaron á Estéban todo lo quél llevaba, diciendo quel Señor lo mandó así; y en toda esa noche no nos dieron de comer, ni de beber. Y otro dia, el sol de una lanza fuera,[4] salió Estéban de la casa, y algunos de los principales con él, y luego vino mucha gente de la cibdad, y como él los vió, echó á huir y nosotros tambien; y luego nos dieron estos flechazos y heridas y caimos; y cayeron sobre nosotros otros muertos, y asi estuvimos hasta la noche, sin osarnos menear, y oimos grandes voces en la cibdad y vimos sobre las azuteas muchos hombres y mujeres que miraban, y no vimos mas á Estéban, sino que creemos que le flecharon como á los demás que iban con él, que no escaparon mas de nosotros. Yo, visto lo que los indios decian, y el mal aparejo que habia para proseguir mi jornada como deseaba, no dexé de sentir su pérdida y la mia, y Dios es testigo de cuanto quisiera tener á quien pedir consejo y parescer, porque confieso que á mi me faltaba. Díxeles que Nuestro Señor castigaria á Cibola y que como el Emperador supiese lo que pasaba, enviaria muchos christianos á que los castigasen; no me creyeron, porque dicen que nadie basta contra el poder de Cibola; pediles que se consolasen y no llorasen, y consolélos con las mejores palabras que pude, las cuales seria largo de poner aquí. Y con esto los dexé y me aparté, un tiro ó dos de piedra, á encomendarme á Dios, en lo cual tardaria hora y media; y cuando volví á ellos, hallé llorando un indio mio que traxe de México, que se llama Márcos y díxome, "padre, estos tienen concertado de te matar, porque dicen que por tí y por Estéban han muerto á sus parientes, y que no ha de quedar de todos ellos hombre ni muger que no muera. Yo torné á repartir entre ellos lo que me quedaba, de ropa y rescates, por aplacallos, y díxeles que mirasen que si me mataban, que á mi no me hacian ningun mal, porque moria christiano y me iria al cielo, y que los que me matasen penarian por ello, porque los christianos vernian en mi busca, y contra mi voluntad, los matarian á todos. Con estas y otras muchas palabras, que les dixe, se aplacaron algo, aunque todavia hacian gran sentimiento por la gente que les mataron. Roguéles que algunos dellos quisiesen ir á Cibola, para ver si habia escapado alguno otro indio, y para que supiesen alguna nueva de Estéban, lo cual no pude acabar con ellos. Visto esto, yo les dixe que, en todo caso, yo habia de ver la Ciudad de Cibola, y me dixeron que ninguno iria comigo; y al cabo viéndome determinado, dos principales dixeron que irian comigo, con los cuales y con mis indios y lenguas, seguí mi camino hasta la vista de Cibola, la cual está sentada en un llano, á la falda de un cerro redondo. Tiene muy hermoso parescer de pueblo, el mejor que en estas partes yo he visto; son las casas por la manera que los indios me dixeron, todas de piedra con sus sobrados y azuteas, á lo que me paresció desde un cerro donde me puse á vella. La poblacion es mayor que la cibdad de México; algunas veces fuí tentado de irme á ella, porque sabia que no aventuraba sino la vida, y esta ofrescí á Dios el dia que comencé la jornada; al cabo temí, considerando mi peligro y que si yo moria, no se podria haber razon desta tierra, que á mi ver es la mayor y mejor de todas las descubiertas. Diciendo yo á los principales, que tenia comigo, cuán bien me parescia Cibola, me dixeron que era la menor de las siete cibdades, y que Totonteac es mucho mayor y mejor que todas las siete cibdades y que es de tantas casas y gente, que no tiene cabo. Vista la dispusicion de la ciudad, paresció me llamar aquella tierra el nuevo reino de San Francisco, y allí hice, con ayuda de los indios, un gran monton de piedra, y encima dél puse una cruz delgada y pequeña, porque no tenia aparejo para hacella mayor, y dixe que aquella cruz y mojon ponia en nombre de D. Antonio de Mendoza, visorey y gobernador de la Nueva España por el Emperador, nuestro señor, en señal de posesion, conforme á la instruccion; la cual posesion dixe que tomaba allí de todas las siete cibdades y de los reinos de Totonteac y de Acus y de Marata, y que no pasaba á ellos, por volver á dar razon de lo hecho y visto. Y asi me volví, con harto mas temor que comida, y anduve, hasta topar la gente que se me habia quedado, todo lo mas, apriesa que pude; los cuales alcancé á dos dias de jornada, y con ellos vine hasta pasar el despoblado, donde no se me hizo tan buen acogimiento como primero, porque así los hombres como las mugeres, hacian gran llanto por la gente que les mataron en Cibola. Y con el temor, despedíme luego de aquella gente de aquel valle, y anduve el primero dia diez leguas; y ansi anduve á ocho y á diez leguas, sin parar hasta pasar el segundo despoblado.

Volviendo, y aun que no me faltaba temor, determiné de allegar á la abra, de que arriba digo que tenia razon, donde se rematan las sierras; y allí tuve razon que aquella abra va poblada muchas jornadas á la parte de Leste, y no osé entrar en ella, porque como me paresció que se habia de venir á poblar y señorear estotra tierra de las siete cibdades y reinos que digo, que entonces se podria mejor ver, sin poner en aventura mi persona y dexar por ello de dar razon de lo visto. Solamente ví, desde la boca de la abra, siete poblaciones razonables, algo lexos, un valle abaxo muy fresco y de muy buena tierra, de donde salian muchos humos; tuve razon que hay en ella mucho oro y que lo tratan los naturales della en vasijas y joyas, para las orejas y paletillas con que se raen y quitan el sudor, y ques gente que no consiente que los de estotra parte de la abra contraten con ellos: no me supieron decir la causa por qué. Aquí puse dos cruces y tomé posesion de toda esta abra y valle, por la manera y órden de las posesiones de arriba, conforme á la instruccion. De allí proseguí la vuelta de mi viaje, con toda la priesa que pude, hasta llegar á la villa de San Miguel, de la provincia de Culuacan, creyendo hallar allí á Francisco Vazquez de Coronado, gobernador de la Nueva Galicia; y como no lo hallé, proseguí mi jornada hasta la cibdad de Compostela, donde le hallé. Y de allí luego escrebí mi venida al Ilustrísimo Sr. Visorey de la Nueva España, y á nuestro Padre Fray Antonio de Cibdad-Rodrigo, provincial, y que me enviasen á mandar lo que haria. No pongo aquí muchas particularidades, porque no hacen á este caso; solamente digo lo que ví y me digeron, por las tierras donde anduve y de las que tuve razon, para dalla á nuestro padre provincial, para que el *la* muestre á los padres de nuestra órden, que le pareciese ó en el capitulo, por cuyo mandado *yo fuí, para* que la den al Ilustrísimo señor visorey de la Nueva España, á cuyo pedimento me enviaron *á esta jornada.*[5] — *Fray Márcos de Nìza, vice-comissarius.*

LEGALIZACION.
En la gran cibdad de Temixtitan, México de la Nueva España, dos dias del mes de Setiembre, año del nascimiento de Nuestro

Señor Jesucristo de mill y quinientos é treinta é nueve años, ante el muy Illmo. Sr. D. Antonio de Mendoza, visorrey é gobernador por S. M. en esta Nueva España, y presidente de la Audiencia y chancillería Real, que en ella reside, estando presentes los muy magníficos señores licenciado Francisco de Ceiños, oidor por S. M. en la dicha Real Audiencia, y Francisco Vazquez de Coronado, gobernador por S. M. en la provincia de la Nueva Galicia, y en presencia de nos Juan Baeza de Herrera, escribano mayor de la dicha Real Audiencia y de la Gobernacion de la dicha Nueva España, y Antonio de Turcios, escribano de SS. MM. y de la dicha Real Audiencia; parecio el muy reverendo padre Fray Márcos de Niza, vice-comisario en estas partes de las Indias del mar Océano, de la órden de Señor San Francisco, y presentó ante S. S. y ante nos los dichos escribanos y testigos y uso escriptos, esta instruccion y relacion[6] firmada de su nombre y sellada con el sello general de las Indias, la cual tiene nueve hojas, con esta en que van nuestros signos; y dixo y afirmó y certificó ser verdad lo contenido en la dicha instruccion y relacion, y pasar lo en ella contenido, para que S. M. sea informado de la verdad de lo que en ella se hace mencion. Y S. S. mandó á nos los dichos escribanos, de como así la presentaba y declaraba el dicho vice-comisario, lo asentásemos al pié della y lo diésemos por fée, signado con nuestros signos. — Testigos que á ello fueron presentes: los susodichos, é Antonio de Almaguer y Fray Martin de Ozocastro, fraile de la misma órden. — En fée de lo cual, yo el dicho Juan Baeza de Herrera, escribano susodicho, fice aquí este mio signo á tal, + en testimonio de verdad. — Juan Baeza de Herrera. — E yo el dicho Antonio de Turcios, escribano susodicho, que á lo que dicho es presente fuí, fice aquí este mio signo á tal, + en testimonio de verdad. — Antonio de Turcios.

NOTES

1. *Coleccion* de Muñoz, tomo LXXXI.

2. Está escrito *ron.*, que tambien pudiera leerse *relacion.*

3. Como antes.

4. Es decir, que el sol estaba en el horizonte á la altura de una lanza, á poco de haber salido.

5. Las palabras que van de cursiva son las que cubre, en los tres últimos renglones del original, un sello de cera blanca, ovalado y de cuya leyenda sólo se halla inteligible. . . . . . *generalis commissariatus omnium Indiarum.* Parece, pues, que solo falta la palabra. *sigillum.*

6. Ron.: Aquí seguramente es *relacion,* y probablemente lo mismo siempre, pues la voz *razon* está algunas veces con todas sus letras.

✳ THE JOURNEY OF FRAY MARCOS ✳

José Cisneros

The Journey of
Fray Marcos de Niza

by
Cleve Hallenbeck

Illustrations and Decorations
by
José Cisneros

University Press in Dallas
1949

TO MY DAUGHTER

JUANITA POMONA HALLENBECK

···Contents···

ILLUSTRATIONS

Hawikuh

ARIZONA

NEW MEXICO

Sr. Carlos

Cascabel

CHIHUAHUA

Bacoachi

Baviacora

Corazones
Matape
Tepupa

SONORA

DURANGO

Minas Nuevas

Vacapa

Petatlán

Sinaloa

Gulf of California

Culiacán

Old Culiacán

SINALOA

N

CIBOLA

Kwakina
Zuñi Creek

Modern Zuñi
Halona

Matsaki

Kiakima

Hawikuh

Kyanawa

J. CISNEROS

The Road to Cíbola

Indian Towns .... △
Spanish Towns 1539 ...... □
Modern Towns .... ○

····Historical Background····

N sketching the historical background of Friar Mark's journey in search of the "Seven Cities of Cíbola," we shall have to go back eight centuries and begin with a medieval legend that dates from the year 1150 A.D.

In that year the Moors captured the city of Merida, in Spain, and—so runs the legend— seven bishops of the Church and their followers, fleeing *en masse* from the Moorish conquerors, reached the seaport of Lisbon and, taking ship, boldly sailed away into the western ocean, seeking a legendary group of islands known as "The Blessed Isles," where they might re-establish themselves.

After a long and stormy voyage, during which they more than once were swept out of their course, they came to a large and beautiful island, whereon they landed, burned their ships and founded seven settlements. They named the island Antilia.' With the passage of time their settlements grew into seven great, rich, and beautiful cities that became known in Latin Europe as "The Cities of the Seven Bishops" or "The Seven Cities of Antilia."

How all this information was carried back to Europe, the legend conveniently neglects to advise us: a failing characteristic of most legends. One Portuguese navigator claimed, however, that he had seen the paradisaical island, whereon crystal-clear rivers flowed over golden sands, and had heard of the cities, but had not visited them. (Neither did he bring home any of the sand, although it seems that a man of any intelligence would have loaded his ship with it and gone back for more.) Other rovers of the seas also claimed to have learned of the island and its great cities, but were not agreed upon its geographic location, except that it lay somewhere in or beyond the Sea of Darkness—the Atlantic, which, incidentally, was not called the Sea of Darkness because it was dark, but because the sun set beyond it.

The legend has some variants—thus, one version has the Seven Cities located in seven great caves—but the version I have briefly recited is the most common one. The first part of it—the flight and embarkation of the refugees—may be true.

After Columbus' discovery of the West Indies in 1492, it was believed by many people that one of the larger of those islands would prove to be Antilia. The name Antilles, now applied to the West Indies, is a reminder of that belief. When exploration proved that none of the islands contained any cities larger than squalid Indian *rancherías,* the legend, refusing to die, transferred the Seven Cities to some part of the vast, unknown mainland of the New World, and it was believed that eventually some lucky or daring explorer would find them or learn of their whereabouts.

Meantime, during the years 1515 to 1521, Hernando Cortés carried out his picturesque conquest of the Aztec portion of Nueva Espagna (New Spain), as Mexico was then called. In 1522 he founded Zacatula, on the west coast, and thus in three years had a band of settlements from coast to coast across New Spain.[2]

For a few years Cortés was the dominant figure in this realm he had won for the crown of Spain. After having established colonies on the west coast, he began exploring the Gulf of California, with ships built at Zacatula. His efforts in that direction, however, had met with little success.

In 1527 an *Audiencia*[3] was created, partly to look after the civil affairs of New Spain and partly to hold the ambitious Cortés in bounds. Three years later one Nuño de Guzmán, then president of the *Audiencia,* came forward with an interesting story. While at the colony of Pánuco, near the east coast, he had been told by an Indian from farther north of seven large, populous, and rich cities that lay forty days' journey to the north, beyond a vast treeless region and "between the two oceans." The Indian said that when he was a boy he had visited those cities in company with his father, who was a trader.

This story does not come down to us direct from Guzmán, but through Pedro de Castañeda, who recorded it some thirty years later. Castañeda, a trustworthy chronicler, doubtless reported the story as he heard it, but we do not know how much Guzmán may have added to the Indian's tale. When it will serve the Indian's interests to lie, he will lie as willingly as does his white brother, but otherwise he tells the truth as he sees it. This native doubtless told the truth according to his standards, for to a nomadic savage the pueblos of New Mexico were large and rich cities. But we can not know to what pueblos he referred, for there were, at the time, three or more groups of seven pueblos each within New Mexico, and another in Arizona. I believe Guzmán's informant had in mind the Piro pueblos that lay east of the Manzaño Mountains.[4]

People of New Spain at once identified these "cities" with the long-sought Seven Cities of Antilia, and interest in the old legend flamed up anew. But the country to the north of the occupied zone of New Spain was vast and unknown, and the Indian's information was sufficiently vague. He must have told Guzmán that the big cities lay to the northwest rather than to the north, for the pueblo district was in fact northwest of Pánuco, and Guzmán, in seeking them, crossed to the west coastal district before turning north.[5] He took along about four hundred Spaniards and nearly a thousand Indians. Somewhere near the present site of Culiacán he for some unknown reason turned eastward, but was brought to a halt by impassable mountain barriers, and failed in three attempts to force a passage. At this juncture his health failed, and the enterprise had to be suspended. Meanwhile he carved out a new province for himself—the province of Nueva Galicia, corresponding roughly to the modern Mexican states of Nayarit and Sinaloa—establishing Compostela as his capital and founding San Miguel de Culiacán, some three hundred miles farther north, as an outpost for use as a base for further operations northward.

Finally, in the summer of 1536, he was arrested on the charge of having aided and abetted the enslavement of Indians. He was tried and convicted, and upon his appeal to Spain his sentence was confirmed. But he was still at Compostela, ruling there as governor of Nueva Galicia, when occurred an important event in the history of New Spain.

One of Guzmán's henchmen, named Alcaraz, on a slave-catching expedition just above the Rio Sinaloa, was startled, one day in April 1536, by the arrival of four apparitions coming out of the north—three lean, sun-browned Spaniards and a swarthy Moor, scantily dressed in deerskins and badly in need of the services of a barber.

They announced themselves as Álvar Nuñez Cabeza de Vaca, Castillo Maldonado, Andrés Dorantes and Estévan,[6] the Moor, and reported that they were the sole survivors of Narváez' ill-starred expedition that, eight years before, had disappeared in the forests of Florida and thereafter had not been seen or heard of.

The four wanderers were escorted on southward to San Miguel de Culiacán, and there they told their story to the *Alcalde* of the town, Melchior Díaz.

Narváez' three hundred men, they said, had penetrated far inland when they were compelled, by sickness, lack of food, and attacks by Indians, to retreat. After the loss of about fifty men from illness and the arrows of the natives, they regained the coast at a bay that they later named *Bahía de los Caballos* (Bay of the Horses), because they there killed and ate their horses (this later was identified as Apalachicola Bay). The ships that had been instructed to patrol the coast for them failed to appear, and in desperation these men constructed five crazy barges, hoping to sail coastwise to Spanish settlements on the east coast of New Spain. They of course had no idea how far they would have to go, for the extent of the Gulf coast was unknown.

After more than a month of very slow progress and great suffering, the barges were separated by the outrushing torrent of a mighty river (the Mississippi); then the craft were caught in a storm and eventually were hurled upon the coast. Narváez and two of his crew, remaining on one of the barges, were carried out to sea and that was the last that was seen of them.[7]

Within a year all but four of the unfortunate men had died of starvation or had been wantonly killed by the Indians. The four survivors were held in slavery by the bestial, inhuman coastal tribes for six years. Then, managing to escape, they fled inland. They found the inland tribes much more humane: these regarded the Spaniards as great magicians, and relayed them, with guides, from village to village. The Spaniards practiced "faith healing"[8] on ailing Indians along the way, and their reputation as beneficent "children of the Sun" ran far ahead of them.

It was the desire of these wanderers to reach the Spanish settlements at Pánuco, but because of their horror of falling again into the hands of the brutal coastal tribes, and their ignorance of how much farther westward the coast extended, they refrained from turning southward so long as the rivers they crossed flowed southward (thus indicating, to them, that the coast still was south of them). At the Pecos River they refused to heed the advice of their guides to take a trail running southwestward from there, although it was the one they should have followed, for it would have saved them a thousand miles of weary traveling through desert country.

Thus they crossed western Texas and southern New Mexico. Reaching the Gila River in southwestern New Mexico, they saw that now the drainage was toward the South Sea (the Pacific), and so they swung southward through southeastern Arizona, and then through Sonora to the Yaqui River. There they were told by Indians of a party of Spaniards farther on, and they hastened to overtake them. From the time they escaped their captors until they reached the Yaqui River they traveled about three thousand miles through country never before seen by any European. Incidentally, at the time they decided to turn southward, they were farther from any white settlement than they were before they began their long trek, and were twice as far from their objective (Pánuco) as they were at the start.

For pathos, tragedy, and bleak misery, the story that these men told, and afterward published,[9] is a classic in the annals of mankind. So far as my reading goes, it is without a parallel: Homer's *Odyssey* cannot compare with it, for it was the truth. Yet the only thing in that epic of suffering and fortitude that aroused more than a passing public interest was what would appear to us an item of commonplace information. While with a certain tribe of Indians (later identified as the Ópatas, of the Sonora Valley in Sonora) they were told that to the north, in or beyond a mountainous region, was a group of towns of very big houses and many people, with whom the Ópatas traded, exchanging seashells, parrot feathers, and deerskins for turquoises, "emeralds" (malachites), and cotton blankets. To Estévan, who was serving as spokesman for the party, the Indians pointed out the trail leading to those towns. It was, of course, the group of Zuñi pueblos in west-central New Mexico to which the Ópatas had reference.

Contrary to what our eastern-bred historians are prone to write, those men told no tall tales of what they had seen or heard. What the Ópatas told them must have been the truth, for what the men reported having been told was the truth. To the Ópatas, the northern pueblos did contain very big "houses": they are big even to us of today, and a town of five hundred or more inhabitants did contain "many people" as compared to the Ópata villages with their two hundred to three hundred souls each.

Cabeza de Vaca and his companions must have learned more, and told the viceroy more, of those towns than Cabeza de Vaca gives in his written narrative, for that document is much condensed and covers in a few thousand words the events of eight years. But there is no evidence whatever that in reporting this information they ever varied from the truth, for both the written accounts are obviously honest. They did not state the number of towns, although it is probable that the Ópatas told them how many there were in the group.

Before Cabeza de Vaca, and even before Guzmán, we find some evidence in Spanish documents that a little vague information, hardly more than rumor, of the terraced-house culture to the north had filtered down from tribe to tribe to the Spaniards of New Spain. Probably even the Aztecs knew something of the pueblo district, although, since trading among the Indians was usually only from tribe to contiguous tribe, any information of the pueblo country would have been relayed perhaps half a dozen times before it reached as far as Mexico City. Such shadowy rumors, however, served more to keep the old legend alive than definite information would have done, for nothing shackles man's imagination so effectively as facts. Consequently, all sorts of wild conjectures were current as to what might be found in the intriguing north country.

Now Cabeza de Vaca not only had heard of the elusive cities, but had been shown the road leading to them. They were no longer at large on the continent, for many people believed that the Seven Cities of Antilia, the seven that Guzmán had been told of, and the group of which the Cabeza de Vaca party had been informed were the same. Hence the excitement produced throughout New Spain by that one paragraph in Cabeza de Vaca's narrative. The more intelligent class, of course, were very skeptical of the old legend. But New Spain was infested by idle adventurers who had come to the New World seeking wealth and fame, and to these no story was too improbable to be believed. Wealth had been found in Mexico, and again in Perú, so why not, they argued, in the vast north country?

The more sober class, on the other hand, including the viceroy, the practical Antonio de Mendoza,[10] believed that Cabeza de Vaca's story of populous towns of large houses was worth investigating. The thing was practicable, now that the route to them had been revealed. Moreover, Mendoza had another motive for taking action on the matter.

The colonial Spaniards, however, took things leisurely unless there was urgent necessity for haste. Even in the search for gold and for natural resources to exploit and dissipate, they lacked the frenzied rush of the Anglos. Also, there was a good deal of squabbling, and even litigation, among the candidates of both New Spain and Old Spain as to who should have the privilege of leading an *entrada* into the north. There were many claimants, and we are told that the Council for the Indies,[11] in Spain, after examining the credentials of the various aspirants, declared that each had proved the complete incapacity of all the others. So none was approved.

In New Spain there were a few men who were qualified, through experience, prominence, and financial resources, to organize and equip an expedition. Chief of these were Viceroy Mendoza, Cortés, Guzmán, and Alvarado. But Guzmán, arrested and dismissed from his post as governor of Nueva Galicia, was thereby removed from the picture; Alvarado had been shunted off on another mission; Cortés had royal authority for coastwise explorations only; Mendoza lacked authority to undertake or authorize any expedition looking to the occupation of new lands, other than the peaceful penetration by missionary friars.

So a year and a half elapsed after the arrival of Cabeza de Vaca before anything definite was attempted. In the meantime Cabeza de Vaca and Maldonado had returned to Spain, and with the exception of the slave Estévan, Dorantes was the only one remaining in New Spain who knew the road to the big-house towns. Late in 1537 he also was about to take ship for Spain when Mendoza persuaded him to remain for the purpose of conducting a small reconnaissance into the north country. Mendoza promised him a squad of mounted men and a number of friars and agreed himself to finance the enterprise. But somehow the scheme fell through: Mendoza later reported to the Crown that he knew not why it had come to nothing.

Then the viceroy was spurred into action by the activities of Cortés and De Soto. The former was preparing to explore the coast clear to the head of the Gulf of California. The latter was organizing an expedition in Spain to penetrate the continent from the east, and his efforts to enlist Cabeza de Vaca showed that he too wished to reach the supposed "Cities of Antilia."

Mendoza then hit upon the idea of employing a friar for the job, and so giving it the color of a purely missionary exploration. Thus he would not be exceeding his authority. If such preliminary reconnaissance revealed the elusive seven cities, or any other country worth occupying, steps could then be taken toward possessing it. At the moment, the important thing was to be the first to establish a claim to the country.

For this purpose he selected a Franciscan friar named Marcos de Niza.[12] It appears that Marcos had been recommended for the mission by his father provincial, Fray Antonio de Ciudad-Rodrigo, and perhaps also by Bishop Zumárraga who had been instrumental in bringing Marcos to New Spain from Guatemala. Marcos was claimed by Fray Antonio to be a proficient cartographer and cosmographer and to possess other special qualifications for the task in hand.

Mendoza also purchased the slave Estévan from Dorantes, so that he, knowing the road, might serve as a guide for the friar; and he arranged for a number of Indians, who also knew most of the road, to accompany Marcos in the capacity of porters, servants, and interpreters. Some of these were Indians who had accompanied the Cabeza de Vaca quartet southward nearly three years before. They knew Estévan and, since they had learned Spanish in the interim, were able to serve as interpreters. Altogether, the friar was furnished with a quite impressive retinue, and he himself chose as a personal companion a fellow friar named Honoratus.

Marcos and Estévan were conducted by Francisco Vázquez de Coronado[13] to San Miguel de Culiacán—then still a lone outpost three hundred miles north of any other Spanish settlement—and on the way, at Guadalajara (then known as Tonalá), Coronado delivered to Marcos the viceroy's written instructions. My translation of these instructions, and of the friar's formal acknowledgment, follows.

DON ANTONIO DE MENDOZA

Instructions of Viceroy Mendoza

FIRST: as soon as you arrive at the province of Culiacán, you shall exhort and encourage the Spaniards who reside in the *villa* of San Miguel, to treat well the Indians that are at peace, and not to employ them for heavy or prolonged labor, assuring them [the Spaniards] that if they comply, they shall have favors and remuneration from His Majesty for the hardships they there have undergone and in me they will have a zealous advocate; but if they do the contrary, they shall be punished and regarded with displeasure.

You shall give the Indians to understand that I send you in the name of His Majesty, to see that they be treated well, and that they may know that he grieves because of the injuries and wrongs which they have suffered,[14] and that henceforth they shall be well treated, and those who do them evil will be punished.

Likewise, you shall assure them that they no more will be made slaves, nor removed from their lands, but that they will be left free thereon, without hurt or damage; and that they should lose their fear and recognize God, Our Lord, who is in heaven, and the Emperor, who is placed by Him on the earth, to rule and govern it.

And since Francisco Vázquez de Coronado, whom His Majesty has appointed as governor of that province [New Galicia],[15] will go with you as far as the *villa* of San Miguel de Culiacán, advise me how he manages the affairs of that town in that which concerns the service of God, Our Lord, and in the conversion and good treatment of the natives of that province.

And if, with the aid of God, Our Lord, and the grace of the Holy Spirit, you shall find a route to go farther on and to enter the country beyond, you shall take with you Estévan Dorantes, as a guide, whom I order to obey in all and by all that you command him, as he would

[9]

myself; and if he does not do so, he shall incur jeopardy and the penalties which befall those who do not obey the persons who have authority from His Majesty to command them.

Also, the said governor, Francisco Vázquez, took with him the Indians who came with Dorantes,[16] and some others that it has been possible to recover from those parts, in order that, if to him and to both of you it may seem advisable that you take some [of them] in your company, you shall do so and may employ them as you see is suitable to the service of Our Lord.

You shall always arrange to travel as securely as may be possible; and inform yourself in advance if the Indians are at peace or if some are at war with others, that you give them no occasion to commit any violence upon your person, which would be cause for proceeding against them and administering punishment, and thus, instead of doing them good, it would be to the contrary.

You shall take much care to observe the people who are there,[17] if they be many or few, and if they are scattered or live in communities; [note] the quality and fertility [of the soil], the temperature[18] of the country, the trees and plants and domestic and feral animals which may be there, the nature of the ground, whether rough or level; the rivers, if they are large or small, and the minerals and metals which are there; and of the things of which you may be able to send or bring specimens, bring them or send them, in order that His Majesty may be advised of everything.

Inquire always for information about the coast of the sea, that of the North as well as that of the South,[19] because the land may become constricted and in the country beyond some arm of the sea may enter the land beyond. And if you come to the coast of the South Sea, on the points that enter the water[20] bury, at the foot of some prominent tree outstanding for size, letters concerning what may appear to you noteworthy, and on such tree whereunder is placed the letter, make a cross so that it may be discerned. Likewise, on the largest trees at the mouths of rivers and in situations suitable for harbors, make the same sign of the cross and leave letters, because, if we send ships, they will go advised to look for this sign.

You shall arrange to send information by Indians, telling very particularly how you fare and are received, and what you find.

And if God, Our Lord, is so served that you find some large settlement, where it appears to you there is a good situation to establish a monastery[21] and to send friars to undertake the conversion, you shall send information by Indians or return yourself to Culiacán. Send such information with all secrecy, in order that whatever is necessary can be done without commotion, because in bringing peace to the country which may be found, we look to the service of Our Lord and the good of the inhabitants.

And although all the land belongs to the Emperor, our Lord, you, in my name, shall take possession of it for His Majesty, and you shall execute the signs and the acts of possession that appear to you to be required for such case, and you shall give the natives to understand that there is a God in heaven and the Emperor on the earth to command and govern it, to whom all have to be subjected and to serve.

Don Antonio de Mendoza

··Certification of Fr. Marcos de Niza··

I, FRAY MARCOS DE NIZA, *of the order of Saint Francis, affirm that I received a copy of these instructions,[22] signed by the most illustrious lord, Don Antonio de Mendoza, viceroy and governor of New Spain, the which were delivered to me, by order of His Excellency and in his name, by Francisco Vázquez de Coronado, governor of this New Galicia, which copy is being taken from those instructions de verbo ad verbum,[23] and with them compared and corrected; which instructions I promise faithfully to fulfil, and neither go against nor exceed them in anything therein contained, now or at any time; and as I thus will obey and fulfil them, I sign hereto my name, the 20th day of November of the year 1538, in Tonalá, which is in the province of New Galicia, where were given and delivered to me the said instructions in the said name.*

Fray Marcos de Niza

Two and a half months elapsed, however, before everything was ready. I find no mention of the cause of the delay: it may have been due to the tardy receipt of some of the supplies, or the nonarrival of some of the Indians who were to accompany Marcos. Possibly warmer weather was awaited, for while February at Culiacán is quite balmy, it may have been feared that winter still held on in regions to the north.

In the meantime, in February, Marcos and Estévan made a short preliminary trip eastward from Culiacán to an Indian village called Topira (on the site of modern Topia), returning to Culiacán about the first of March. The stage was now all set for the revelation to the world of the mystic Seven Cities that for three centuries had intrigued the imaginations of men. Early in March Marcos bade goodbye to civilization and, with his entourage, started northward, backtracking the route that Estévan had followed southward three years before.

Thereafter nothing was seen or learned of Marcos until, about three and a half months later, he appeared at Compostela (the first settlement south of Culiacán), traveling alone, and with a wonderful story to tell of what he had seen and heard. Shortly thereafter, he presented a written account of his journey, prepared after his arrival at Compostela. This narrative appears to have been written from memory, for he made no mention of having kept a journal during his travels, although he had carried writing materials.

I now yield the floor to Marcos, and in what follows permit him to tell his own story of his journey.[24]

NARRATIVE OF FRAY MARCOS

FRAY MARCOS DE NIZA

·•Narrative of Fray Marcos·•

WITH THE AID AND PROTECTION of the Most Holy Virgin Mary, Our Lady, and of the Seráfico,[25] our father Saint Francis, I, Fray Marcos de Niza, a professed friar of the order of Saint Francis, in compliance with the instructions above contained,[26] from the Illustrious Lord Don Antonio de Mendoza, viceroy and governor for His Majesty of New Spain, departed from the *villa* of San Miguel,[27] in the province of Culiacán, Friday, the seventh day of March,[28] year of one thousand five hundred and thirty nine, taking with me as companion the Father Friar Honoratus, and also taking with me Estévan de Dorantes, a black,[29] and certain Indians of those which the said Lord Viceroy liberated and purchased for this purpose, the which were brought to me by Francisco Vázquez de Coronado, governor of New Galicia, and with many other Indians from Petatlán and from the town that is called Cuchillo,[30] that would be fifty leagues[31] from the said *villa* [of San Miguel]. These came to the valley of Culiacán showing great joy, because it had been proclaimed that the Indians are free men, the said governor having previously sent word to them to inform them of their liberty, and to assure them that they would not be made slaves nor warred upon nor mistreated, telling them that this was the will and command of His Majesty.[32] And with the company that I have said, I took my way toward the town of Petatlán, receiving on the way many hospitalities and presents of food, roses and other things of this sort, and huts that they built for me of mats and brush in

[15]

those districts where were no people.[33] In this town of Petatlán
I rested three days, because my companion, Fray Honoratus,
was seized with illness, and I found it advisable to leave him
there. So, conforming to the said instructions, I pursued my
journey, wherein I was guided by the Holy Spirit, though I was
unworthy. And with me went the said Estévan de Dorantes, the
black, and some of the freed Indians and many people of the
region, arranging for me, in all places that I reached, much
hospitality and celebrations and triumphal arches. They gave
me of the food they had, though it was little because they said
they had three years without rain, and because the Indians of
that region think more of hiding themselves than of planting
crops, through fear of the Christians of the *villa* of San Miguel,
who until then had been accustomed to go there to make war
and slaves.[34] On all this road, which would be for twenty-five
or thirty leagues [after leaving Petatlán[35]] I saw nothing worthy
of being placed herein, except that to me came Indians from
the island that had been visited by the Marqués del Valle;[36]
these informed me that it was an island and not, as some would
say, the mainland; and I saw that they passed to the mainland,
and from the mainland back to the island, on rafts. The distance from the island to the mainland may be half a sea league,
a little more or less.

Also, there came to see me Indians of another island,
larger than the first one, and farther away; from these Indians
I received information of thirty other, small, islands occupied
by people having little food, except two which they said had
maize. These Indians wore, hanging from their necks, many
shells of the kind that contain pearls. I showed them a pearl
that I carried as a specimen, and they told me that such were
found in the islands, but I saw none of them.[37]

I pursued my way through a *despoblado*[38] for four days, Indians from the islands I mentioned as well as from the towns that I have passed, going with me, and at the end of the *despoblado*[39] I reached other Indians who marveled at seeing me, as they had no knowledge of Christians,[40] because they have no dealings with those below the *despoblado*. These Indians gave me many receptions and much food, and they tried to touch my robe, calling me *Sayota*, which would be to say, in their language, "man from Heaven." Through my interpreters,[41] I made them understand, the best I could, the tenor of my instructions, which is [to impart to them] the knowledge of Our Lord in Heaven and of His Majesty on the earth. And always, by every means I had, I sought information of a country of numerous settlements and of people more enlightened than those which I had encountered; but I learned nothing more than that, as they told me, the country beyond [inland], four or five *jornadas*[42] from where the ranges of mountains ended, contained an extensive and level valley[43] wherein they said were many and very large settlements, wherein were people possessing cotton garments. Showing them some metals that I carried in order to learn of the metals of the country, they took the piece of gold and told me that they had vessels of that metal among the people of the valley, and that there they wore, hanging from their ears and noses, certain round ornaments of gold, and that they had some small golden plates (*paletillas*) with which they scrape themselves to remove their sweat. But as this tract is away from the coast [i.e., inland] and my instructions are not to depart farther from it, I decided to leave it [the valley] until my return, because then I would be able to see it better (or, "see more of it"). And so I went on three days through country inhabited by the same tribe,[44] by whom I was received the same as by those before. I then came to a fair-sized settlement that they called Vacapa, where they made me a great reception and gave me much food, of which they had an abundance because their land is irrigated.[45] From this settlement to the sea [the coast of the Gulf of California] is forty leagues, and as I found myself so far removed from the sea, and as it was two days before Passion Sunday, I decided to stay there until Easter, in order to learn more about the islands of which I said, above, I had been told. So I sent Indian messengers by three routes to the sea, charging them to bring me people from the coast and from some of those islands, that I might inform myself of them. On another route I sent Estévan de Dorantes, the black, whom I instructed to follow to the north for fifty or sixty leagues, to see if by that route he would be able to learn of any great thing such as we sought; and I agreed with him that if he received any information of a rich, peopled land, that was something great, he should not go farther, but that he return in person or send me Indians with this signal, which we arranged: that if the thing was of moderate importance, he send me a white cross the size of a hand; if it was something great he send me one of two hands; and if it was something bigger and better than New Spain, he send me a large cross.[46]

And so the said Estévan, the black, departed from me on Passion Sunday after dinner (or, "after eating"), while I stayed on in this settlement which, as I say, is called Vacapa. And after four days there came messengers from Estévan with a very large cross, of the height of a man, and they told me on the part of Estévan that I should at once ("on the hour") depart and follow him, because he had reached people who gave him information of the greatest thing in the world; and that he had found Indians who had been there, of whom he was sending me one.

This Indian told me so many wonderful things of the land that I forebore to credit him until I should have seen them or have more information of the place. He told me that it was thirty *jornadas* from the place where he had left Estévan to the first city of that country, which city he said was called Cíbola.[47] And as it appears to me worth placing in this paper that which this Indian, whom Estévan sent me, said of the country, I will do so. He affirmed and said that in that province were seven very great cities, all under one lord; that the houses, of stone and lime, were large, the smallest being of one story with a terrace above, and others of two and three stories, and that of the lord had four, all joined under his rule, and in the porches (*portadas*) of the main houses were worked many designs of turquoises, of which, he said, there was a great abundance, and that the people of those cities went very well clothed. Many other particulars he told me of these seven cities, as well as of other provinces farther away, each of which, he said, was much greater than the seven cities; and in order to comprehend it as he knew it, I asked him many questions, and I found him to be of very good intelligence.

I gave thanks to Our Lord, but deferred my departure in pursuit of Estévan de Dorantes, believing he would await me as I had arranged with him, and also because I had promised the messengers whom I had sent to the sea that I would await them; for I proposed always to treat truthfully the people with whom I dealt. The messengers arrived on Easter Sunday, and with them were people from the coast and from the islands which, as I said before, are poor in food, though populated. These wore shells on their foreheads and said that such contain pearls. They informed me that there were thirty-four islands, near to each other, whose names I place in another paper,[48] wherein I give the names of the islands and settlements. The people of the coast say they have as little food as those of the islands, and that they trade among themselves by means of rafts. They say that the coast goes almost directly to the north. These Indians of the coast brought me shields of cowhide, very well made, so large that they cover them from feet to head, with some holes above the handle in order to be able to see from behind them: they are so thick (or "strong") that I believe a crossbow arrow would not pass through them.

This day there came to me three Indians, of those that are called *Pintados*,[49] their faces, chests and arms all decorated; these are in a district to the east and they border on a people who are next to the seven cities.[50] They told me that having heard of me, they had come to see me, and, among other things, they gave me much information concerning the seven cities and the provinces that Estévan's Indian had told me of, in the same manner that Estévan's told me. And so I sent back the people of the coast; and two Indians of the islands said they wished to go with me seven or eight days. And with them and with the three *Pintados* that I mentioned, I left Vacapa the second day of Easter[51] by way of the road that Estévan had followed, from whom I had received other messengers, with another cross the size of the first one he sent, urging me to hurry, and declaring that the land we sought was the best and greatest thing of which he ever had heard. Those same messengers told me in detail, without differing on any point, that which the first one had told me, except that they told me much more and gave me a clearer description.

And so I traveled that day, the second day of Easter, and two other days, traveling the same *jornadas* as had Estévan, at the end of which I reached the people who had given him information of the seven cities and of the country farther away, the which told me that from there it was thirty *jornadas* to the city of Cíbola, which is the first of the seven, and I had the account not only from one, but from many: and very particularly they told me of the grandeur of the houses and the style of them, just as the first one had. They told me that beyond these seven cities are other kingdoms that they call Marata and Ácus and Totonteac. I wished to know for what they went so far from their homes, and they told me that they went for turquoises and for cowhides and other things; and of both they had a quantity in that town. I also wished to know what they exchanged for what they obtained, and they told me, with sweat and with the service of their bodies; that they went to the first city, which is called Cíbola, and there served by digging in the ground and in other labor, and that [in payment] they were given cowhides, which they had there, and turquoises. All the people of this town wear fine and beautiful turquoises hanging from their ears and from their noses, and they say that these [turquoises] are worked into the principal doorways (*portales*) of Cíbola.

They told me that the form of clothing of the people of Cíbola is a cotton shirt reaching to the instep of the foot, with a button at the throat and a large tassel that hangs from it; the sleeves of the shirt being of the same width above as below: to me it appeared like the Bohemian [gipsy] dress. They say that they go girt with belts of turquoises, and that over these they wear the shirts: some wear very good blankets (*mantas*) and others cowhides,[52] very well processed, which they hold to be the better clothing and of which that country, they say, has a very great quantity. The women, likewise, go clothed and covered to the feet in the same manner. These Indians received me very well, and took great care to learn the day I left Vacapa,[53] so as to take food and shelter for me on the road. They brought me their sick, that I might cure them,[54] and tried to touch my robe. I recited the Gospel over them. They gave me some cowhides so well tanned and dressed that they appeared to be the work of men of much culture, and they said that all these had come from Cíbola.[55]

Next day I continued my journey, taking with me the *Pintados*, who did not want to remain behind. I reached another settlement where I was very well received by its people, who tried to touch my robe, and they informed me of the land which was my destination, as particularly as I had been told before, and they told me how people from that village had gone four or five *jornadas* with Estévan Dorantes. Here I came upon a large cross erected by Estévan to indicate that the news of the good country always increases, and he left word for me to hurry on and that he would await me at the end of the next *despoblado*. Here I erected two crosses and took possession, in compliance with instructions, because it appeared to me that this was a better land than that which I had passed,[56] and so it was proper to perform there the acts of possession. And after this manner I continued for five days, always finding well-populated settlements where I was received with great hospitality and receptions and where I found many turquoises and cowhides, and the same report of the country. They all spoke to me of Cíbola and that province as people who knew that I was going in search of it and they told me how Estévan had preceded me; and from him I there received messengers who were natives of that town, and who had gone some distance with him; and always he overloaded my hand (*cargándome la mano*)[57] in speaking of the grandeur of the land and urged me to make haste.

Here I learned that after two more *jornadas* I would reach a *despoblado* of four *jornadas* extent, in which there was no food more than was provided by making me shelters and carrying food: I went on, expecting to meet Estévan, because he had sent to tell me that he would await me. Before reaching the *despoblado*, I came to a fresh, cool town,[58] irrigated, where came to meet me a considerable number of people, men and women, clothed in cotton [garments] and some covered with cowhides which in general they hold to be better garments than those of cotton. All in this town wear *encaconados*[59] of turquoises which they hang from their noses and ears, and which they call *cacona*. Among them came the lord of that town and his two brothers (or "two of his brothers") very well clothed in cotton and *encaconados*, and each with necklaces of turquoises on his neck, and they brought me much meat of deer, coneys[60] and quails, and maize and meal, all in great abundance. They offered me many turquoises and cowhides and very handsome bowls and other things, of which I took nothing, for such has been my custom ever since I entered country wherein they have no knowledge of us. Here I had the same account as before of the seven cities and the kingdoms and provinces. I was dressed in a habit of dark woolen cloth of the kind known as Saragossa, which was given to me by Francisco Vázquez de Coronado, governor of New Galicia, and the lord of this town and other Indians touched the habit with their hands and told me that there was a great deal of that material in Totonteac, and that the natives in that place were clothed with it. At this I laughed and declared that it could not be so; that the blankets that those people wore were made of cotton; and they replied, "Think you that we know not that what you wear and what we wear is different? Know that in Cíbola all the houses are full of this cloth that we wear, but in Totonteac they have some small animals from which they take the fiber with which they make cloth like yours." I was surprised, because I had not heard of any such thing before arriving here. I desired to inform myself very particularly of it, and they told me that the animals are of the size of the two Castilian greyhounds that Estévan had with him: they said they had many of them in Totonteac, but I could not learn what genus of animals they were.[61]

The next day I entered the *despoblado*,[62] and where I had to go to dine, I found huts and sufficient food, near an *arroyo*; and at night I found huts and similar food again; and so it was for the four days that I continued through the *despoblado*. At the end of them [the four days] I entered into a valley very well occupied by people, where in the first town[63] there came to me many men and women with food. They all wore many turquoises that they hung from their noses and ears, and some wore necklaces of turquoises like those which I said were worn by the chief and his brothers of the town on the other side of the *despoblado*, except that those wore only one loop (*vuelta*) while these wore three and four, and had very good blankets (*mantas*) and cowhides: the women were similarly dressed, with turquoises on their noses and ears and very good skirts (*naguas*) and blouses (*camisas*).[64] They had as much knowledge of Cíbola as in New Spain they have of Mexico or in Perú of Cuzco. They particularly described the style of the houses and of the city and its streets and plazas, like people who had been there many times. They wore handsome articles that they had obtained from there through their services, like those before. I told them that it was not possible that the houses were of the style that they described to me, and to make me understand, they took soil and ashes and mixed them with water, and showed me how they placed the stones and how the edifice was built up, placing stones and mortar until it reached the required elevation. I asked them if the men of that country had wings to mount these stories;[65] they laughed and explained to me the ladder as well as I could explain it, and they took a stick and placed it over their heads and said that that was the height, story to story. Also, I was given an account of the woolen cloth of Totonteac, where they said the houses are like those of Cíbola, but better and many more, and that the place was very great and had no end.

Here I learned that the coast turns to the west very strongly (or "very abruptly") though until I entered the first *despoblado* that I passed, the coast ran always to the north. As a change in the direction of the coast was a matter of importance, I wished to learn of it, and so I went to view it, and saw clearly that, in latitude thirty-five degrees, it turns to the west; with which I was no less gratified than with the good news that I had of the country [ahead].

And so I returned to continue my journey, and was in that valley five days. It is well populated with splendid people, and so well provided with food that it would suffice to feed more than three hundred of horse;[66] it is all irrigated and is like a garden; there are compact villages[67] to every half league and quarter of a league.[68] In each town I had a very long account of Cíbola, and they spoke so particularly to me of it, like people who went there each year to gain their livelihood.

Here I found a man, a native of Cíbola, who told me he had fled from the person whom the lord had placed there in Cíbola,[69] for the lord of these seven cities lives and has his home in one of them that they call Ahacus, and in the others he has placed persons who rule for him. This native of Cíbola is a man of good disposition, somewhat aged and much better informed than the natives of this valley and those before. He told me that he wished to go with me in order that I might obtain his pardon. He informed me particularly of it, and told me that Cíbola is a large city, that it has many people and streets and plazas, and that in some parts of the city there are some very large houses that have ten stories, and that in these the chiefs assemble on certain days of the year. He said the houses are of stone and lime, in the form that I was told of by those before, and that the porches and fronts of the principal houses are of turquoises. He told me that the other seven[70] were of the style of this city [Cíbola] but some were larger, and that the most important one is Ahacus. He said that to the southeast is a kingdom that they call Marata, which used to have very many large settlements; that all have these houses of stone and stories, and that those [towns] were and still are at war with the lord of the seven cities, through which war this kingdom of Marata is greatly reduced in numbers, but still is on top and continues the war with the others. And he also told me that, to the southeast, is a kingdom that they call Totonteac,[71] which he said is the biggest in the world and with the most people and riches; and that they dress in clothing of that from which is made this that I wear, and other more delicate material which they pull from the animals that previously had been described to me; and that the people had much culture and were different from those that I thus far have seen. Also, he said that there is another very large province and kingdom that they call Ácus, because there are Ahacus and Ahacus;[72] with the aspiration it is one of the seven cities, the most important one, and without the aspiration, Ácus, is a kingdom and province in itself. He told me that the garments that they have in Cíbola are of the style that I had been told of before; he said the people of that city sleep in beds high above the floor, with bed clothing (*ropas*) and with canopies (or, "awnings") over the beds. He told me that he would go with me to Cíbola and beyond, if I wished to take him along. I was given the same account in this town by many other persons, but not in such detail.

I traveled in this valley three days,[73] the natives preparing for me all the feasts and rejoicings that they could. Here in this valley I saw more than two thousand cowhides,[74] extremely well processed. I saw a much larger quantity of turquoises and turquoise necklaces, in this valley, than in all [the country] I had passed before; and they said that all these came from the city of Cíbola, of which they have as much knowledge as do I of what I hold in my hands; and they have the same knowledge of the kingdoms of Marata and of Acus and of Totonteac.

Here in this valley they brought me a hide, half as large again as that of a large cow, and they told me it was from an animal which has only one horn on the forehead, and that this horn is curved toward the chest, and that from there it turns out in a straight point which, they say, has so much strength that nothing, no matter how hard, would fail to break if struck by it. They said that there were many of these animals in that [other] country: the color of the hide is like that of a goat and the hair is as long as the finger.[75]

Here I received messengers from Estévan,[76] who told me on his part that he had already entered the last *despoblado*,[77] and was very happy, because he was going more assured of the grandeur of the country; and he sent to me to tell me that, since he separated from me, he had never caught the Indians in any lie, and that until there [i.e., up to that time] everything had been found as they said it would be, and so he anticipated finding the rest. And I also hold this for certain, because it is true that, from the day I first learned of Cíbola, the Indians told me of all that until today I have seen, telling me always the towns that I would find along the way and the numbers of them, and, in districts where there were no people, telling me where I would have to eat and sleep, without having erred on one point. Having traveled, from where I first had news of the land until today, one hundred and twelve leagues, it seems to me not inappropriate to record the great truthfulness of these people.

Here in this valley, as in the other towns I passed, I placed crosses and performed the acts of possession that were proper, conforming to the instructions. The natives of this *villa*[78] asked me to rest myself with them for three or four days, because there was the *despoblado* four *jornadas* from there, and from the beginning of it until arriving at Cíbola made fifteen long days of travel; and they wished to prepare food and to dress themselves properly for it. And they told me that more than three hundred men had gone from there with Estévan, the black, to accompany him and carry his food, and many wished also to go with me, to serve me and because they expected to return rich men. I acknowledged the favor and told them to prepare quickly, because with my desire to see Cíbola, each day seemed to me a year.

And so I remained three days without going forward, during which I continually informed myself of Cíbola and of all the other places, and I did nothing but take Indians apart and question them, each one by himself, and all agreed in their accounts, and told me about the great number of the people and the arrangement of the streets and the grandeur of the houses and the style of the porches, just as those before had told me.

After the three days had passed, many people assembled to go with me; from these I chose thirty chiefs, very well dressed with their necklaces of turquoises, some of them having five or six loops; and with these I took the people necessary to carry the food for them and for me, and was ready for the road.

For my *jornadas*,[79] I entered the *despoblado* the ninth of May, and thus we went: on the first day, by way of a very wide and much-used road, we arrived for dinner at a spring (*agua*) where the Indians had erected a sign for me; and, to sleep, at another spring where I found a hut which they had made for me, and another built for Estévan to sleep in when he passed this way, and old huts and many signs of fire, made by people who passed to Cíbola over this road. And in this way I traveled twelve days, always well supplied with food of deer, hares,[80] and partridges, of the same color and flavor as those of Spain, although not so large but a little smaller.

At this point[81] there arrived an Indian—the son of a chief among those who had gone in the company of Estevan, the black;—he was fatigued, his face and body covered with sweat. He showed profound grief in his person, and he told me that at one *jornada* before reaching Cíbola, Estévan sent messengers [ahead] with his calabash, as he was accustomed to send notice ahead so that they might know he was coming.[82] The calabash[83] carried some rows of cascabels and two feathers, one white and the other red. When they arrived at Cíbola, before the ruler that the lord [of the seven cities] had placed there, and gave him the calabash, he, as soon as he took it and saw the cascabels, with much wrath and anger flung the calabash to the ground and told the messengers to be gone immediately, saying that he knew what people those were; that they [the messengers] should tell them not to enter the city; otherwise all would be killed. The messengers returned and told Estévan what had passed; he told them that was nothing, that those who exhibited irritation received him the better; and so he pursued his way until he reached the city of Cíbola, where he found that the people would not consent for him to enter within. They placed him in a large house that was outside the city, and presently took from him all that he carried, his trade-articles and the turquoises and other things that he had received along the road from the Indians. There he was that night, without their giving anything to eat or to drink to him or to those who were with him. The next day in the morning this Indian was thirsty and left the house to drink from a stream (*río*) that was nearby. From there, a moment later, he saw Estévan running away, and after him followed the people of the city, and they killed some of those who were with him; and when he saw this, this Indian retreated, under cover, up the stream and then crossed over to reach the road of the *despoblado*.

With this news, some of the Indians who were with me began to weep. With the evil tidings, I feared I would be lost, and I feared not so much to lose my life as not to be able to return to give information of the greatness of the country, where God, Our Lord, could be so well served and his holy faith exalted, and the royal patrimony of His Majesty augmented. But with all this, I consoled them the best that I could, and told them they ought not to give entire credit to that Indian; but they, with many tears, told me that the Indian had told nothing that he had not seen. So I withdrew from the Indians to commend myself to Our Lord and to supplicate him to guide this matter as might best serve Him, and to enlighten my heart. This done, I returned to the Indians and with a knife cut the ropes of the bundles of clothing and trade-articles that I carried, which until then I had not opened nor given anything to anyone, and distributed that which I carried among all the chiefs, and told them not to fear and that they should go along with me; and so they did.

Upon resuming our journey, one *jornada* from Cíbola, we met two other Indians of those who had gone with Estévan; they arrived covered with blood and with many wounds, and at their arrival they and those that were with me began such a weeping that from compassion and fear they made me cry also, and there was so much outcry ("so many voices") that I was not able to inquire of them about Estévan, or of what they had suffered. I entreated them to be silent that we might learn what had happened, and they replied, "How can we be silent, since we know that of our fathers, sons and brothers, of those who were with Estévan, more than three hundred are dead? And we dare no more to go to Cíbola, as [we were] accustomed." Nevertheless, I tried to pacify them the best I could, and rid them of fear, although I was not without need of some one to rid me of it. I asked the Indians who were wounded about Estévan and what had happened. They remained a while without speaking a word to me, weeping with those of their towns. Finally, they told me that when Estévan arrived at one *jornada* from the city of Cíbola, he sent his messengers with his calabash to Cíbola, to the lord, to make it known to them that he was coming to make peace [i.e., in peace] and to cure them. When they gave him the calabash and he saw the cascabels, he angrily threw the calabash to the ground and said: "I know these people, for these cascabels are not of the fashion of ours; tell them to turn back at once; if not, no man of them will remain [alive]," and thus he remained much enraged. And the messengers returned, but feared to tell

Estévan of what had happened; however, they [finally] told him, and he told them that they should have no fear; that he wished to go there, because, although they had answered him badly, they would receive him well. So he went on and arrived at the city of Cíbola just before the setting of the sun, with all the people who went with him, which would be more than three hundred men, not counting the many women; and they [the Cíbolans] would not consent for him to enter the city, but [put them] into a large house with good apartments that was outside the city, and they presently took from Estévan all that he carried, telling him that the lord so ordered, and "in all that night they gave us nothing to eat or to drink. The next day, when the sun was a lance-length high,[84] Estévan went from the house and some of the chiefs with him, and at once there came many people from the city and, when he saw them, he began to flee and we with him. Immediately they gave us these arrow-strokes and gashes and we fell, and upon us fell some dead men. And so we remained until night, without daring to move. We heard loud voices in the city, and on the terraces we saw many men and women watching. We saw no more of Estévan, but we believe that they shot him with arrows as they did the rest who were with him, of whom there escaped none but us."

In view of what the Indians told, and the bad prospects for continuing my journey as I wished, I could not but sense their loss and mine, and God is witness of how much I wished to have some one of whom to beg counsel and assistance, for I confess that it seemed to me I was at fault. I told them that Our Lord would punish Cíbola and that when the Emperor learned what had happened he would send many Christians to chastise them; but they did not believe me, because they say that none can withstand the might of Cíbola. I begged that they be comforted and not weep, and I consoled them with the best words I could, the which would be too long to place here. And after telling them this, I then withdrew a stone's throw or two, to commend myself to God, therein tarrying an hour and a half; and when I returned to them, I found, crying, one of my Indians[85] who was called Mark, and whom I had brought from Mexico, and he told me, "Father, these people have plotted to kill you, because they say that through you and through Estévan their kinsfolk are dead, and that there will not remain, of them all, a man or woman who will not die" [i.e., if they continue on to Cíbola]. I proceeded to distribute among them what I still had of garments and trade-articles, to pacify them, and I told them to observe that if they killed me, they would do no evil to me, because I would die a Christian and would go to heaven, and that those who killed me would suffer for it, because the Christians would come in search for me and, against my will, kill all of them. With these and many other words that I spoke I appeased them somewhat, although they still felt great resentment because of the people that were killed. I asked that some of them should go with me to Cíbola, for to see if any other Indian had escaped and to learn anything new of Estévan, but I could do nothing with them. In the end, seeing me determined, two chiefs said that they would go with me. With these and my own Indians and interpreters, I pursued my journey until within sight of Cíbola, which is situated on a plain at the skirt of a round hill. It has the appearance of a very beautiful town,[86] the best that I have seen in these parts. The houses are of the fashion that the Indians had described to me, all of stone, with their stories and terraces, as it appeared to me from a hill where

I was able to view it. The city[87] is bigger than the city of Mexico. At times I was tempted to go to it, because I knew that I ventured only life, which I had offered to God the day I commenced the journey. At the end I feared [to do so], considering my danger and that, if I died, I would not be able to make a report of this country, which to me appears the greatest and best of the discoveries.[88] Saying to the chiefs who had come with me how beautiful Cíbola appeared to me, they told me that it was the least of the seven cities, and that Totonteac is much bigger and better than all the seven, and that it has so many houses and people that it has no end. Viewing the situation of the city, it appeared appropriate to me to call that country the new kingdom of Saint Francis; and there, with the aid of the Indians, I made a great heap of stones, and on top of it I placed a cross, small and light because I had not the equipment for making it larger, and I announced that I erected that cross and monument in the name of Don Antonio de Mendoza, viceroy of New Spain, for the Emperor, our lord, in token of possession, conforming to the instructions, which possession I proclaimed that I took of all the seven cities and of the kingdoms of Totonteac and of Acus and of Marata, and that I went not to them in order to return to give account of what I did and saw.

And so I returned, more satiated with fear than with food, and with the greatest haste I could went to overtake the people I had left behind. I overtook them after two days of travel and went with them until past the *despoblado*, where[89] they did not make me so good a reception as the first time,[90] because the men, as well as the women, made great lament for the people who were killed at Cíbola. And with fear I hurried immediately from the people of that valley,[91] and went ten leagues the first day, and then eight, and then ten leagues, without stopping until past the second *despoblado*.[92]

Returning, and still not rid of fear, I determined to approach the gorge where the mountain ranges ended, of which I said before I had information,[93] and there I had information that the valley was peopled many *jornadas* to the eastward, but I dared not enter it, because it appeared to me that we have to go to occupy and dominate that other country of the seven cities and the kingdoms that I spoke of; that then (or, "at that time") we could see it better, without placing my person in jeopardy, and leaving it in order to give an account of what I had seen. I saw only, from the mouth of the gorge, seven settlements of fair size, at some distance a valley farther below, very green and of very good land,[94] from which arose many smokes: I was informed that in it is much gold, and that the natives of it trade in vessels and jewels for the ears, and little plates with which they scrape themselves and remove the sweat, and that these people do not consent that those of the other part of the valley trade with them: they were unable to tell the reason for that. Here I placed two crosses and took possession of all the gorge and valley after the manner and ritual of the possessions above, conforming to the instructions.

From there I turned back to my journey, with all the haste I could, until I arrived at the *villa* of San Miguel, of the province of Culiacán, expecting to find there Francisco Vázquez de Coronado, governor of New Galicia, and as I did not find him, I continued my journey to the City of Compostela, where I found him. And from there I presently wrote of my arrival to the most illustrious lord, the viceroy of New Spain, and to our Father Friar Antonio de Ciudad-Rodrigo, Provincial, asking him to send me orders what to do.

I do not place here many details, because they have nothing to do with the case: I only tell what I saw and was told me of the countries where I went and of those of which I was given information, for to give it to our Father Provincial, so that he might show it to the Father of our Order, who may advise him, or to the Assembly[95] at whose command I went, that they give it to the Most Illustrious Lord, the Viceroy of New Spain, at whose request they sent me on this journey.

Fray Marcos de Niza, vice-commissary

·· Certification of the Minister Provincial ··

I, FRAY ANTONIO DE CIUDAD-RODRIGO, *friar of the order of the Minorites and Minister Provincial, for the time being, of the province of the Holy Evangel of this New Spain, affirm that it is true that I sent Fray* MARCOS DE NIZA, *priest, friar, presbyter and religious, and in all virtue and religion such that he was esteemed by me and my brethren of the governing deputies,[96] who take counsel in all things arduous and difficult, he was approved and held suitable and sufficient for making this journey and discovery because of the aforesaid sufficiency of his person [and] for being learned, not only in theology, but also in cosmography, in the art of the sea [navigation], and when it had been discussed and decided that he should go, he went with another companion, a lay brother who was called Fray Honoratus, by the command of the lord Don Antonio de Mendoza, viceroy of this said New Spain, and His Excellency gave him all the equipment and supplies that were needed for the said road and journey; and these instructions that here are written, the which I saw and which His Excellency communicated to me, asking me what I advised, and as they appeared good to me, were given to the said Fray Marcos by the hand of Francisco Vázquez de Coronado; the which he received willingly and executed faithfully, as in fact has appeared. And as that which is above is the truth and there is no falsehood in it, I have written this belief and testimony and signed it with my name. Dated in Mexico [City], the 26th day of August, in the year 1539.*

Fra. Antonio de Ciudad-Rodrigo, Minister Provincial

···Legalization of æNiza's Report···

IN THE GREAT CITY of *Temixtitán, Mexico,*[97] *of New Spain, on the second day of the month of September, in the year of the nativity of Our Lord Jesus Christ, one thousand five hundred and thirty nine, before the very illustrious lord, Don Antonio de Mendoza, viceroy and governor for His Majesty in this New Spain and president of the* Audiencia *and royal chancery, [and] who resides in this said city, and being present the very magnificent lords, the licentiate Francisco de Ceinos, Judge for His Majesty in the said royal* Audiencia, *and Francisco Vázquez de Coronado, governor for His Majesty in the province of New Galicia, and in the presence of us, Juan Baeza de Herrera, Chief Secretary of the said royal* Audiencia *and of the government of the said New Spain, and Antonio de Turcios, secretary to Their Majesties and of the said royal* Audiencia: *appeared the very reverend father, Fray Marcos de Niza, vice-commissary in these parts of the Indies of the Ocean Sea,*[98] *of the order of Saint Francis, and presented before their lordships and before us, the said secretaries and witnesses, the said writings, these instructions and Relation, signed with his name and sealed with the general seal of the Indies, the which have nine leaves with this in which go our signatures,*[99] *and he said and affirmed and certified to be true the contents of the said instructions and Relation, and that what is contained therein occurred, in order that His Majesty may be informed of the truth of that which therein is made mention. And their lordships ordered us, the said secretaries, that as it was presented and declared to be such, by the said vice-commissary, we attest the same at the foot thereof and that we declare it for the truth, signed with our signatures. Witnesses that were present: the above-named, and Alamaguez and Fray Martín de Ozocastro, friar of the same order.*

IN FAITH *of which I, the said Juan Baeza, the aforesaid secretary, affix here my seal as such, in testimony of truth.*

Juan Baeza de Herrera　　[Seal]

AND I, *the said Antonio de Turcios, aforesaid secretary, who was present at what here is said, affix here this, my seal, as such in testimony of truth.*

Antonio de Turcios　　[Seal]

[37]

ESTÉVAN DE DORANTES

··Analysis of the Narrative··

FOREWORD

IN my examination of the friar's narrative and journey, occasional references to the sequel—Coronado's expedition—will be unavoidable. Hence, I submit this brief preliminary sketch of that expedition as far as it is intimately connected with our subject.

Immediately upon the friar's return to Mexico with his account of what he had seen and heard, Viceroy Mendoza began action toward organizing a military *entrada*,[100] and placed his protégé, Coronado, in command. There was no lack of recruits, nearly all of whom furnished their own equipment, some of them mortgaging or selling all their property to that end.

In the meantime Captain Melchior Díaz, *Alcalde* of Culiacán, was sent northward with a small squad, in the autumn of 1539, to test Marcos' account. He got as far as the Gila River, where he was compelled by severe winter weather to turn back. As far as he went the natives along the way—perhaps the same Indians whom Marcos had interviewed—gave him a very unattractive picture of the "Cities of Cíbola," but an entirely truthful one. His report, however, was withheld from the men of Coronado's gathering forces.[101]

I may mention in passing that Mendoza had no authority for Coronado's expedition. Royal permission had been requested, but certainly was not received before the expedition started, and so far as I can learn was never received.

In February, 1540, the start was made from Compostela. There were about three hundred Spaniards and seven hundred Indian servants, together with a herd of livestock. Marcos was taken along, but not to serve as a guide.

Progress was so slow, because of the artillery and the herd of livestock taken along, that Culiacán was not reached until April. Leaving the main force there to follow later, Coronado with a picked force of eighty men pushed on, with Marcos in tow.

After a toilsome journey of about three more months, and with his men exhausted and short of food, Coronado reached the first of the "Cities of Cíbola"—the Zuñi pueblo of Hawikuh—and found it to be, not a magnificent city with gem-encrusted façades, but only a miserable little Indian pueblo. The Indians there, noting the small number and weakened condition of the Spaniards, put up a fight. They were speedily subdued, however, although they had been reinforced by warriors from the other pueblos. They possessed no gold or gems, but they did have a store of corn, which was a godsend to the famished Spaniards. The other Zuñi pueblos submitted without opposition, but all were equally poor. A small squad sent to the seven Moqui pueblos (Marata) found them to be no better than those of Cíbola.

Great was the rage of the soldiers against Marcos because of this grotesque anticlimax to their expectations. So bitter were the curses and anathemas hurled at him that Castañeda, a chronicler of the expedition, "prayed God to spare him from them." He was sent back in disgrace to New Spain: probably only his holy calling saved his life.

Further exploration showed Totonteac to be the pueblos of the Rio Grande drainage, but while numerous and in a better country than that of the Zuñi and Moqui tribes, they possessed no riches, and instead of being one "kingdom" were of five different linguistic groups.

About Coronado's subsequent search for the fabled golden Quivira we here have nothing to say, save that when in eastern Kansas he was so close to De Soto that he encountered Indians who had seen the latter.

In 1542 Coronado returned, crestfallen and disillusioned, to New Spain. He resumed his duties as governor of Nueva Galicia, but soon after was dismissed from the post. The charge against him was ostensibly misconduct of his office, but the real cause of his dismissal was his mistreatment of the Indians of New Mexico. The old friendship between him and Mendoza was disrupted, for Mendoza feared that the failure of his expedition to achieve any noteworthy results would bring down the displeasure of the Crown upon himself. It appears, however, that the viceroy succeeded in clearing himself.

The expedition destroyed for all time the romantic old myth of the Seven Cities. Thereafter, it was never revived. But for the one brief year the "Seven Cities of Cíbola" were talked of throughout the civilized world.

The "cities" were pitifully insignificant to have stirred up so much commotion and to have given rise to those gorgeous stories that even today intrigue the American school boy. The six of them—there were but six—would have no more than filled an ordinary city block, and any one of the larger pueblos to the east—Ácoma, Taos or Pecos—could have contained their combined populations with room to spare. The Zuñi tribe was in fact the most insignificant, numerically, of the half-dozen pueblo tribes.

In the order of their size, the "cities" were, in 1581, Hawikuh with 118 family quarters, Matsaki with 104, Kiakima with 75, Coaquina with 60,

Halona with 44, and Acana with 40. Matsaki is the Ahacus of Marcos' narrative.

With the single exception of Hawikuh, these are now mere jumbles of sand-mounded stones, unrecognizable as the remains of human habitations. Hawikuh, being on an elevation, has not been buried so thoroughly, and its ground plan is easily traceable. Somewhere at the base of its ridge rest the ashes of Estévan the Moor, who won fame by dying.

These pueblos were abandoned about two and a half centuries ago, when their people united and built the pueblo of Zuñi. That name, pronounced "Soon'-ye," is the name by which the cities of Cíbola were known to the Ácoma Indians. It was adopted by the Spaniards for the new pueblo, though the country thereabouts was known as Cíbola to the end of Spanish rule.

THE JOURNEY

It is conceded by all students that Marcos' "City of Cíbola" was the Zuñi pueblo of Hawikuh, as it is called today—the southwesternmost of the Zuñi group of six villages and the first one reached on the trail coming up from the San Pedro. That it was the one reached by Estévan and that he was killed there Coronado learned the following year.

Whether Fray Marcos actually saw that pueblo, or even entered New Mexico, is a question that has been revived and argued from time to time, neither side ever conceding defeat. Some prominent historians have declared in the friar's favor; others, equally competent, have flatly denied his claim. Those of his contemporaries best qualified to judge decided adversely and branded Marcos "The Lying Monk."

In recent years the question has been reopened by two well-known scholars.[102] In the past the subject has been of interest to the layman also, for it originally involved the question of what white man first set foot within Arizona and New Mexico, as well as that of whether the friar's narrative should be taken seriously by the historian. It appears, however, that as yet no student has had the time to make a really serious study of that account and test its accuracy throughout.

Until a few years ago I was of those who regarded the friar's claim as valid,[103] but I had merely accepted the verdicts of Bandelier, Bancroft and Winship; and beyond a single reading of Marcos' *Relación* some twenty-five years ago, I had not concerned myself with testing his pretensions. Since I knew, at that time, little of the country and nothing at all of the native peoples involved, and had then no acquaintance with the route that Marcos followed or with the factors that control foot travel on the primitive Indian trails, it was inevitable that I should overlook even the outstanding discrepancies in his narrative.

Other writers, defending that document, point to the "undeniable air of plausibility which permeates the *Relación*." It does carry an atmosphere of plausibility. But that I think is mainly due to the almost entire absence of figures: there is but one figure of speech in the entire story. Its author recites the most exciting things in a most prosaic way. But that was his style, and it argues neither for nor against the narrative's credibility.

That "air of plausibility" disappears from large portions of the story as one acquires acquaintance with what I call the "nondocumentary" evidence that we now have available. Some parts of the account we know are true; other parts have been proved false, and to the rest we have to attach the question mark, for when a document is proved false in part, the conscientious student must question everything therein that is not supported by other evidence. Thus we have to question most of what Marcos recorded from the time he left Culiacán, northbound, until he showed up at Compostela three and one-half months later.

Baldwin declared, in 1926, that "Fray Marcos de Niza (Friar Mark of Nice) was the first white man who *indisputably* set foot on the soil of New Mexico"[104] (italics his). That assertion always seemed to me rather rash in view of the fact that at the time Baldwin was writing the friar's claim had been flatly denied by several eminent students and branded as highly dubious by many others. Moreover, no claim is indisputable unless it stands *proved*, and the Marcos claim is supported by no evidence whatever save his own word.

Dr. Carl O. Sauer conclusively showed, in 1932,[105] that Cabeza de Vaca entered southwestern New Mexico and skirted the Colorado Plateau, and seven years later I demonstrated that he also crossed the Sacramento Mountains of that state.[106] So with regard to Marcos, now certainly stripped of the distinction of having been the first white man to enter either Arizona or New Mexico, the only question remaining to be answered is whether or not he fabricated parts of his narrative, including all that portion having to do with the last stage of his supposed journey to Cíbola.

The following discussion is mainly an examination, concurrently, of the friar's narrative and of the arguments that have been advanced in support of and against its veracity, together with some additional evidence, hitherto overlooked, that bears upon the question. I am not a professional historian, but during the last quarter-century I have acquired a thorough acquaintance with the topography and other details of the country through which the disputed portion of the friar's journey lay.

Familiarity with the pertinent historical documents is not of itself sufficient qualification for a competent analysis of the *Relación* of Fray Marcos, or, for that matter, of any of the journals and accounts of the sixteenth-century expeditions into our Southwest; and several otherwise well-qualified students have gone grievously astray in assuming that it is enough.[107] Acquaintance with the terrain, the streams and other watering places, the trail routes,[108] the flora and fauna, and the ethnic traits of the native peoples along the way is equally essential. Dr. Sauer mentions[109] a good illustrative case in the narrative of Cabeza de Vaca, where the latter, in speaking of the native village that he named Corazones, says "By it is the passageway to many tribes that are on the South Sea, and if those who seek passage should not enter through it, they will lose their way." That passage is unintelligible to most students, but to one acquainted with the long Ures gorge of the Sonora River, and the trail that leads through it, Cabeza de Vaca's statement is perfectly clear, and moreover enables one to identify the exact site of Corazones.

Also, one must have a sufficient understanding of the various handicaps that beset travelers in those days, if he wishes to *follow,* and not *lead,* those adventuring Spaniards on their way. One familiar only with the documentary evidence will almost surely lead them. Then it is necessary to know at what rate a pedestrian, as well as a mounted man, could travel on the trails that every one of the Spanish expeditions followed, under conditions existing in those days. This is especially important in the study of the journey of Fray Marcos.

Marcos made his journey on foot over unimproved Indian trails, and tramping the old trails of the Southwest is real work. I have covered hundreds of miles on them, afoot and mounted. Often the trail one follows is uphill and downhill in tiring repetition. The pathway as a rule is rough, sandy or filled with loose detritus that affords poor traction. Where minor streams are followed the trail crosses the water all too frequently—I know of one that crosses twenty-eight times in twenty-six miles[110]—so that the traveler has either to wade or to take a long, rough detour through rocky or brushy hills. By the time one has traveled fifteen miles under such conditions he has done a fair day's work, although he may have covered an air-line distance of no more than a dozen miles. I know from experience that after one has spent a week or so on the mountain trails of our Southwest, the feel of smooth, level ground underfoot and the knowledge of just where and when one's foot will land at every step afford a positively luxurious sensation that does not wear off for two or three days.

On a smooth, packed road, a well-seasoned walker can set a pace of twenty-five or thirty miles a day and keep it up. But I know of not one of the pioneer pedestrians who ever averaged as much as twenty miles a day for any long journey in this region: not even such sinewy men as Kino and Garcés, who were quite different from the aging Marcos. There were always delays due to illness and blistered feet, sprains and other injuries, rainstorms, snow, howling winds, dust storms, temperature extremes, flooded streams, etc. In the sixteenth century much additional time was lost in repairing clothing and equipment, seeking food and water, and inquiring about trail routes. Many trails bypassed some watering places because the terrain forbade the laying of a trail beside the water: this fact necessitated side trips. I here recall one eighty-five-mile stretch of trail along which only one of seven watering places (springs) was beside the road.[111] I know from my own observation and experience that for a tolerable pedestrian on a march of a week or more on the trails of the semiarid Southwest, even today an average of sixteen miles a day is fair going, twenty miles a very good pace, and twenty-four miles an exceptionally fast rate that I doubt could be maintained for a week under summertime conditions.[112]

On horseback travel is not much faster than afoot, for there are few places on an Indian trail where a horse can move faster than a walk without risk of breaking a leg, or his rider's neck.[113] Twenty-five miles a day is a good average for even a mountain-bred horse, and thirty miles is an excellent average. The best I ever did was twenty-six miles. That was on a trail that had been improved by the Forest Service, and there was no stop for lunch. None of the mounted Spanish *entradas* into our Southwest ever averaged over fifteen miles a day. Espejo's troop, well mounted with several horses to the man, averaged hardly fifteen miles a day on the comparatively easy Pecos Valley trail. Coronado, mounted and in moderate haste, consumed two and one-half months in covering three-fourths of the distance that Marcos claimed to have covered, on the same trail, in little over one month.

Indians could travel faster and farther than Europeans, and it is a mistake of large proportions to assume, as a majority of students have done, that the white man's *jornada* is equal to that of the Indian. The latter is a notoriously tireless walker, as was demonstrated so forcibly during Crook's campaign against the Apaches, when his Indian scouts were still fresh and unwearied after a forced march that prostrated the best athletes among his white troopers. Thirty miles a day is to be considered only a fair day's march for an Indian when traveling on a peaceful mission in his own affairs, and when in haste he can maintain a rate of better than fifty miles a day on his own trails. But it is to be noted that when he is employed by others his rate of travel is likely to be governed by selfish considerations, and may be anything from one mile to fifty miles a day.[114]

The route that Estévan followed, trailed by Marcos as far as the Sonora Valley—the "Road to Cíbola"—was followed as far as the Gila River by Melchior Díaz a few months later, and, a year later, for its full length, by Coronado. Three years before Marcos, it had been traveled from the Sonora Valley southward by the Cabeza de Vaca party, and even before that it had been covered by Spanish parties as far north as the Yaqui River. Eventually it became the *Camino Real* to the north."[5] Hence its general course is known, and it is possible to trace it in some detail.

In Bandelier's time, and indeed up to comparatively recent years, the friar's veracity has been impugned chiefly upon his gross misrepresentation of the "City of Cíbola." That was the most outstanding of his falsehoods, and the one most easily exposed. It remained for Dr. Sauer to raise the question of the man's ability to make the return trip from Cíbola within the time at his disposal.

But here we have to know, first of all, how far he would have had to travel; and so far as is known, only a portion of the trail he followed is still in use and practically unaltered. The roads that follow the general course of the friar's route can not be utilized here, for they have materially shortened the distance. The road-builder removes, cuts through, fills up, or bridges barriers and impediments that the original trail had of necessity to detour. All the help we get from the friar himself is the information that his course lay farther inland than the barren coastal belt, and that he traversed alternate occupied and unoccupied districts. As far as he traveled, he does not give us one identifiable point anywhere on or near his route: identifiable, that is, from his narrative alone. Nevertheless, I think we can trace his course in some detail with a measure of confidence.

First, from the Yaqui Valley on northward to the upper end of the Sonora Valley, the original trail still exists and is in use for nonvehicular travel to this day. So that part of the route can be charted exactly. Then from the Yaqui River back to the Mayo, we know that Marcos must have followed the Cedros and Chico valleys: there was no other way for him to go. Also, once he had reached the upper Sonora Valley, there was but the one route that he could have followed as far as the middle San Pedro Valley. So, from the Mayo River to the middle San Pedro, we can trace his actual course with certainty.

We are left with the 230-mile portion of his route, from Culiacán to the Rio Mayo, and the part from the middle San Pedro to Cíbola, a distance of about 275 miles.

As regards the first of these two uncertain stretches, we know only that Marcos crossed the Rio Fuerte a considerable distance from the coast. We get very little help from the *relaciónes* left by other users of that route. One can, however, trace the *most practicable route* between Culiacán and the Fuerte, and since every trail of which I have any definite knowledge invariably followed the most practicable course, I see no reason why the one that Marcos here traveled should have been the only exception to the rule. Hence, I have so charted it.

The other stretch, from the middle San Pedro to Cíbola, is complicated by the fact that from near the site of Cascabel there were two routes to the Gila, equally feasible. One of these followed the San Pedro to the Gila; the other skirted the Galiuro and Santa Teresa mountains, reaching the Gila about opposite the mouth of San Carlos Creek. From the Gila to Zuñi there were three practicable routes, all of about the same length.

The distances traveled by Marcos between different points on his route, as well as the total distance covered, remain to be ascertained as closely as possible, and I find the old Spanish estimates unsatisfactory. They are in too-round numbers, sometimes are contradictory, and often are obviously erroneous. They were based upon the assumption that a horse, carrying a mount, covers one league per hour: hence it is obvious that in rough country distances would be overestimated, while they were likely to be underestimated where the going was easy.

I here submit, for reference and comparison, three sets of estimated distances: (1) Spanish values, reduced to miles, allowing 3.1 miles to the league; (2) distances calculated for me by Mr. Lew Kennedy, an experienced cartographer of the U. S. Geological Survey, who has been over the ground; and (3) estimates made independently by myself, for which I charted the route on the most detailed topographic maps available.[116]

	(1)	(2)	(3)
Mexico City to Compostela	330	525	515
Compostela to Culiacán	310	305	310
Culiacán to Rio Fuerte	186	180	180
Rio Fuerte to Bacoachi	404	385	390
Bacoachi to Gila River	264	225	235
Gila River to Hawikuh	264	225	215
Totals, Compostela to Hawikuh	1427	1320	1330

The one Spanish estimate of the distance from Mexico City to Compostela is grossly erroneous, perhaps because of a typographical error. Spherical triangulation, I find, gives the "beeline" (air-line) distance as 388 miles, and the road was so vermicular that it must have been one-third greater than that. Sauer states the distance as "all of five hundred miles," and that is a conservative estimate. As illustrative of the difference in Spanish estimates, Castañeda makes the distance from Culiacán to Cíbola 300 leagues; the *Relación Postrera de Cívola* makes it "more than 300 leagues," and *Traslado de las Nuevas* makes it "350 long leagues." Yet these three authorities traveled the road together. Actually, the distance is very close to 330 leagues. I may add that Jaramillo makes it 300 leagues from Culiacán to the Gila River, which is about 70 leagues short of Cíbola. The *Relación del Suceso* makes it 150 leagues from Culiacán to Corazones, which is quite close to Castañeda's estimate of 150 leagues from Culiacán to the lower end of the Sonora Valley.

Distances from Bacoachi to the Gila, and from the Gila to Cíbola, as submitted by Coronado's men, are much too great, perhaps because the going was slow. Or maybe Coronado did not follow as direct a course as was practicable for pedestrians.

I submit here my calculations of a few additional distances that the reader might find helpful:

	Miles
Culiacán to Petatlán	65
Petatlán to Vacapa	115
Vacapa to the *despoblado* between the Yaqui and Sonora rivers	245
Distance across that *despoblado* by the route Marcos followed	60
The Sonora Valley	85
Despoblado between Sonora and San Pedro valleys	100
San Pedro Valley	135

In what follows, I shall use my own estimates. They are no more than close approximations, but cannot be sufficiently in error to invalidate any argument based upon them.

In discussing the friar's journey, I shall divide his outbound trip into three stages and deal with each stage separately, as nearly as may be practicable: (1) from Culiacán to Vacapa, (2) from Vacapa to a certain thickly-populated valley, and (3) from that valley to the man's farthest north. Students today are not agreed upon the terminal point of any one of these stages, and it is one of my aims definitely to pin each one down, if not to a certain spot, at least to a very limited area.

The trip from Culiacán to Vacapa was made in eleven days of travel, broken by a three-day rest at the Indian village of Petatlán, which was four-elevenths of the distance, in traveling time if not in miles, between the two terminal points.

The location of Vacapa is one of several points on the friar's route upon which students have not agreed. Bandelier[117] placed it at or near the present Matape, between the Yaqui and Sonora rivers and some 430 miles above the original site of Culiacán, and his followers seem inclined to insist upon that locality, although some have placed it even farther north.[118]

I am unable to accept Bandelier as sufficient authority on this question. He is said to have been well acquainted with Sonora, but his tracing of the route of Cabeza de Vaca betrays either carelessness or insufficient acquaintance with the region, for he entirely ignores the practicable trail routes, sends the man over impassable mountains and through deserts that even the Indians avoided, and misses the true site of Corazones by a wide margin. It appears probable, therefore, that he was mistaken as regards the true site of Vacapa. In fact, some twenty years later he confessed insufficient knowledge of the region.[119]

Moreover, his chronology is faulty. He has Marcos reaching Vacapa "about the middle of April," although the friar himself recorded that he reached that village *"dos días antes de la Domínica de Pasión"* —"two days before Passion Sunday"—and Passion Sunday, in 1539, was on March 23. Therefore he reached Vacapa on March 21. Bandelier's carelessness with his calendar here invalidates his whole argument, for while Marcos could easily have reached Matape by mid-April, he simply could not have done it by March 21. To arrive there on that date he would have had to travel thirty-nine or forty miles a day. The same objection lies against every proposed location for Vacapa above latitude 28°; the distance was too great to be covered by a pedestrian in eleven days.

Possibly Bandelier was influenced by the friar's statement that Vacapa was forty leagues from the sea. Matape does not fall far short of that, and no point on the route below the Rio Yaqui, except perhaps the place where Marcos crossed the Fuerte, was anything like that far from the coast. But how did Marcos know the distance? Neither he nor any other white man had ever traveled it. He had no means of estimating it except that the Indians he had sent to the coast were absent sixteen days. He may have credited them with five leagues per day, which was about his own rate. But there is no knowing at what rate they traveled on this assignment, or how many days they spent visiting with the coastal and insular people. As I have pointed out, an Indian, when employed by others, will travel leisurely unless he has some incentive to hurry. Marcos gave these Indians no reward; hence it is not probable that he had promised them any, and in that case they would have taken plenty of time, just as a child would do. They were Indians of the country and so not subject to his orders as were those of his escort. Besides, it looks suspicious that these Indians, sent by separate routes to different points on the coast, should all return at the same time. The three routes would have differed in length.

Or, again, it may be that Bandelier and others were misled into placing Vacapa too far north by the fact that Marcos' account permits him only four days between Culiacán and Petatlán, with the remaining seven days spent between Petatlán and Vacapa. If Petatlán was where most historians have placed it—on the site of modern Sinaloa—it would in fact have been about four-elevenths of the distance between Culiacán and Matape. Bandelier failed to note the astonishing speed that would have been required of Marcos.

I myself can not accept that location for Petatlán. I note that Bancroft also looks askance at it. Marcos would have had to travel at an impossibly fast rate—some thirty-two miles a day—to pass from Culiacán to Sinaloa in four days, but that appears a moderate pace in comparison with the rate of forty miles a day that he would have had to maintain between Sinaloa and Matape.

Samaniego, operating for Nuño de Guzmán, in 1531 reached what is believed to be the Sinaloa River, and found thereon a rather large village which he named Petatlán because the houses were built of reed mats. Two years later, Diego de Guzmán noted the same village, identifying it as Petatlán.

That sounds like satisfactory evidence. But Castañeda recorded[120] that Petatlán was twenty leagues (62 miles) above Culiacán, and Jaramillo[121] placed Petatlán four *jornadas* (60 or 65 miles) above Culiacán and three *jornadas* (45 or 50 miles) *below the Rio Sinaloa*. Both these men, with Coronado's expedition, passed over the route in 1540 and again in 1542, and were in a position to know. Moreover, their estimates are in practical agreement, and they place that village exactly where I would place it—near the present site of Mocorito—on the assumption that the friar traveled at a fairly uniform and reasonable rate between Culiacán and Vacapa.

There is a possibility that the village of Petatlán may have moved to the south between 1533 and 1539. Other Indian villages moved occasionally. Since six years elapsed between the visit of Diego de Guzmán and that of Marcos, while only one year elapsed between Marcos and Coronado, the testimony of Castañeda and Jaramillo is to be preferred over that of Samaniego and Guzmán.

If, however, the identification of Petatlán and Sinaloa be insisted upon, then Marcos, as well as Jaramillo and Castañeda, must have mistaken some other village for that one. Except for size, all the Indian towns in that region looked much alike: all used *petates* (mats) in the construction of their homes. And the natives thereabouts did not know the village by its Spanish name. They called it Moretia. Neither Marcos nor his fellow friar had ever seen it before. Probably they never had talked with anyone except Estévan who had seen it, and Estévan did not know its name. So, unless there was something other than the name and appearance of the town that would have enabled Marcos to identify it, he could easily have been mistaken.

Dr. Bloom, apparently in an effort to find more time for this stage of the friar's journey (Culiacán to Vacapa), cites a letter written by Coronado and dated from Culiacán March 8, 1539, wherein Coronado states that Marcos "proceeded farther inland on the seventh of last February."[122] Bloom argues from this that Marcos made a mistake of one month in the date of his start northward, and really set out on February 7 instead of on March 7 as he records. Given that additional month, Marcos could easily have reached Matape by the twenty-first of March.

But Coronado's letter had reference, not to the friar's start northward on his assigned mission, but to the short preliminary trip, already mentioned, that he and Estévan made in February to "Topira" (a village about seventy miles inland from Culiacán, on the site of modern Topia) from which they returned about a week before starting northward: a sort of warming-up jaunt, so to speak. In the same letter Coronado speaks of the preparations he was making to visit Topira and test the friar's report thereon.[123]

Dr. Carl O. Sauer, who is well acquainted with the region traversed by Marcos and with the ethnic features and history of the Indian tribes, places Vacapa near the Rio Fuerte, or "twenty-five to thirty [miles] southeast of Alamos,"[124] which would be about ninety-five miles from the coast by way of the river trail. There certainly was a native village called Vaca or Vacapa in that vicinity. I believe it was in the valley of the Fuerte, for Marcos says all the land thereabouts was irrigated. There were, however, other irrigated tracts between the Rio Fuerte and the Rio Mayo. To have reached the place in eleven days of travel from Culiacán would have required a rate of about sixteen miles a day; but since the trip was broken by a three-day rest at Petatlán and was the first stage of the journey, sixteen miles a day would not have been too much to expect of the old friar.

It will be remembered that at a village forty or fifty miles (three days' travel for Marcos) above Vacapa, the natives informed him that from there to Cíbola was a thirty-day journey (for them). Marcos was twice given this information, so it was probably correct. To Hawikuh from a point forty or fifty miles above the Rio Fuerte would have been a normal thirty-day march for Indians, but from Matape to Hawikuh would have been no more than twenty Indian *jornadas*.

Again, four easy days' travel from Matape would have taken Marcos to the thickly-populated Sonora Valley; yet according to his account he reached no such peopled valley for about three weeks after leaving Vacapa, and then did enter a valley that is unmistakably identifiable as that of the Rio Sonora.[125]

According to the friar's account, he spent eleven traveling days between Culiacán and Vacapa, and thirty-nine between Vacapa and Cíbola. Hence, if Vacapa be identified with Matape, he averaged thirty-nine miles a day as far as that point, then only fourteen miles a day for the rest of his outbound journey—or if, as I believe, the supposed third stage of his journey was never traveled, then only six or seven miles a day. Those students who have placed Vacapa so far north apparently have failed to note the astonishing change of pace that would have been required there. But if we place Vacapa beside or near the Rio Fuerte, we find that a reasonable pace is permitted throughout.

So I find Sauer's location for that village in accord with all the evidence, and Bandelier's location, as well as all other locations beyond the Rio Mayo, irreconcilable therewith. I would place it in the Fuerte Valley (as Sauer did in his first analysis of Marcos' account) instead of a little distance farther north. The *exact* location is of little moment.

Next, we have the friar's second stage, from Vacapa (i.e., from the Rio Fuerte) to the northern end of a well-settled valley that has been identified as that of the San Pedro River by some students and as that of the Sonora River by others. This stage of the journey was one of some 625 miles if the former location is correct, and of 390 miles if the latter. According to Marcos, it occupied twenty-nine days (April 7 to May 5) or thirty-two days if we include his three days' rest at the end of the valley.

I would place the village that was three *jornadas*—for Marcos—above Vacapa, in the vicinity of Minas Nuevas, but not beyond the Rio Mayo. That would have been about three days' travel above the Rio Fuerte, and he says he made the trip in three days. For convenience, I shall refer to that village hereafter as "Minas Nuevas," meaning only that it was somewhere in that vicinity. At this point we lose track of the calendar, for Marcos records no more dates until May 9. He reached Minas Nuevas at the end of April 9.

As regards the valley he entered toward the end of this stage of his journey, I find that except for one small item of very dubious validity, all the evidence points directly to the Sonora Valley.

Marcos could not have reached the lower San Pedro within the time fixed by his narrative. He says he left that valley on May 9, and since he accounts for eleven days spent therein, he must have reached it by April 28. So the journey would have required twenty-four miles a day if he traveled every day, or twenty-seven miles daily if he rested on Sundays, as he almost certainly did. Too, this does not allow for any other days on which no traveling was done. At his previous rate of progress, this stage, if it extended to the lower San Pedro, would have occupied forty-two days. But it would have required only fifteen miles a day to reach the upper Sonora Valley, and that is about what should be expected of the man.

His descriptive notes exactly fit the Sonora Valley, and do not in any particular fit the San Pedro Valley, or any other district that he could have reached anywhere on his route. "Well populated with splendid people," surplus food production "enough for three hundred of horse" (as a permanent garrison), "irrigated and . . . like a garden, . . . *barrios*[126] to every half league and quarter of a league"—these notes cannot by any stretch of the imagination be made to apply to the San Pedro and its people (the Sobaipuri Pimas), for they were casual farmers, their crop lands were in small and widely-scattered patches, they did not practice irrigation, and the term *barrios* could not properly be applied to their rambling communities. One of the chroniclers of the Coronado expedition said they did not even live in villages.

The valley is the only one that Marcos mentions, although he traversed others. Hence he must have been impressed by it. The Sonora Valley and its people similarly impressed all the early explorers who saw it, beginning with Cabeza de Vaca. Its people were of a higher culture than any others Marcos encountered, and the valley itself is the most beautiful district in all north-western Mexico.

Marcos says first that he traveled five days in that valley: later he seemingly corrects this to three days. I entirely agree with Bancroft[127] that he meant three *more* days. He could not have passed from twelve miles below Baviacora to Bacoachi (the limits of the Ópata villages in the Sonora Valley) in five days without increasing his pace, by one or two miles per day, over what it previously had been; yet one would assume that he here traveled quite leisurely, both from the amount of local gossip he records and because anyone naturally would proceed slowly through that interesting region, especially if, like Marcos, he was fond of eating. According to him, he stopped at every village to erect crosses and to make detailed inquiries about Cíbola, and if the villages were half as numerous as he represented, he must have reached four or five every day. He could easily have spent eight or more days in the Sonora Valley, not counting his three-day rest at its upper end.

At the northern end of the valley he described, Marcos had traveled, he says, 112 leagues from the village that I call Minas Nuevas. From Minas Nuevas to Bacoachi by trail is between 105 and 110 leagues. So, if he here was at the upper end of the Sonora Valley, he made a very good estimate of the distance he had come. But had he been at the lower Sobaipuri settlements on the San Pedro, his distance would have been approximately 180 leagues. One traveling a route for the first time, especially if on foot, will almost invariably overestimate the distance he has gone, but will rarely or never underestimate it. This is a matter of common experience. Yet, if Marcos here was on the lower San Pedro, he *under*estimated his distance by 65 or 70 per cent! Had he been on the middle San Pedro, where some students place him, his estimate still would have been too small by 45 or 50 per cent.

The Indians of the last village in that valley told him, he says, that from the beginning of the *despoblado* in front of him to Cíbola was a journey of fifteen long days.[128] They would not have called it a fifteen-day march, long or short, from the Gila to Hawikuh. It was between 215 and 225 miles by trail, or a normal week's journey for Indians.[129] But from the upper Sonora Valley to Hawikuh would have been a fifteen-day trip for them.

We may further note that while the Indians at Minas Nuevas told Marcos it was thirty ordinary *jornadas* thence to Cíbola, he now was informed that from the beginning of the *despoblado* facing him to Cíbola was fifteen *long jornadas*. Hence he must have been less than half way. But on the Gila he would have been three-fourths of the way from Minas Nuevas to Hawikuh. It seems highly improbable that the Indians would have called the entire distance thirty *jornadas*, and the last one-fourth of it fifteen *long* ones. Incidentally, we may note that Marcos spent almost a month (April 10 to May 8, inclusive) getting over those first fifteen *jornadas*, which must have been comparatively short ones if he had still fifteen long ones to go.

On entering the *despoblado* that now confronted him, Marcos says he traveled over a very wide, well-traveled road. Such a road was easily possible through the Cananea uplands—in fact, other writers have remarked it—but no such road was possible in the rough terrain above the Gila River, as Coronado discovered the next year. The "roads" there were all single-path trails, and most of them remain so today.

If Marcos here was on the Gila, then he forgot entirely to mention crossing the *despoblado* between the Ópata and the Sobaipuri settlements, although the passage would have taken him six days at his normal rate of travel. Marcos had mentioned in some detail the crossing of the two smaller *despoblados* he had thus far traversed, so why should his memory have been absolutely blank as regards this one?

Finally, placing him on the lower San Pedro at the end of the second stage of his journey introduces a dilemma from which there is no escape, for it requires that he travel at an impossible rate on one or the other of the two stages: the first stage if we place Vacapa at or near Matape, the second if we place that village near the Rio Fuerte.

To sum up: Placing the end of the first stage at Matape and of the second at the Gila River, as the Bandelier school has done, not only runs counter to the evidence but requires that Marcos march at an impossibly fast rate through the first stage. Placing the end of the first at the Rio Fuerte and of the second at the upper end of the Sonora Valley conforms to the evidence and permits the friar a reasonable, fairly uniform pace throughout.

We come now to the third and last stage of the outbound journey, and the evidence compels me to believe that Marcos traveled no more than one *jornada* of that stage.

Up to this point I find no reason for questioning his veracity as regards his progress and what he saw of the country and people along the road: this excepts, of course, his pretended side trips to the coast. He thus far had no discernible motive for falsifying his itinerary, and the meager data he recorded concerning the country and the Indians along the way agree pretty well with what we since have learned from other sources. There can be no doubt that he backtracked the Cabeza de Vaca route as far as the upper Sonora Valley.[130]

But from here on until he reached Culiacán on his return trip I regard his account as mostly fabricated. Sauer, at this point, says "The rest of the account of Fray Marcos I consider impossible,"[131] and it is true that his narrative is now so obviously falsified that we can only weigh probabilities in trying to determine where he went and what he did.

While in the Sonora Valley, Marcos received his last message from Estévan, reporting that he then (at the time he dispatched his messengers and not, as some writers assume, at the time they reached Marcos) was traveling in the last *despoblado* between him and Cíbola. All students agree that the Moor was in the unpeopled region between the Gila River and the Zuñi pueblos. The friar apparently believed, or wished others to believe, that the *despoblado* that lay just ahead of him and the one Estévan had entered were the same. Had this been true, then, since Marcos was four *jornadas* from *his despoblado* at the time he heard from Estévan, the latter would have had a lead of but eight days, and it may be that Marcos supposed the man was no farther ahead than that. He does not, however, actually say, or report the Indians as saying, that the *despoblado* just ahead of him was the last one or the one Estévan was crossing.

Here enters the question of how far in advance Estévan really was. There is no knowing, but we may as well digress for a moment to examine the probabilities. The friar's partisans evidently believe that the black man had a lead of no more than four or five days. With this belief I emphatically disagree.

It is obvious, from what Marcos recorded, that Estévan was in great haste. He was restive under the slow plodding pace of the old friar. It was largely his eagerness to get on faster that induced Marcos to turn him loose at Vacapa. Thereafter, every message he sent back, if correctly reported by the friar, urged him to hurry along, because the greatest country in the world lay ahead.   He was in such haste that he ignored the instruction to stop and wait if he learned of any important country ahead, although he had been ordered by the viceroy to obey the friar in all things. He even disregarded his own promise to wait "at the end of the next *despoblado*."

The reason for his haste is clear enough. He, an obscure slave, a mere chattel, now had the opportunity to win freedom and fame by being the discoverer of that new country of populous towns and big houses, of which he had learned three years before. He made the most of his opportunity, just as any one else in his situation would have done.[132]

But it is equally obvious that Marcos, while he too was in eager haste, took the journey rather leisurely, perhaps of necessity because of his age. He spent sixty-three days, twenty-two or more of which were devoted to resting and to visiting with the natives, in covering a distance of about 570 miles. Bloom says that Marcos "evinced considerable skepticism of him [Estévan] and his messages,"[133] and certainly those hurry-up communications never once accelerated the friar's pace.

So I think we may credit Estévan with *at least* five miles per day more than Marcos, or an average of twenty or more miles a day, inclusive of Sundays, although he probably did not travel on the Sabbath, since he was a Christian Moor.

So Estévan had a lead of fifteen days, or of some three hundred miles, over Marcos at the time the latter left Vacapa.[134] He would have gained some 150 miles more up to the time Marcos received his last message, and 60 miles on top of that during the three days that the friar was taking his ease in that last Ópata village. This, without counting any other days on which Marcos did no traveling, would have given the black man a lead of at least 510 miles, which is about 60 miles more than the trail distance from that village (Bacoachi) to Hawikuh. So Estévan would have been well on his way through that last *despoblado* before the friar entered the Sonora Valley, and could easily have reached Hawikuh several days before his final message reached Marcos. We can check this from the friar's own account. From the Gila to a point four *jornadas* (for Marcos) below Bacoachi would be about 280 miles. Estévan's messengers would have covered that distance in ten days, and during that time he himself would have advanced 200 miles farther toward Cíbola. This would indicate that at the moment those messengers reached the friar, Estévan had a lead of about 460 miles. To this add the 60 additional miles he would have gained while Marcos was resting, and we have 520 miles separating the two men at the time Marcos resumed his journey.

Assuming that both friar and Moor traveled at about the rates I have assigned them, Estévan would have been entering the Sonora Valley at the time Marcos left Vacapa, would have reached the Gila River while Marcos still was in the Yaqui Valley, and would have reached Cíbola about the time the friar entered the Sonora Valley.

That many students believe Estévan had a lead of only four or five days may be the result of a mistranslation of one sentence in the friar's account. Thus, Baldwin renders *"de allí había ido gente con Estéban Dorantes cuatro ó cinco jornadas"* as "Some persons had gone from there with Stephen Dorantes, four or five days previously." That really is an inexcusable error. A word-for-word translation of that passage is "from there had gone people with Estévan Dorantes four or five *jornadas*," or, in more usual English, "people from there [i.e., from that village] had gone four or five *jornadas* with Estévan Dorantes." That certainly cannot be taken as meaning that Estévan had passed through that village only four or five days before.[135] The Indians who accompanied him might have been back in their village many days before Marcos showed up; and they had certainly returned, else how could it have been known how far they had traveled with Estévan? Marcos reports that very often Indians of the villages he was passing through joined his company and traveled long distances with him before turning back, and the same doubtless was true in the case of Estévan. When the Cabeza de Vaca party passed over that route, going south, large numbers of Indians thus joined the party, and one whole village of Pimas accompanied him clear down into Cahita territory and there re-established themselves.

If Marcos ever inquired of the Moor's messengers how far ahead Estévan was, he nowhere mentions it; and if he had inquired he would probably have misinterpreted the information given him. To illustrate: suppose that at the time Marcos left Vacapa, Estévan was three hundred miles ahead, with the friar moving fifteen miles, Estévan twenty miles and Indian messengers thirty miles a day, which perhaps was not far from their actual rates. From Marcos to Estévan would have been thirty *jornadas,* for Indians, while from Estévan to Marcos would have been only seven *jornadas.* In that case the friar, who I think had not sufficient intelligence to allow for the fact that both he and Estévan were moving forward, would have assumed that the black man was only seven days ahead, when in fact he would have been twenty-two *jornadas,* for Marcos, in the lead.

It is not likely that the Moor ever suspected how far he had outdistanced Marcos, for the latter never once sent any message ahead to him. Estévan had repeatedly urged the friar to make all the haste possible, and probably believed that Marcos was following at top speed. The messengers that Estévan sent to Marcos, being Indians of the country, of course returned to their homes after fulfilling their mission. It would hardly have been practicable for Marcos to send anyone to Estévan, for unless they hurried the messengers would not have gained more than ten miles a day on him.

It is *possible,* of course, that Estévan may have stopped once or twice to await Marcos and then, impatient to resume his journey, started on after a day or so. But the friar certainly does not suggest anything of the sort, and the few reports he mentions having received from the villagers along the way speak of the Moor as *passing through* only. Had he tarried long at any village, except to sleep, the natives would surely have told Marcos of it. In short, there is no evidence that Estévan ever wasted a day, and he may have had a greater lead over the friar than I have credited him with.

At the beginning of the friar's supposed third stage, we run against one of the most puzzling statements to be found in his narrative. At one village— apparently the town where Estévan's last message reached him—he says the Indians told him that four *jornadas*[136] farther on he would reach a *despoblado*, and that accordingly he waited there for three days while the villagers were preparing food, and themselves, for the trip across the unpeopled region.

If he still had four days of travel through occupied country, as had to be the case if he still was four days from the *despoblado*, then why take on provisions here? Such food as could not be procured in the *despoblado* would have been taken on at the *last* village, for Indians are not so industrious as to carry burdens unnecessarily. And why should three *days* have been spent preparing food? Three *hours* would have more than sufficed, I think; for all the food except corn meal, of which they had an abundance on hand, would have been obtained as they crossed the *despoblado*. Indians never carried along food that was procurable en route, and the foods that Marcos names—venison, hares and partridges (quail)—were plentiful, and of course the escort was equipped to bring down game. Also, the Indians who desired to accompany Marcos would have needed no more than thirty minutes in which to get ready: he gives the impression that they only put on their turquoise necklaces, but they would also have donned tough moccasins.

The most plausible explanation that suggests itself is that Estévan's messengers reached Marcos somewhere near the middle of the Sonora Valley— perhaps at the lower end of the Arispe basin—and the natives there, perhaps upon inquiry from him, informed him that he had four *jornadas* to go before reaching a *despoblado*. Assuming this to be the *despoblado* that Estévan was crossing, Marcos continued his journey to the last village (Bacoachi) and there took his three-day rest. Certainly there would have been no sense in his resting up for the crossing before he reached the beginning of it.

Marcos makes no mention of having traveled a single day between the village where provisions were taken on, and the *despoblado*: on the contrary, immediately after speaking of the arrangements for the crossing, he says "I entered the *despoblado* the ninth of May," etc. Several other students have reached the same conclusion as myself, and I note also that Herrera, in his excellent paraphrase of the Marcos *Relación*, has the friar entering the *despoblado* immediately upon leaving that village. Perhaps others, like myself, are unable to picture Marcos entering an unoccupied district four days before reaching it.

Bloom says, "Fray Marcos states that he entered that 'last despoblado' on May 9th," but, as already noted, the friar does not *say* it was the last one, although he does leave the reader with that impression.

I also find that if the friar rested on Sundays—and even nonreligious travelers observed the Sabbath in those days unless their haste was very urgent —thirty of the thirty-two days from April 7 to May 8, inclusive, are accounted for. And, as Wagner has observed, there were apparently other stops indicated but not specifically mentioned. It is probable, for example, that Marcos spent a day in the village where he got his first details on Cíbola. So, if his last recorded date (May 9) is correct, he had at most only two days, and perhaps no time at all, for that hypothetical four days' stretch.

Again, his rate of travel will hardly allow for those four additional days. We find that for the first stage of his journey he averaged about sixteen miles a day, and some fifteen while crossing the *despoblado* between the Yaqui and Sonora rivers. One's pace usually slows down a little as the days pass, but allowing him sixteen miles a day after leaving Vacapa and permitting him no rests except on Sundays, we find that he still would not have reached the Sonora Valley until April 28. Counting backward from his May 9, we find that he did enter that valley on April 28. He accounts for eleven days spent in the Sonora Valley, which takes him up to and including May 8. So where had he the time for four more days of travel before May 9?

Several absurdities result from the assumption that Marcos here was on the San Pedro four *jornadas* from the Gila River, although that appears to be the prevailing view among the friar's champions. For instance, by the time Esté-van's messengers would have reached Marcos, the Moor would have had a lead of eight *jornadas,* and would have gained three more while Marcos was spending those three days "taking Indians apart." Yet Marcos, according to his own account, reached Cíbola no more than a day after Estévan, assuming that the latter was killed in the morning as Marcos claimed was reported to him.[137] If we are to rely on the friar's word about this, he in twelve days gained eleven days on Estévan, and but for that three-day rest would have reached Cíbola a couple of days ahead of the eager black man! Or if, as Marcos claimed, he traveled twelve days over the *despoblado* before he learned of the death of his avant-courier, the latter must have spent twenty-three days between the Gila and Cíbola—a rate of less than ten miles a day: rather slow going for a vigorous man who was in a hurry and nearing his goal.

Of course, the friar's claim of having reached Cíbola is fraudulent. Except for his mention of the excellent road he followed and the huts and remains of fire he saw the first day, his narrative contains not one word about the country or the people beyond the Sonora Valley. His route would have led him, for a week, through the Sobaipuri villages of the San Pedro Valley, but he does not mention them coming or going. (He probably would have sought advance information about them from his escort, had he realized that the *despoblado* confronting him was *not* the last one between him and Cíbola.)

Above the Gila he would have encountered wild and impressive scenery that sticks permanently in the memory of whoever traverses it. He would have ascended the Colorado Plateau where majestic mountains tower into the clouds; he would have passed on trails cushioned with pine needles through heavy pine forests with their cathedral-like dimness and quiet; he would have entered the haunts of the white-tail and black-tail deer, the dusky grouse, the tassel-eared squirrel, the turkey, the wolf, the brown bear, the lynx and the puma, and three or four of these would have been new species to him. In the smaller canyons of the Colorado Plateau, at that time of year, he would frequently have heard the warning buzz of the rattlesnake. He would have threaded deep canyons and cleft-like passes where twilight reigns at midday. Then, beyond the mountains, he would have tramped over grassy hills and mesas, the home of the antelope, coyote, prairie dog and jack rabbit. While all this region was a *despoblado*, the higher portions of it have a greater annual rainfall and a more varied flora and fauna than any other district on the friar's route above the Rio Mayo. Between the San Pedro Valley and the Colorado Plateau the climate changes from subtropical to cool-temperate: a fact that no traveler, in the spring, could fail to observe and remember.

Yet all Marcos has to say of that wild and diversified region is, "I traveled twelve days."[138]

He would have had to ford the Gila River to reach Hawikuh, and in the spring, swollen by the melting of the winter's accumulation of snow on its mountain shed, the Gila is a mean stream to cross, even on a horse—as I know from experience—and difficult not only because of its volume but because of its current. Where Marcos would have crossed, it has nearly thirty times the gradient of the Mississippi. When more than waist-deep it cannot be waded, because the current takes one off one's feet. At such times it cannot be crossed at all unless one swims and drifts with the current until he finds a landing place where he can climb out. The trails crossed where landing was feasible on both sides, but in times of high water an inexperienced swimmer would almost surely be carried below the landing place. Marcos failed to mention any stream of Sinaloa or Sonora, but that may have been because in those states the rivers normally are at their lowest in spring and then easily ford-able—the smaller ones are even dry. The Gila, however, is normally at its highest in spring.[139]

Marcos evidently represented Cíbola as being much farther west and south than it actually was. The latitude he assigned to the head of the Gulf of California is really the latitude of Cíbola. If Coronado had with him equipment necessary for determining latitude, as he doubtless had, then after reaching Cíbola he must have assumed that the head of the Gulf was directly westward.

At no time after his pretended view of the head of the Gulf does Marcos give us any idea of the direction in which he traveled. Many students credit him with data that they really obtained from Cabeza de Vaca and Castañeda. Eliminate those two, and Jaramillo, and we would be at a loss to know where the friar went. We have clear evidence of this in the fact that after Coronado departed on his expedition, additional supplies and equipment for his men were sent by ship to the head of the Gulf of California, which was more than four hundred miles air-line, and perhaps five hundred by trail, from Cíbola. Naturally, Coronado did not get the supplies. Maps of the time also reflect this error. One map places Cíbola about in the position of Tucson, Arizona. It must have been based upon the Marcos *Relación,* for the operations of Díaz, in connection with the Coronado expedition, clearly showed the great discrepancy between the friar's representations and the facts.

I believe that Estévan met his death before May 5, for the reason that he could very easily have reached Hawikuh before that date—twenty miles a day would have taken him there by May 3—and Marcos, if he got as far as the present international boundary, would have had to begin his retreat not later than May 15 to be able to reach Compostela by the latest date that the evidence will tolerate. Presumably it took Estévan's Indians no more than ten days to get back to Marcos with the news of his death, for they evidently hurried— Marcos says the first one to reach him arrived exhausted, and it takes better than fifty miles a day to wear down an Indian. Only forty-eight miles a day would have taken them from Hawikuh to the Arizona-Sonora line in eight days. Therefore the news must have reached Marcos within some three days after he resumed his journey, and in that time he could hardly have passed the present international boundary.

I find some supporting data in the presumably dependable portion of Marcos' narrative. Since it was fifteen long Indian *jornadas* from Bacoachi to Hawikuh, and only a week's journey from the Gila to Hawikuh, it is obvious that from Bacoachi to the Gila was eight *long jornadas*. Estévan was at or beyond the Gila when he dispatched his final message. Since the messengers had no special incentive to hurry, we may set a *minimum* of eight days for their trip back to Marcos. Therefore it must be that Estévan reached Hawikuh one or more days before those Indians found Marcos, was dead before his message was delivered, and had been dead three or more days at the time the friar resumed his journey.

This is on the assumption that Marcos was at Bacoachi when the messengers reached him. If, as I am convinced, he was four *jornadas* below Bacoachi, then Estévan was killed three or four days before those messengers reached Marcos, and had been dead for some nine days at the time the friar started across the *despoblado* above Bacoachi.

We may even go farther and still remain well within the bounds of plausibility. For a vigorous man like Estévan, twenty-three miles a day would have been less remarkable than were the eighteen miles a day that Marcos appears to have maintained on his homeward journey, for the Moor traveled under comfortable temperature and weather conditions, while the second half of the friar's homeward trip was made under the great heat of June; and even the heat of the latter half of May, below the Sonora Valley, is devitalizing. At twenty-three miles a day Estévan would have reached Hawikuh April 27, and the returning runners, by covering only forty miles a day, would have reached the Sonora Valley by May 8. Since Marcos says he did not start across his *despoblado* until May 9, it is easy to believe that he did not leave the Sonora Valley at all, but turned back from Bacoachi immediately upon learning of the death of Estévan. Neither Díaz nor Coronado found any evidence that he went any farther north than the Sonora Valley.

Marcos' mention of the wide, well-used road he followed in leaving that valley, and the huts and remains of fires he saw along its course, is not to be accepted as conclusive evidence that he traveled it, although of course it is possible that he did make a start on it. He makes it clear throughout his account that he always inquired of local Indians concerning the road ahead, and all the information he here records about the trail could have been, and doubtless was, obtained from the people of that last village, even if Marcos did subsequently continue his journey for a day or so.

Indians advise me that shelter-huts—usually no more than brush-thatched structures open on one or more sides—were to be found along every trail leading through hot, treeless districts. In fact, I have seen some of them myself. They were erected, not as shelters against rains and storms, but to furnish travelers a midday respite from the intense heat of summer.[140] Such shelters would not have been needed along the road to Cíbola above the Gila River, for there nature provided shady places enough. Also, the climate of the Colorado Plateau is much cooler than that of southern Arizona and the *despoblados* of Sonora and Sinaloa. Remains of fires would have been found along the way through every *despoblado* that Marcos crossed. So all he records regarding the road above Bacoachi he could have anticipated, from previous experience, without a word of information from the natives.

He says that only three of Estévan's escort reached him. What probably happened is that immediately after the killing of the Moor, three of the swiftest runners were dispatched to carry the news back to Marcos. They knew that the friar was coming, for Estévan had occasionally sent messengers back to him. The rest of the company of some sixty (*not* "more than three hundred men" and "many women" as Marcos wrote) followed the runners at a more leisurely pace. This, anyhow, is exactly what one would expect Indians to do in the circumstances. One of the three couriers seems to have outdistanced the other two by a couple of hours. Marcos retreated before the rest of the Moor's escort arrived, and so saw none but the three. Nevertheless, all of them came home.

It is even possible that Estévan's escort left Hawikuh before he was killed. The fact that they were dismissed, while his interpreter was detained along with him, suggests that the Moor was still under investigation at the time; and it is to be noted that none of the three runners reported having seen Estévan dead. Also, the temporary detention by the Cíbolans of a few of the younger members of the Moor's company, as hostages, suggests that they had not yet finished scouting the country for signs of a war party.

Marcos claimed, however, that he did reach the environs of Cíbola and viewed the city from a hilltop. I will speak of his description of the place presently: here I may point out another absurdity resulting from the assumption that he told the truth. All but two of his Ópata contingent deserted him, he says, when he was one day's journey from Cíbola: they turned homeward and he, with the rest of his escort, went on and viewed the wonderful city. Two days after he started back, he overtook the deserters. Hence, he must have traveled the equivalent of four Indian *jornadas* in two days, and so must have covered about sixty miles a day. Bloom, in his defense of Marcos, unintentionally makes the matter even worse. In the belief that the friar spent fifteen days crossing that last *despoblado,* he places him three days' journey from Cíbola at the time his Ópatas deserted him.[141] The deserters, therefore, would have been six days in advance when Marcos started home, going two more before he overtook them. He therefore would have covered eight Indian *jornadas* in two days, or some one hundred twenty miles a day! It will not do to argue that those Ópatas sat down and awaited his return, for, according to him, they did not believe he would live to return, and, besides, they had become alienated from him. They would have headed straight for home and would have wasted no time on the way.

So much for the third stage of the friar's outbound journey: a stage that never was traveled.

We may now examine his return journey. I will assume for the moment that he did reach Hawikuh, and reached it on May 22 (thirteen days after he left the Sonora Valley), in accord with his narrative, and see to what the assumption leads.

He says he started back filled more with fear than with food, and there can be no question that he was perturbed by the death of Estévan. From the time he reached the first Ópata village (Bacoachi) until he had passed the second *despoblado* (the uplands between the Sonora and Yaqui rivers) he says he did not stop (i.e., made no daytime stops for rest), and for the first three days covered a total of twenty-eight leagues. Farther down the trail, he says, he made a side trip to the mouth of a valley that was four or five Indian *jornadas* off his route.

His fear, however, appears to have been intermittent. According to his story, he fled in fright from Cíbola, but after overtaking his unfaithful and now hostile Ópatas, he traveled with them until he reached their village. There fear again smote him, and "with fear" he "hurried immediately from the people of that valley," making the impossible record of eighty-seven miles in three consecutive days.

The date of his arrival at Compostela he judiciously refrained from recording: in fact, he suppressed all dates after learning the fate of Estévan. But we can fix the latest date, within reason, at which he reached Compostela.

From that place to Mexico City was about 520 miles by the roads then used, and if we do not go beyond his account for evidence, that road was traveled three times: twice by the friar's messenger and once by himself. Presumably both had horse transport, but the roads at that time were hardly more than mule trails winding about through mostly broken or mountainous country, and twenty-five miles a day would have been a fair pace for one not riding post. So far as I can learn there were no post-houses along that route, and no places where one could depend upon obtaining a remount. However, I will allow thirty miles a day, for good measure. Fifty-two days would thus have been consumed from the time Marcos reached Compostela to the time he arrived at the capital.

Since it is established that Marcos reached the capital before August 26 (the date of the first certification of his written report), he must have arrived at Compostela at least fifty-two days earlier, or not later than July 4. This leaves him forty-three days between Cíbola and Compostela, and from that we must deduct eight or ten days for the side trip he claimed to have made, leaving him, at most, only thirty-five days. Since the distance from Cíbola to Compostela was some 1,330 miles, the friar would have had to average a minimum of thirty-eight miles a day if he traveled every day, or of forty-four miles if he rested on Sundays.

Such a pace, on that trail, would have been impossible even for a mounted man unless he had a fresh remount for each day. For Marcos, a man of advanced years, half that rate would have been most remarkable, for he would have been slowed down by the heat and, during the last half of his journey, by rising or flooded streams.

Bloom says, "Nor can I conceive of Fray Marcos staying in Compostela while an advance messenger went on to Mexico City and returned."[142] What the friar wrote was this: "From there [Compostela] I presently wrote of my arrival to the most illustrious lord, the viceroy of New Spain, and to our Father Friar Antonio de Ciudad-Rodrigo, Provincial, asking him [Rodrigo] to send me orders what to do."

Why was he asking that orders be sent to Compostela if he did not intend to await them? He had no authority to proceed of his own volition to the capital; besides, had he gone on, he stood a chance of missing his messenger on the road, for there were detour or alternate routes on the road to Mexico City. The most-used road was the one passing through Guadalajara.

But the friar does not actually say he awaited his courier. His *Relación* terminates with the dispatching of the man, and for what afterward happened we have to depend upon other sources. Thus, while Marcos found Coronado in Compostela when he arrived there, there is good evidence that Coronado was in Mexico City about the middle of July, and it may be that he took upon himself the responsibility of conducting Marcos to the capital at that time. Castañeda wrote that Coronado, upon hearing the friar's story, "without stopping for anything, . . . set off at once for the City of Mexico, taking Friar Marcos with him."[143] Castañeda was in a position to know: his home was in Compostela.[144]

It appears from this evidence that Marcos must have reached Compostela by June 25 *at the latest,* for while a seasoned horseman like Coronado could have made the trip to the capital in fifteen days by taking along remounts, he could not have done it if he had Marcos in tow. I do not believe that the friar, unaccustomed to the saddle, could have *endured* more than twenty-five miles a day. Marcos riding with Coronado would have been much like Dumas' Friar Gorenflot keeping pace with Chicot. He would have needed three weeks, at least.

Both Sauer and Bloom cite a letter written by Coronado to the Crown and dated as from Compostela, July 15, 1539. Therein he submits a brief summarization of the expedition undertaken by Marcos and Estévan, not forgetting to mention the part he played in it, and states that "it pleased God that they should reach a very good land, as Your Majesty will see from the *Relación* of Fray Marcos and by that which the viceroy is writing to Your

Majesty." In the next sentence he speaks of the "grandeur" of the land Marcos describes.

In that letter Coronado made no mention of the death of Estévan. This omission is taken by Bloom to indicate that Coronado had not yet talked with Marcos; i.e., that the latter had not yet reached Compostela. Bloom argues[145] that Coronado might have received news of the *prospective* discovery from messengers dispatched by Marcos while en route northward.

It would have been an act of stupidity on the part of Coronado to have thus revealed to the king the hostility of the Cíbolans, and that probably was one of the "details" that he said he was leaving up to the viceroy. Coronado himself aspired to win renown and perhaps fortune by leading an armed expedition to the Cities of Cíbola, and he must have known that if the belligerent attitude of the Cíbolans were revealed to the Crown, the contemplated *entrada* would promptly receive the royal veto. Since Marcos was representing Cíbola as having a homicidal population in excess of that of Mexico City, and as being but one of seven cities "under one lord" (and therefore united in warfare), the conquering of those cities would be an expensive undertaking, and one of doubtful outcome. Besides, Charles V was decidedly opposed to all attempts to "pacify" the Indians by force.

So Coronado must have decided to leave so delicate a matter to the viceroy. Perhaps Mendoza even dictated what he should say to the Crown; I cannot doubt that that triumvirate of schemers—Mendoza, Coronado and Marcos—got their heads together in determining what to tell the king.

While Marcos had been instructed to send back reports on the country as he advanced, there is not even a suggestion that he did so in his narrative, nor in any other document that I have seen, and this would not have been the only one of his instructions that he totally ignored. Bloom says[146] that it would be surprising if Marcos did not send off his first hearsay reports on the country during his long stay at Vacapa. It would surprise me to learn that he at any time did comply with this instruction. His utter disregard for most of his instructions is so obvious that if we *must* believe he complied with this one, some shred of evidence to that effect should be produced.[147]

Any information dispatched while en route northward, however, could have told Coronado nothing of the actual "discovery," and Coronado's letter speaks of the wonderful country *discovered* by the friar, and not of a country of which he had only been told. So Coronado certainly had seen and talked with Marcos prior to the date of that letter. As Sauer has pointed out, the general tone of the document indicates that it was not freshly-received news that he was transmitting; for that news formed but a part of what was an official routine report, in which Coronado in effect declares that the friar's account has already been written and that the viceroy's is in course of preparation.

Coronado, then, could not have known that Mendoza was at work on his report unless he had seen the viceroy. This means that he was in Mexico City at the time. We have sufficient evidence that after learning of the friar's "discovery" he did hasten to the capital to confer with Mendoza. Even without any supporting evidence, the known intimacy between the two would lead the student to assume that Coronado did that very thing.

Sauer suggests that Coronado's letter was written in Mexico City and dated as from Compostela. I accept that as a fact, since Compostela was his official post. Then, as today, the heading of a letter meant no more than "send replies to this address." Except when he was on an officially approved or directed tour, Coronado probably headed all his correspondence as from Compostela. His absence from Compostela on this occasion had not been officially authorized in advance, and the *Audiencia,* or the Council for the Indies, might have been inquisitive as to what business he had so far from that city.

There remains the bare possibility that Coronado, in hurrying to the capital, took along the friar's report but left him at Compostela. If his report was prepared overnight, this would have allowed him to about June 30 to arrive at Compostela. It is probable, however, that the compilation of the account occupied him several days.

Another item of evidence that has been overlooked by the friar's defenders, and that escaped me until it was brought forward by Sauer—although as a professional climatologist I should have seen it immediately[148]—is the change, toward the end of June, from the dry to the wet season, with the resulting rise in the streams, especially in Sinaloa and Nayarit. These, in the spring very low, or in the case of the smaller ones practically dry, rise to high and often flood stages by July, and continue so through that month and usually through August. The rainy season there arises from the same conditions that produce the prolonged monsoon rains of India. This condition is more pronounced in Nayarit and southern Sinaloa than to the north. In those two states are six or more streams that Marcos could hardly have forded after June, and the natives had no boats. Yet he mentions no such conditions during his return journey.

In the preceding I have reference to the friar's chronology, but it is to be remembered that he was using the Julian calendar, which was ten days behind the Gregorian. Thus, June 30 on his calendar is July 10 on ours. The official climatic data for Mexico show the rainy season beginning about the end of June, which means the middle of June on the Julian calendar.

I have perhaps said enough to establish pretty closely the latest date at which

Marcos could have arrived at Compostela, but I might mention another letter, written by Cortés to Mendoza from the former's home at Cuernavaca, on August 6, 1539. This letter has been cited by Wagner as evidence that Marcos had not based his report on the north country upon information previously obtained from Cortés as the latter claimed. Wagner established his point, but he did not extract all the juice from that letter. It was written in reply to one from Mendoza informing Cortés of the marvelous discovery effected by Marcos, and in it Cortés states that he had been hoping for some official confirmation or denial of the story that had been going around concerning that discovery, which up to that time he had not credited. It is clear from that letter that Mendoza at the time was planning the conquest of the cities of Cíbola, and had asked Cortés' suggestions thereon. The viceroy would hardly have begun definite plans until after he had conferred with Marcos. Hence the latter must have reached Compostela by June 20 if he there awaited orders from the capital, and in any event it appears that he reached Mexico City by August 5, or at least three weeks before the initial certification of his report.

Bloom, assuming that Marcos reached Cíbola, states[149] that "it is quite unnecessary to picture Fray Marcos as rushing along at forty miles a day. Half that speed during the return to Compostela would have sufficed," and "even this average was not essential." I fail to see how he arrived at that astonishing conclusion. Even using his own inclusive dates (May 25 to July 10) for the trip, Marcos would have had to average thirty-five miles a day if he made that side trip—and Bloom does not deny that he made it—or of twenty-eight miles a day if he kept continuously to the homeward trail, *without a day's rest or delay anywhere* between Cíbola and Compostela. At twenty miles a day, and marching every day, he would not have reached Compostela until July 30, or August 7 if he made the side trip that he claimed.

Bloom suggests that Marcos may have improved his daily mileage by traveling at night and resting in the daytime. I have no doubt that he did rest in the shade during the midday heat. Even the natives did not travel during the hottest hours of the day: not only the natives, but the animals and insects remained quiescent in the shade. But man cannot sleep under air temperatures of 105 to 115 degrees. And I doubt that Bloom himself ever tried stumbling along an unimproved trail in the dark. I have done so—just once—when delayed in getting back to camp. It is about the most temper-testing work I have ever done. Those trails were not paved, lighted thoroughfares. They are bad enough in the daytime, when one can see where he steps.

In my own foregoing calculations of the speed that would have been required had Marcos really reached Cíbola, I go beyond reason in making concessions in his favor. Thus, I allow for no stop at Culiacán, although surely upon reaching that haven after his thousand-mile marathon from Cíbola Marcos would have relaxed for a day or two. His statement that he did not stop between the northmost Ópata village and the end of the next *despoblado* is a virtual concession that he did occasionally rest a day or so afterward: I do not allow for that. I allow for no time lost at Compostela between his arrival and the departure of his courier; I permit this messenger no delay on the road or in Mexico City; I start the friar toward the capital the moment his messenger returns and assume that he himself lost not a day en route, although one unaccustomed to the saddle could not have held the pace that I set for him regardless of the roads or the endurance of his mount; I assume that his report was examined, edited and certified overnight. Is there anything more that I could allow him in order to give him more time for travel? On the contrary, it is almost certain that *at least* eight or ten days should be deducted from the time I have allowed him.

Now we may consider the return trip as it probably *was* made. We may attack the problem experimentally by assuming that the friar's farthest north was the present Arizona line, and that he reached Compostela by July 4. He therefore must have turned back not later than May 12, assuming that his last recorded date (May 9) is correct. It is known that he did not make the side trip that he claimed to have made; hence he had forty-nine days for covering a distance of about 940 miles. This would have required an over-all average of nineteen miles a day, or twenty-two miles if he rested on Sundays. He would thus have spent some thirty-three days in reaching Culiacán, whereas on his outbound trip he consumed fifty-one days if we exclude all weekdays on which no traveling was done, or sixty-seven days over-all.

But since, especially during the last half of the return trip, he would have been much retarded, not only by the enervating heat but by flooded streams and inundated lowlands, that still seems too fast a pace for him. Sauer says that after June the lowlands of northern Nayarit are inundated, with a dozen coast-plain valleys flooded. He has been there, and should know. My own ramblings have never taken me that far south, but Sauer's statement is amply supported by the official rainfall statistics, *which show Nayarit to be, during July, the wettest district on this continent north of latitude 20°.*[15] If, as Sauer says, traffic above Compostela is suspended after June, then surely a pedestrian could hardly have gotten through. Marcos mentions no such conditions, but gives the impression that he had smooth going.

So let us assume that, as appears highly probable from both the documentary evidence and the climate, Marcos reached Compostela by June 25 (July 5 on our calendar). He would not have escaped the rainy season entirely, but probably would have reached Compostela before the streams of Nayarit had risen to unfordable stages. He would still have been subjected to the debilitating heat of June, and I believe that an over-all average of eighteen miles a day—or of twenty-one miles excluding Sundays—would have taxed his endurance to its limit. At any rate, under the conditions then existing, it would have sorely taxed mine in the days when I was a seasoned pedestrian.

I think it very improbable that Marcos turned back before May 9, for if his chronology is correct—and we have no grounds for questioning it—he was at the northmost village of the Sonora Valley at the end of May 8. Now, starting at Compostela and reckoning backward, we find that the friar, to have reached Compostela June 25, at eighteen miles a day, *would have had to start back from the upper end of the Sonora Valley on May 9.* The distance was about 880 miles. So it appears very probable that he started home on the very day he claimed to have resumed his journey toward Cíbola.

Except for a stop at Culiacán, I do not believe that he wasted any *week* day between the time he began his retreat and his appearance at Compostela. While no doubt he was frightened, or at least greatly perturbed, at the start, I think his fear thereafter was mostly pretended. His haste, I believe, was partly due to his anxiety to get in ahead of Ulloa, for so far as he knew, Cortés' man was already at his task. Also, his desire to get back to Compostela ahead of the annual inundation may have helped to keep him moving along as briskly as possible. Then again, he had to pretend even greater haste in order to account for the short time it took him to return from Cíbola: hence his preposterous claim of twenty-eight leagues in three days.

Some of his critics believe that a full month elapsed between his arrival in Mexico City and the first certification of his report. But assuming that he reached Compostela June 25, hardly more than ten days could have thus elapsed if he awaited the return of his courier. But if he accompanied Coronado, he would have had a full month for preparing, editing, and attesting his report. A month's time would have been nothing unusual: there are instances in which two months elapsed between the preparation of a document and its certification.

Aside from the absolute barrenness of his narrative as regards anything seen above the Sonora Valley, Marcos' description of Hawikuh as a very beautiful city, larger than Mexico City, proves that he had not seen that squalid little pueblo, which Castañeda a year later exactly described as "a little unattractive village, looking as though it had been all crumpled up together," and of which he said, "there are cattle ranches[151] in New Spain that make a better appearance at a distance." The friar's defenders, while forgetting to mention the insignificant dimensions of Hawikuh, state that Mexico City at that time may have had a Hispanic population of no more than 2,500. But that city must have contained fully as many resident Indians as Spaniards, which would have raised the total population to 5,000 or more. I believe the capital was even more populous, for while we have no statistics for that time, it was reported as containing 1,500 Spanish families in 1556, and six or seven were usually reckoned to the family.[152] Winship says the population of Mexico City "probably doubled" between the years 1539 and 1556, but even so, a Hispanic population of some 4,500 would be indicated for the former year.

I have seen and examined the site of Hawikuh, the foundation outlines of which were still traceable twenty years ago, and probably are even more prominently revealed now, for excavations have been made there since I visited the place. *I could have kicked a football clear over the "City of Cíbola."* It and its "courtyards" occupied a space about equal to one-third of an ordinary city block, and only one-half that area was occupied by buildings, of which there were six or seven. There are two that may have been joined. Two of the seven were quite small, of no more than half a dozen rooms each: they were on the slope of the hill and I suspect that in one of them Estévan and his party were quartered. The "city" was between 210 and 220 feet wide at its widest part, with an over-all length of about 600 feet. (This is exclusive of the mission buildings, which of course were not there in 1539.)

I have seen the population of Hawikuh variously estimated between 300 and 1,000. Measured by other pueblos whose populations were known, it could have contained no more than 450 or 500 people.[153] And while Marcos remarked how beautiful it was, that little excrescence of mud and stone, in its drab desert setting, must have been about the last word in unkempt ugliness, just as are the smaller pueblos of today. Moreover, Hawikuh was not "on a plain on the skirts of a round hill" ("at the *foot* of a round hill," one translator renders it), as Marcos reported. It was on the top of a low, irregular spur, and the country thereabouts was not a plain.[154] And only in sardonic antiphrase may one speak of that arid, treeless region, which the Zuñians possessed only because no other tribe wanted it, as "the best of all the discoveries" in the New World.

The friar's defenders excuse his whopping falsehoods here by explaining that he had probably expected to find a magnificent city, and that his expectations were reinforced by the distorting and bewitching effects of the evening air. Thus Hammond and Rey say, "Since the rarefied atmosphere of the southwestern deserts is very deceptive, it may be that the pueblo appeared much larger than it really was";[155] Baldwin suggests that here was a case where "distance lent enchantment to the view";[156] Winship naïvely remarks that "all witnesses agree that these light stone and adobe villages impress one who first sees them from a distance as being much larger than they are."[157]

As regards Winship's assertion, I must confess that such has not been my experience, nor the experience of any others whom I have interviewed. The "light stone and adobe" of which the pueblos are constructed is of exactly the same color tone as the ground on which and from which they were built; consequently, notwithstanding the comparative transparency of the desert atmosphere, they do not stand out at all. Unless they exhibit a skyline or have a background of green vegetation they blend into their environment at a few miles' distance. I recollect one that I failed for a while to see at a distance of no more than three miles, although my eyes are good and two companions, who knew its situation, were trying to point it out to me; and even then I discovered it through the *shadows* of its buildings rather than through the buildings themselves. There are several others that I first saw at a distance, or from an elevation, and against the far-flung dimensions of their backgrounds they appeared *smaller* than they afterward proved to be. Others report similar experience. So the alibi proposed by Winship collapses completely.

Neither would exaggerated expectations have the effect that Baldwin ascribes. The effect, I think, would be just the opposite. The pueblos of New Mexico have been attractively advertised throughout the eastern United States. But take some of your eastern relatives on a visit to a few pueblos, as I have done, and some of the expressions you are likely to hear from them are "How insignificant!" "How unkempt!" "How squalid!" "How dirty!" "How unattractive!" "How crude!" Yet their *expectations* had been high, and their disappointment produced a negative reaction.

As regards the effect of the "rarefied atmosphere": the type of refractive phenomenon known as "towering" is the only atmospheric distortion that can alter the apparent size of an object, and it never magnifies the object in a horizontal direction.[158] It can make a thing appear to be taller than it actually is, but not wider. While the ordinary reflection mirage is common in the Southwest, towering is comparatively rare so far as my observation goes: I have seen examples of it but twice in thirty years. It requires for its production a "reversed" vertical temperature gradient and not "rarefaction," and is more common in regions of greater atmospheric density, as at sea level, because the denser the air the greater its refractive power. It produces the *Fata Morgana* (the "castles" of Morgan la Fay) of the Mediterranean coasts and has been observed on other coasts. It is regarded as essentially a marine phenomenon; and since the atmospheric condition required for its production is very unstable, it rarely lasts longer than a few minutes. Often its duration is a matter of seconds. I very much doubt that nature would have been so obliging as to produce this marine phenomenon on a southwestern desert just for the delectation of a marvel-seeking friar. Moreover, had it occurred, Hawikuh would have taken on the appearance of a towering mass of rock rather than of a creation of human hands.

As a matter of fact, under *normal* atmospheric conditions, objects on or near the horizon take on a flattened appearance: they seem to be *lower* than they actually are. Witness the "flattening" of the sun and the moon when they are rising or setting. A square object, on the horizon, appears slightly longer than high. This distortion is not usually recognizable on objects of irregular shape, but it is there, just the same.

The "rarefied atmosphere" of the Southwest is deceptive only in that, because of its transparency, it makes distant objects appear to be nearer and, consequently, *smaller* than they really are, because they subtend a smaller angle than would be the case were they as near as they appear to be. Aside from the automatic comparison of an object with its environs, already mentioned, the *apparent* distance and the subtended angle are the only means the human eye has for estimating the size of the object. So the friar's cause loses rather than gains by blaming the atmosphere for his departure from the truth.

His partisans insist that he viewed Hawikuh from afar; yet they allow him an additional day's travel toward the place after he says he was a day's journey from it. Unless his eyes were sharper than mine, he could not have observed that the structural details were as they had been described to him—and he says they were—at a distance of more than two miles, under normal conditions.

Possibly I have dwelt overlong on this matter, but it is well to leave nothing more to be said on the subject. I have never known a sane man to remain uncognizant of a material fact when that fact obtruded itself nakedly before his eyes; therefore, either the friar lied, or his narrative is a document that should interest the psychiatrist rather than the historian.

H. W. Haynes,[159] after an examination of Marcos' *Relación*, concludes that "he fairly deserves the epithet of 'the lying monk'." J. G. Shea,[160] objecting, says "Haynes follows his [Marcos'] real narrative and does not note a single statement as false or bring any evidence to show any assertion untrue." So, in addition to what I already have set forth, I shall endeavor, in what follows, further to supply the deficiency of which Shea complains.

I may say first that the friar's critics are divided into two schools: those who believe him a deliberate liar, and those who consider him mentally unbalanced and therefore not responsible. Of the latter group, Wagner is a prominent representative. He sums up thus:

What he heard from the Indians in southern Sonora . . . was substantially correct. He simply magnified everything he heard, one turquoise became a hundred, a small town became a great city and everything else in proportion . . . Men were crazy for gold. The first great gold rush of which there is any record [in Perú] was at its height.

In such an overcharged atmosphere men will believe anything that promises gold . . . Someone is always forthcoming to provide the story. To stamp such people as unmitigated liars is not to the point, they are simply the victims of their own imaginations or hallucinations; what they wish to see or hear, that they see or hear.[161]

But Wagner adds that if Marcos saw Cíbola, "it was in a vision, something not at all unlikely in such a case."

I myself am convinced that Marcos was just a plain liar. Hallucination or an overwrought imagination cannot explain his pretended visits to the coast, his suppression of all dates after learning of the death of Estévan, his assertion that certain Indians had no knowledge of Europeans, his pretense of having penetrated unknown country early in his journey, etc. There is too much of such deliberate falsehood in his narrative to permit the charitable hypothesis that he was mentally off balance—too much "method in his madness," in fact. His having "provided the story" and his gross magnification of the information given him by the natives do not imply a disordered imagination: if they do, then every fiction writer is demented.

Baldwin says, "Friar Mark had been given many glowing accounts of the greatness of Cíbola by the Indians."[162] Such a positive assertion should be supported by evidence more trustworthy than the friar's word. Lacking that, it should be amended to read, "Friar Mark *claimed* that he had been given many glowing accounts." *I do not believe that any Indian told him anything that was not true.* It is beyond reason to suppose that the natives told the unembellished truth to those passing that way before and right after Marcos, and lied so outrageously to him in between. The supposition simply does not make sense. Baldwin here appears to have overlooked the friar's repeated assertions that the Indians all along his way had proved absolutely truthful as regards what he would find ahead. They assumed that he would find Cíbola. So why should they have lied about that place and it only?

It is preposterous to hold that the first information about Cíbola burst like a thunderclap upon Estévan and Marcos at that Cahita village three *jornadas* above Vacapa. Estévan himself, three years before, had learned more about the terraced-house culture than Indians that far south could have told him, for he had gotten his information from the Ópatas who had firsthand acquaintance with the cities of Cíbola, while three other tribes and eight hundred miles lay between the Cahitas and Cíbola. Estévan, as spokesman of the Cabeza de Vaca party, must have learned a great deal more about the Zuñi pueblos than Cabeza gives us in his condensed narrative, for the mere mention of big-house towns would have interested those men and they would have questioned their informants closely. All of this information Estévan doubtless imparted to Marcos before they ever left Culiacán, and Marcos could hardly have learned anything more from Indians along the road, at least until he reached the Ópatas.

Again, if Marcos, as he says, had in his company some Indians that had been purchased and freed from slavery by Mendoza, he had some Cahitas. These must have been drafted to serve as interpreters, for there were plenty of other Indians closer at hand to employ as servants and porters. Marcos says he inquired all along and right from the start, through these interpreters, for information concerning lands peopled by Indians of a higher culture than that possessed by those he was encountering. Yet he pretends that he learned nothing whatever of the cities of Cíbola until he reached the tribe to which those interpreters belonged. They must have known as much about Cíbola as did their tribesmen. How does it happen that they did not themselves give him the information he was seeking?

It was all part and parcel of the friar's pretense that he was in country that no one else ever had seen or heard of, and that he was the first ever to learn of the big towns to the north. Thus, he says that at Vacapa, after dispatching Indians to the coast, he sent Estévan by another route to see if in that direction he might "learn of any great thing" such as they sought—pretending that they were on a roving tour, ready to turn in any direction that promised results. Yet we know that their one objective was the country of which Estévan had learned in 1536, and that neither of them ever departed from the direct route. Marcos did not send Estévan by another route: he simply told him to go on, knowing perfectly well what route the man would follow.

It is quite possible that Estévan did manufacture some intriguing reports, as he sped northward, in an effort to hasten the laggard friar along. But since we have only the latter's word for it that Estévan "overloaded his hand," we cannot know which of the two supplied the fiction. I am inclined to believe it was the friar.

As regards the Moor's eagerness to get on, I have already suggested a reason for his haste; a reason first advanced by one of his contemporaries. And if we can judge from his actions, he was not appreciably disappointed upon finding Cíbola to be only a small pueblo: apparently he had expected nothing more.

Marcos had interpreters with him, but it is possible that he at times misunderstood the Indians, although his years of contact with the natives in Perú and Guatemala should have taught him to evaluate their information correctly. The student of his narrative should have little difficulty in distinguishing between possibly misinterpreted data and pure invention. As an example, we may take a look at the friar's interview with the exiled Cíbolan he found in the Sonora Valley. This Cíbolan, he says, told him that Totonteac was the greatest "kingdom" in the world, and had no end. The pueblo country of the Rio Grande doubtless was the biggest occupied region in that Indian's world, and he probably never had seen the end of it. He told the truth as far as his experience extended. But when Marcos has that same man informing him that Cíbola was a great city of many streets and squares, of ten-story buildings with porches and façades of turquoises, we know that Marcos is lying. For Hawikuh was that man's home, and he knew it to be a very small town, with no buildings over three stories high—a town possessing only a few turquoises, none of them used to decorate walls, porches or doorways.

Several times in his narrative Marcos quotes Indians verbatim and at considerable length: such conversations of course never took place.

It appears from contemporaneous evidence that Marcos did not stick to his story of having reached Cíbola. Accounts of his journey written by brother Franciscans soon after his return do not credit him with the discovery. Castañeda wrote[163] that Marcos turned back immediately upon learning of the fate of Estévan, and I believe that the friar, cornered, confessed that this was the case.

Baldwin declares that "when it comes to a question of his [Castañeda's] word against the Friar's, there is certainly no reason to accept his."[164] But, leaving the friar's narrative out of the question entirely and judging both men by their records, it appears to me that there is every reason to accept the word of the soldier. Castañeda has never acquired any reputation for mendacity. His *Relación* does contain a few misstatements of fact, but these were hearsay and reported as such. Nothing that he recorded as a personal experience has ever, to my knowledge, been questioned by any competent student. Even one of the friar's most violent partisans, C. F. Lummis, has referred to Castañeda as "dyspeptic but truthful."

Marcos, on the other hand, acquired a reputation as a liar before he ever started for Cíbola, and he was afterward branded, throughout New Spain and in Old Spain, "The Lying Monk." His report of his journey to Topira, just before he started for Cíbola, is demonstrably false. Baldwin states that Cortés' accusation—that Marcos in telling of Cíbola was "merely following a practice for which he had become notorious in Perú and Guatemala"—is a "grotesque" charge.[165] Yet that charge has since been substantiated by Wagner, who after a thorough study of the friar's life declared that "the whole history of the man, as far as we know it, clearly indicates that he was given to loose statements and great exaggeration"; and even Baldwin, after stoutly maintaining Marcos' truthfulness, concedes that in his *Relación* are statements "that are open to question."

Again, Baldwin declares that "had he not been over the ground previously, the fact would have become painfully evident as the expedition [Coronado's] proceeded."[166]

But it has never been denied that the man had previously been over the ground as far as the upper Sonora Valley, which is to say, two-thirds of the way to Cíbola. Beyond that point, it appears that his lack of acquaintance with both the land and the people did become apparent on more than one occasion. He had lost the confidence of the leaders by the time the Gila River was reached, for he betrayed no acquaintance with either the Indians or the road. For a reason that is obvious to us, he did not offer to guide a detail to that rich and populous valley he claimed to have seen, or even to point out the trail leading to it, but left Diaz to seek it in vain. As later exploration proved, it had no existence. At the Gila River, Marcos told Coronado that the coast was only five leagues (fifteen miles)[167] away, and that he had seen it; but Coronado learned from the Indians that it was ten *jornadas* (about three hundred miles) distant, as in fact it was. At no time after leaving the Sonora Valley had Marcos any idea how far it was to Cíbola. By pointing out his heap of stones as the expedition neared Cíbola, he could have proved beyond any argument that he had been there; and this he doubtless would have done had there been any heap of stones. When the expedition finally reached Hawikuh, the fact that he had not seen the place did become very "painfully evident," and Castañeda says the most fearful curses were hurled at the friar by the disillusioned soldiers. Coronado finally sent him back to New Spain lest he be killed in spite of his holy garb. If he ever spoke a word in his own defense it is not of record, although an honest man would not have suffered such abuse without protest.

Coronado later reported to the viceroy that "everything the friar said was found to be quite the reverse," and stated, "I can assure you that in reality he has not told the truth in a single thing he said." Coronado here was speaking of what Marcos had told him, and not of the wild stories credited to the friar.

Does not all this render the friar's mendacity "painfully apparent"? What sort of evidence would be acceptable to his partisans if the testimony of his own associates is worthless? Those three witnesses have been accused of bias against the friar, but the charge does not state that this bias developed after, and not before, his untruthfulness was established. Before that, Castañeda and Cortés were neutral and Coronado was quite friendly with Marcos. There can be no question as to what would be the ruling of any civilized court of today on this case.

Criticism of the friar even extended to foreign countries. One old English writer (Heylyn) declares that Marcos' story was "so disguised in Lyes and wrapped up in fiction that the light was little more than darkness."

Even the friends of Marcos are not agreed upon the most important feature of his narrative. Thus, while Bloom declares that "his report is of what he *saw and heard* and does not always clearly distinguish between the two,"[168] Baldwin as stoutly asserts that "all through his narrative he is careful to distinguish between observation and hearsay."[169]

To one acquainted with the character of the southwestern Indians, the tale told by Marcos of the massacre at Hawikuh must appear altogether fishy. Moreover, it is flatly contradicted by what the Indians of that pueblo told Coronado. Marcos has it that over three hundred Ópatas and a large number of their women, who had accompanied Estévan to Cíbola, were slaughtered without putting up a fight.

He claimed that this information was given him by the three survivors, but that claim is not punctureproof. *No Indian ever told a lie that placed the stigma of cowardice upon his own people.*[170] Marcos must take the responsibility for that falsehood upon himself.

The men accompanying Estévan were of course armed: Indians always carried their weapons when on the road. The Ópatas were an aggressive race as compared to the timid Zuñians who never fought except defensively,[171] and Hawikuh hardly could have mustered more than 150 warriors.[172] Yet Marcos would have us believe that twice that many armed Ópata men permitted themselves, along with the women who were accompanying them, to be captured, disarmed, imprisoned and then butchered! Three hundred Ópatas could have captured and devastated Hawikuh, for the next year Coronado, with eighty hunger-weakened men, unable to use their arquebuses and crossbows effectively, captured the pueblo without the loss of a man; and at that, Hawikuh had been reinforced by warriors from the other Zuñi pueblos. Thereupon all the "Cities of Cíbola" surrendered.

The Zuñians would not have attacked even a small squad of Ópatas unless provoked beyond the limit of even their endurance. There was no existing *casus belli* between these two tribes, the Ópatas present were not in war paint and so presumably were on a peaceful mission, and the Cíbolans must have known that an attack on them would bring up an avenging war party from Ópataland.[173]

The Zuñians were suspicious of *all* alien visitors, for they had learned through bitter experience that such were often spies or advance scouts seeking to discover the vulnerable points in their pueblo's defenses. But they were also politic, and were averse to arousing the wrath of any powerful nation like the Ópatas, who outnumbered them several times over. Moreover, they would have been much more suspicious of Estévan's "Mexican" Indians than of the Ópatas. They were acquainted with the latter, through the commerce carried on with them, but the Indians of Estévan's permanent escort were of a strange tribe with which the Cíbolans had never had any previous contact.

While it may be true that Estévan attempted to enter Hawikuh without permission, and otherwise violated pueblo law, I doubt very much that his conduct was as arrogant as it has been painted. His accusers were on the defensive before Coronado, and so would have lied without compunction in order to justify themselves for the slaying of Estévan. The Moor's real offense was his trying to escape. He was under suspicion as a possible spy, and the Cíbolans had not yet decided whether he was a harmless visitor or the agent of some enemy. His attempt to escape served to confirm the latter supposition. It is to be noted that, so far as our evidence shows, he was not tried, sentenced, and executed according to pueblo custom in dealing with malefactors, but was slain while running away.

But the hostility of the Cíbolans would not have extended to Estévan's escort unless they defended him, and this they would not have done, for he was an alien to them also. They doubtless took the neutral stand that "this is no business of ours." The Cíbolans, according to their testimony before Coronado,[74] detained a few boys along with the Moor's interpreter and dismissed the rest of the escort of some sixty men (*not* "more than three hundred men and many women," in addition to his permanent retinue, as Marcos has it). The boys were probably detained as hostages in the event that a hostile force was approaching—several southwestern tribes raided the Zuñians when they felt the need of diversion—but when scouts failed to find any war party the boys were released and sent home, just as Estévan would have been had he waited. Such detention of alien callers was not a hostile act: all the pueblo tribes practiced it, whenever there was any uncertainty in regards to the purpose of the visit. Estévan's interpreter, who was not an Ópata, remained with the Cíbolans and was delivered to Coronado the following year. It appears that they had adopted him into the tribe, for they were reluctant to let Coronado take him away for service as an interpreter.

Except for their charges of gross misconduct against Estévan, I fully credit the account that the Hawikuh Indians rendered to Coronado, for it is just what might be expected: they ran true to established pueblo practice, even to the posthumous slander of their victim.

I may mention also that no chronicler of Coronado's expedition speaks of finding any Ópata women among the Cíbolans, although if the massacre that

Marcos depicted had occurred the women would not have been killed, but would have been adopted into the tribe. Moreover, the testimony of the Cíbolans is supported by the fact that the Ópatas at no time thereafter made mention of any of their people having been slain at Cíbola. They surely would at least have told Díaz of it, for he visited them only five or six months afterward.

Marcos' account of the reception of Estévan's messenger (his interpreter) at Hawikuh also fails to accord with pueblo practice. Here was a *neutral* Indian of an unknown tribe, carrying the symbol of a *hostile* tribe, announcing the approach, with a considerable retinue of *mixed* Indians, of a *black* man who himself was coming as the herald of a *white* man. This incredible information would have raised their curiosity to a high pitch, and certainly their suspicion also, for it was something far outside their tribal experience: they had no idea of what was coming against them and could not guess what it all meant, but their suspicions told them that it meant nothing good for *them*. But if it aroused their anger also, they would have kept that feeling masked. As Marcos has it, when the messenger presented the Moor's symbolical gourd, the representative of the lord of the seven cities, without a preliminary question, dashed it to the ground, exclaiming that it was not one of theirs, exhibited great anger, and ordered the messenger to tell Estévan to retreat at once, or every one of his party would be killed.

This may have been the European's way, but it was not that of the Pueblo Indian except as a last desperate attempt at bluff. In such situations, the Indian does not show his hand until he has exhausted every means of exposing the hand of his opponent. The messenger would have been questioned and requestioned, and at the same time scouts would have been sent out to test his story.

Neither would the ceremonial gourd have been treated so contemptuously. Indians respected the sacred insignia of other tribes, even hostile tribes.[175] To have so dishonored that gourd would have been a challenge and defiance to the tribe using it: an action alien to the pacific character of the Pueblo Indian. Moreover, had the messenger entered the pueblo carrying one of *its own* symbols of religious authority, which none but the *shamans* of their own tribe were permitted to handle, the Cíbolans *would* have had grounds for anger and resentment. In short, pueblo custom was opposite to that depicted by Marcos. It is strange that Bandelier did not note this, although it may be he believed it was the Indian runners, and not the friar, who invented the story. The runners, however, were Ópatas, acquainted with pueblo custom.

It is quite probable, though, that the Cíbolans did send out instructions for Estévan and his entourage not to enter the pueblo. And upon his arrival they doubtless did quarter him and his escort in a vacant building outside the main part of the pueblo, as Marcos reported, for such was the custom with aliens among all the pueblos. This manner of quartering visiting delegations of men is understandable when we remember that in the pueblos the mature males slept in the kivas and only the women and children in the houses. There was little if any surplus room in the kivas; besides, none but people of the tribe were permitted to enter them, and of course no village would quarter visiting men with the women and children. This procedure was also a precautionary measure, for the Indian, always wary of aliens, placed them where they could be watched and guarded against. Where no suitable quarters were available, visiting delegations had to camp outside the town.

After the arrival of Estévan with his story, scouts would again have been sent out to look for Marcos and his company. He could not have come within a day's journey of the place, on any route or on no trail at all, without being discovered and constantly watched, and his every move would have been reported back to the war chief of the pueblo. Yet he was never found by any Zuñian.

Again, Marcos says that the pair of fugitives returning from Hawikuh told him they had "played possum" all day in a pile of dead men and then, at night, made their getaway. He does not say that these two had been scalped, but scalped they certainly would have been, along with the dead men around them. Fortunately for those two, Marcos did not know of this practice of the pueblo tribes, so he neglected to remove their scalps.

He does say they had been sorely wounded by arrows, but that is another fiction of his. His narrative abounds in discrepancies that a superficial examination does not reveal. In this case, for instance, according to his story he was only one day's journey for him (about fifteen miles) from Cíbola when the first runner reached him. That Indian had left Cíbola soon after sunrise, and sunrise, in late May in that latitude, is before 5:00 A.M. So the Indian, traveling at only a normal pace, would have reached Marcos by noon, or if he was in a hurry, by 10:00 A.M.

Yet the two wounded Indians, who did not leave Cíbola until after dark, presumably reached Marcos only an hour or two after the first one, and certainly before evening. Therefore, if Marcos told the truth, we have to believe that lying sorely wounded and bleeding for a whole day rendered those two Indians so fleet of foot that they outran time and arrived several hours before they started.

Moreover, Marcos packs an incredible amount of action into that one day. It was, as we have observed, well along toward midday when the first runner arrived. A delay of an hour or two ensued, and then, just as Marcos was resuming his journey, the two wounded ones showed up. A longer delay, probably of three or four hours this time, followed. So it must have been about midafternoon when he again started on. Yet he had time enough, that day, to travel the one *jornada* to Cíbola, feast his eyes on the city for quite a while, erect his big pile of stones, and travel some distance on his way back, all before nightfall. It will not serve to argue that these doings may have been spread over two days. Marcos has not one minute's break in the action from the time the first runner arrived to the time he started homeward from Cíbola.

And I may mention in passing that while Marcos reports the first Indian as saying he had gone to a near-by stream to get a drink, there was no stream nearer Hawikuh than Zuñi Creek, several miles to the west. The rainy season in that region does not begin until June, so let us not argue that there may have been water running in some near-by arroyo.

We may dismiss the whole story of what happened at Cíbola as a romance erected by Marcos upon the one fact that Estévan had courted death and had been accommodated. But what a fiction-writer the friar would have made: what a mass of intriguing detail he could build around the simplest kind of "plot germ"! Clearly, he missed his true calling.

The truth probably is, as I have already suggested, that with the killing of Estévan, or possibly with his arrest, his escort sent those three runners on ahead to break the news to Marcos. That they felt any alarm is very unlikely, and if they commented among themselves upon his downfall, their remarks probably were, in effect, "He invited his own fate: he was no magician at all, but only a very foolish fellow." Nor is it at all likely that the news carried back to Marcos produced any emotion, other than disappointment, in his own escort. Why should it? They simply started back with him, if in fact they (the Ópatas) had yet left their native village. No doubt they were disillusioned with respect to the friar, whom they now must have esteemed a coward, since he feared to go on. Their disappointment over the ignominious termination of the promised adventure was no doubt partly assuaged by Marcos' distributing among them all the dry goods, trinkets, etc., that up to that time he had not disturbed. But if I understand the character of the Ópatas aright, it is more likely that they took than that he gave. Or it may be that he forestalled them by giving before they had the chance to take.

Incidentally, his purpose in taking all those bales of merchandise on his journey is obscure, for he himself says he had not opened one of them, or given Indians a single article, until he unloaded the whole consignment upon the Ópatas.

His statement that thirty *chiefs* (*principales*) from the last Ópata village accompanied him toward Cíbola is manifestly absurd. The largest of the

Ópata towns could not have mustered that many *shamans*. I doubt that even the largest of the New Mexico pueblos could have rounded up as many as thirty, yet they possessed about every imaginable kind of functionary. Then not all the village officials would have absented themselves, and some, says the friar, had accompanied Estévan.

Going back over the friar's path, we find several additional detours from the way of truth. Thus, at some point between Petatlán and Vacapa—somewhere near the Rio Sinaloa—he claims to have visited the coast. The best route between Petatlán and Vacapa was nowhere nearer than eighteen or twenty miles from the coast, and he mentions no side trip. He was at the time far above the latitude of the island (Guayaval) that he claims to have seen. Wagner suggests that he got this information later, from some one who had been with Cortés, which is not improbable.

Somewhere between the Sinaloa and Fuerte rivers Marcos says he reached Indians who were astonished to see him, having had no previous knowledge or news of "Christians." That is a lie, direct and obvious. Not only the Indians of that district, but all those along his way as far as the upper Sonora Valley had seen Europeans. Cabeza de Vaca and his companions had traveled that same route three years before and crowds of natives had accompanied them, relaying them from village to village. Before that, slave-catching squads operating under the license of Nuño de Guzmán had thrice spread "knowledge of Christians" as far north as Cumuripa in the Yaqui Valley. Right here in the district of which Marcos was speaking, Cabeza de Vaca had found the Indians fleeing to the mountains to escape a more intimate "knowledge of Christians," and they had taken him and his companions along, to save them also from the Christians. None of the tribes encountered by Marcos was nomadic. All lived in permanent villages and tilled the soil. Those he says were amazed to see him were there when the squads of Alcaraz and Diego de Guzmán were introducing "knowledge of Christians" into that region. Hence it will hardly serve as a defense of the friar to argue that the Indians he found here were newcomers from afar. And while he refrains from mentioning it, he must have been told of the comings and goings of Alcaraz and the passage of Cabeza de Vaca at every village on his road, for it was characteristic of Indians to remember and speak of such initial contacts with the white man.[176]

The friar's object in this particular deception was, of course, to convey the impression that thus early in his journey he had penetrated country never before entered by any European.

His claim of having visited the coast from the Sonora Valley is also demonstrably false. He spoke of this "visit" as though the trip occupied only a few hours, although at the time he could not have been within one hundred miles of the Gulf.[177] Since his own course had lain northwestward, while he entertained the erroneous belief that the coast trended directly northward, it is possible that he now believed the shores of the Gulf of California lay only a short distance to the west, although there was a mountain range west of the Sonora Valley. I believe, however, that he made inquiry of the Indians and then deliberately falsified what they told him. If they told him in what direction the coast trended, they surely also told him its distance in *jornadas:* this information he suppressed. His supposed error of four or five degrees in the determination of his latitude I believe to have been deliberate. The Indians probably told him how far it was, in *jornadas,* to the head of the Gulf, and he guessed that this would be in about latitude 35°. Thus he would convey the impression that he had actually reached the head of the Gulf. It may be that this item was introduced into his narrative after his return, in order to support a claim that he was there ahead of Cortés' man, Ulloa.

Baldwin, in his defense of Marcos, says[178] that perhaps his meaning is "after inquiry, I perceived" that the coast turned abruptly from northerly to westerly (which, by the way, it did not). What Marcos wrote is this: "As a change in the direction of the coast was a matter of importance, I wished to learn of it, and so I went to view it, and saw clearly that, in latitude thirty-five degrees, it turns to the west." If the alibi offered by Baldwin is valid, then why may we not also assume that when Marcos declared he had looked upon Cíbola and found it to be a very beautiful city, he really meant, "after inquiry (among the Indians of Sonora) I perceived that it was a beautiful city, larger than Mexico City"? Incidentally, this statement of Baldwin's does not harmonize too well with his earlier assertion that Marcos was always "careful to distinguish between observation and hearsay."

Bloom inquires[179] why, if Marcos here lied about having visited the coast, he did not also claim to have blazed trees and left letters, as he had been instructed to do. I do not think the reason is far to seek. Viceroy Mendoza had informed him, in his written instructions, that such marks would be watched for by any vessels sent up the coast. The friar doubtless hesitated about recording a lie that could be so easily and promptly exposed. In fact, he must have known before his departure that Cortés then was fitting out ships for coastwise exploration to the head of the Gulf of Mexico. So far as Marcos knew, those ships were already on their way, and in fact they did set sail before he got back to Mexico. Their commander, Ulloa, was in Cortés' pay and therefore antagonistic to Mendoza, and so would have kept a good eye out for evidence that Marcos had preceded him. Hence Marcos would have been a fool to record that he had left evidence of his presence unless the evidence was there. He must many times have regretted his stupidity in recording that he had left evidence of his presence (his heap of stones) at Cíbola, for it was not there.

Others have insisted that Marcos must have visited the coast because he had been *instructed* to do so. Such students have not examined the viceroy's instructions carefully. Marcos was *not* instructed to visit the coast. He was told to "inquire always for information" about the seacoast, and, if perchance he came to the coast, to leave evidence of his presence.[180] He could have obtained information from the Indians, and clearly all the information he did get was from that source. The rest he invented.

Besides, supposing that he *had* been directed to see the coast in person: would this have been the only one of his instructions that he ignored? Of fifteen specific instructions, he complied with two, partly observed three, and ignored *ten*. Perhaps the reader will permit me to summarize them here, omitting the preliminary instructions concerning what he was to do at Culiacán before starting on his journey, although we have no evidence that he complied even with those.

Instruction	Degree of Compliance
To take possession, in the name of the viceroy, of any new country discovered.	Fully complied with, and even greatly exceeded.
To avoid friction with the Indians along the way.	Complied with.
To observe the native people, their habits, etc.	Ethnic notes superficial and fragmentary.
To obtain information about the coast.	Three hearsay or faked reports, each of which was erroneous.
To take note of the animal life, domestic and wild.	Ignored except for bare incidental mention of three species he ate.
To observe the topography, terrain, etc.	Ignored, except for mention of a valley and some distant mountains.
To note the kinds of trees and other forms of plant life.	Not a tree or other plant mentioned.
To observe the quality and fertility of the soils.	Not a word about the soils, although he must have seen many different types.
To observe the climate.	No element of climate even mentioned.
To observe the streams, their size, etc.	Not a stream even mentioned.
To take note of the mineralogy and metallurgy.	No mention of any mineral or metal of the country.
To leave evidence of his visits wherever he reached the coast.	Necessarily ignored, since he never once visited the coast.

Instruction	*Degree of Compliance*
To send back samples of what he found (i.e., of minerals, metals, food plants, pelts, manufactured articles, etc.)	Totally ignored.
To send back reports as he progressed.	Totally ignored in so far as there is any evidence.
To send or bring back, *secretly*, information of any large town that he found.	This positive instruction was grossly violated.

Does that record look like a faithful compliance with the instructions, as the friar's father provincial certified? One is tempted to believe that Marcos' disregard for most of his instructions was deliberate, for no man with eyes and ears could have failed to note some of the interesting things that he must have encountered, the reporting of which was directly provided for in those instructions.

So far as the results are concerned, Marcos had but four instructions:

1. *Take possession of everything you see or hear of.*
2. Spot a good location for a military outpost.
3. Be on the lookout for signs of material wealth.
4. Whatever you see or fail to see, bring back an intriguing report.

Yet in acknowledging receipt of those instructions, Marcos wrote: "I promise faithfully to fulfil [the instructions] and neither go against nor exceed them," etc.

Baldwin states that Marcos' narrative "conforms pretty accurately with what we know of the ethnology and topography of the region over which he traveled."[181] Why not? What the man said of the topography cannot fail to conform to what we know, for he said nothing. As regards topography, his account would fit any coastal region of the United States quite as well as it fits Sinaloa and Sonora. Were it not that others traveled the same route, both before and after Marcos, we would have no idea where he went after he left Culiacán. Strip our documentary material of what Cabeza de Vaca, Díaz, Castañeda and Jaramillo wrote, and nothing would be left to the friar's credit.

Then there is no reason why his meager ethnological notes should not conform to what we know, for it is not denied that he got as far as northern Sonora, while beyond that point all he has to say of the ethnology is "I traveled twelve days." That, as Baldwin observes, conforms to what we know.

The man's energies seem to have been devoted mainly to gathering and embellishing stories of Cíbola, and from the time he first heard of the place until he started home, nearly all of his time was devoted to such puerilities. He was interested in what lay somewhere else rather than in what met his eyes.

He gives the names of all pueblos he *heard* of, but names only one of the native villages he *saw*. Cabeza de Vaca, writing six years after having traveled that route, does better than Marcos, although he was but a starveling wanderer intent on getting back to civilization, while Marcos' journey was ostensibly one of geographic exploration, in which work he was claimed to be especially proficient. With an exceptional opportunity to contribute to geographical and ethnological knowledge, he babbled only of Cíbola. Credited by his superior, Provincial Fray Antonio, with being learned in cosmography, he betrayed not the slightest acquaintance with any branch of that far-flung science. Fifty-one times he wrote "he said," "they said," and "they told me," but he wrote "I saw" only four times—*and each of the four times he lied.* His report is the most glaringly incompetent specimen of its kind I have yet found in the annals of the Spanish frontier.

Next after Cíbola, eating seems to have claimed most of Marcos' attention. It appears that he had a regular midday "dinner"—though every experienced hiker knows it is better to pass up the noon meal—and sent servants on ahead, not only to prepare the dinner, but to erect a shelter wherein he could dine in comfort and perhaps take a siesta afterward. This is traveling de luxe. He says nothing of a silver dining service or wine, but I should not be surprised to learn that he had both: he certainly had a large enough entourage of porters and personal servants.

His claim of having broken his return journey to visit a rich and thickly-populated inland valley was proved false the next year. Díaz found nothing but two small, impoverished villages, and nothing better was ever found by anyone else.

Marcos says the Indians all along the way from where he first heard of Cíbola, including the one Cíbolan exile, told him there were *seven* cities. Castañeda reported seven, while Jaramillo reported six. Both were writing from twenty-year-old recollections, and probably neither had seen all the Zuñi pueblos. Castañeda may have been but repeating the number that he had heard from the lips of Marcos. At any rate, Gallegos, who visited each one and recorded its native name, says there were only six, and Hodge has proved[182] that there were no more than this.

Certainly not *all* the Indians along the friar's road would have been mistaken as to the number. But Marcos probably knew the old legend of the Seven Cities, and certainly knew that Guzmán had reported having been told of seven rich cities somewhere in the unknown north country. So he reshaped the testimony of the Indians to fit the legend and the Guzmán story. In fact, Castañeda declares that Marcos claimed it was the Guzmán group of seven cities he had discovered.

Then there is the name "Cíbola." It is said to be an Aztec term, meaning "buffalo." I believe Marcos was acquainted with it and its meaning before he ever started on his journey.

The Zuñians' own name for that southernmost pueblo was Aguico, Allico or Hawikuh—the exact pronunciation of Indian words is impossible in the orthoëpy of any European tongue—and they called their group of pueblos Shi-woh'-nuh. If Marcos believed those pueblos to be in the great buffalo range of which the Spaniards in New Spain had vaguely learned from Indians, it is quite possible that he traced a resemblance between "Shiwohnuh" and "Cíbola." Both Coronado and Castañeda recorded that Cíbola (or Cívola) was the name, not of a single pueblo, but of the whole group, so they too must have fancied a resemblance between the two names. Zuñians of today, however, maintain that their pueblos were never known as Cíbola until they were so named by the Spaniards, and as they pronounce the word "Shiwohnuh" I find very little suggestion of "Cíbola."

The point is that Marcos has the Indians all along his road—the Cahitas, the Nebomes (southern Pimas), the Ópatas, and the one Cíbolan he met, speaking of the first Zuñi pueblo as *Cíbola*. Bandelier, who was qualified to speak with authority on the subject, says[183] that the names applied by Indians to themselves (i.e., to their own villages or tribes) were always different from the names by which they were known to other tribes. We find abundant proof of this in the ethnology of the Southwest, although sometimes names are similar, as for example the names Ácus, Ácco, and Ácoma, applied to the Ácoma pueblo.

So each of the tribes encountered by Marcos would have had its own name for Hawikuh, or for Shiwohnuh, and the one Cíbolan Marcos interviewed would alone have the correct names.

It is the same with the names Totonteac and Marata. Marcos has each tribe using those names. Incidentally, Coronado found that the Zuñi Indians had never heard of any place called Marata, and that they said Totonteac was a salt lake or saline.

The Isleta Indians today have a word, *si-bu'-la-da'*, meaning "buffalo," that may have been derived from the Aztec term, but I know of no tribe anywhere in our Southwest or in Sonora who have any similar word.

The friar's story of the Cahita and Ópata Indians journeying to Cíbola and there performing manual labor in exchange for turquoises is a bit of unintentional humor on his part. We can picture those people sweating under the direction of the Zuñians about as easily as we can fancy the Roman legionaries journeying to Cornwall and there laboring for the Britons in exchange for tin. I doubt that the Cahitas ever saw one of the Zuñi pueblos. The Ópatas traded directly with the Zuñians, exchanging parrot feathers, sea shells and deerskins for turquoises, malachites, cotton blankets, etc. They did the necessary traveling, because the Zuñians were too timid to venture far afield; and if they were like other aggressive tribes, then if the Zuñians refused to trade, the Ópatas took.

It has been suggested by others that perhaps what the Indians tried to tell Marcos is that they dug in the ground for the turquoises, and he interpreted this as a gardening operation. But no turquoises were produced anywhere near the Zuñi country. The Zuñians themselves obtained them in trade from pueblos of the Rio Grande Valley and beyond, where they were mined.

Marcos' object in this prevarication was probably to depict the Cíbolans as a race of supermen before whom all others had to bow, just as he does when he "quotes" his Ópata escort as declaring that "none can withstand the might of Cíbola." There again Marcos unintentionally gives us a laugh.

There is something curious in his repeated insistence upon the truthfulness of the Indians along his road. No fewer than seven times does he record that the people at successive villages gave him exactly the same information about Cíbola as had all those he had interviewed before, with a trifle more added; and at his last village where, he says, for three days he did nothing but "take Indians apart" to question them, all told precisely the same tale.

He finally says, in effect, that "since these people always told me the exact truth concerning what I would find along my road, they must have told me the truth about Cíbola."

But why all this, if he subsequently saw the place himself?

I also note that during his final soliloquy on the absolute veracity of the natives, he for some reason drops into the present tense. Thus: "From the day I first learned of Cíbola, the Indians told me of all that *until today* I have seen," and again, "having traveled, from where I first had news of the land, *until today*, one hundred and twelve leagues" (italics mine).[184] That paragraph in his narrative is worth examining carefully. It reads as though it were written on the ground, and as though the writer intended going no farther. If so, it was not properly edited afterward.

At times in his narrative, Marcos pretends that he traveled Indian *jornadas*, although he clearly reveals in other parts of the account that his *jornada* was hardly half that of an Indian. He finishes up by pretending to have traveled fifteen long Indian *jornadas* in thirteen days, although he had previously spent a month covering fifteen short ones. It may be that in some instances he remembered his own traveling time between points, and recorded that as the time the Indians said would be required. For example, the *despoblado* between the Yaqui and Sonora rivers: Marcos says the Indians told him it was a four days' trip, and states that he crossed it in four days. The trail he followed is still there, and is about sixty miles long: four days' travel for Marcos, but only two for Indians.

Marcos leaves both his champions and his critics puzzled on three points. One is, why, after he learned of the death of Estévan, was he so anxious that the Ópata contingent of his company go on to Cíbola with him? He did not need them; they had joined his party voluntarily. His escort of Mexican Indians had previously been sufficient, and would have been more than sufficient now, since he had disposed of all his bales of merchandise. The Ópatas, he says, were now hostile to him, and had even planned to kill him. Since he was only one day's journey from Cíbola, they were not needed as guides. Yet Marcos says he spent much time fruitlessly trying to induce them to continue with him, and he did not go on until two of them consented to go with him.

The second point is, what became of his permanent escort? He says no word about them after leaving Cíbola, but gives the impression that he made the return trip alone, except for a short distance traveled with the now hostile Ópatas (whom he had hastened to overtake). Those Mexican Indians lived at points between Cuchillo and Culiacán, and surely returned home. Why did he not travel along with them?

Finally, he says nothing further about his companion-friar, Honoratus, whom he abandoned, presumably ill, at an Indian village sixty miles from any civilized outpost. It seems that a humane man would have arranged with the Indians at Petatlán to carry the sick man in a litter back to Culiacán where he could get medical care and European food. Marcos makes no mention of having stopped to inquire after Honoratus when he passed through Petatlán on his way home. All of which lends some color to the suspicion that the real cause of the separation of the two was a quarrel, with Honoratus refusing to acquiesce in some scheme or other, and turning back to Mexico. He turns up later, well and hearty, in the history of New Spain.

In the foregoing, I have confined my attention mainly to that which Marcos himself recorded and subsequently declared to be the truth, and which therefore can not be dismissed as hearsay. I should perhaps make some mention of what he is reported to have related orally after his return to Mexico. This would not be accepted as valid evidence by any court; nevertheless the charge that he told glamorous tales greatly outshining those of his written report cannot be passed over in silence, for it was made by some reputedly honest men who had no discernible motive for lying. Of these men, I might mention Suarez de Peralta, who wrote a creditable history of the events of 1535-1540. He was in New Spain during that time, and he must have had opportunity to hear Marcos, and even to talk with him. According to Peralta, Marcos represented the arid country he had discovered as "the best in the world," and "according to the way he painted it, this should have been the terrestrial paradise," and "he exaggerated things so much that everybody was for going there and leaving Mexico depopulated."

Others charged the friar with having declared that Cíbola was more than twice as large as Sevilla, Spain, and with having told of pagan temples with altars of pure gold. His written report was not made public, at least not for some time, but it appears that he supplied the lack of a public press himself, and while probably the tales credited to him must be discounted, it cannot be denied that he did talk very freely. Nor were his powers of invention exhausted in his written narrative. Being himself an ecclesiastic, he soon had the pulpits of New Spain resounding with the magnificence of his "discovery." It also appears that he made no effort to counteract or discount any of the wild tales that swept over the country. He was much like a man who deliberately starts a fire, then complacently watches it develop, or even himself fans it into a conflagration.

After his tales of Cíbola were disproved by Coronado, Marcos says nothing in his own defense. His purpose having been achieved, he simply slinks out of the public sight.

There is one thing more to be mentioned of that tissue of misrepresentation. Marcos signed his *Relación,* but he at no time signed any formal attestation of its truthfulness. In the preliminary certification, it was the father provincial who, over his signature, declared the account to be true, and even went so far as to assert that Marcos had faithfully complied with the viceroy's instructions!

There is something even queerer in the second and more formal attestation. It is the only specimen of its kind that I have found in history. Others also declare it unique. It was signed by two secretaries of the royal *Audiencia,* who stated, over their individual signatures and seals, that since Marcos had orally "said and affirmed and certified" the truth of his narrative, they themselves were attesting its truth *because they were commanded to do so* by "their lordships" (Mendoza and Francisco de Ceinos)! So, of the three men who attested the truthfulness of the *Relación,* not one knew whether it was true or not, and two of them signed under compulsion.

Marcos' object in all this deception has been made clear by Dr. Sauer,[185] and I think the reason it escaped detection for so long is that it was *excessively* obvious, like Poe's example of the name that sprawls in big type clear across a printed map.

To discover the friar's motives, as well as to test the genuineness of some of his statements, we occasionally have to go backstage, for in some of the

scenes he probably was only a marionette, with Mendoza and Coronado pull-
ing the strings and ventriloquially furnishing the conversation. It is known
that Mendoza was determined to forestall Cortés in exploring and occupying
the intriguing north country, and he also feared De Soto,[186] who was then
organizing his expedition with the finding of the "Seven Cities" as one of his
avowed objects. A preliminary reconnaissance, under a pretext of geographic
and missionary exploration, by an agent of Mendoza, would give him a prior
claim on the region. While it is clear that the real object was the discovery
of the terraced-house culture of which Cabeza de Vaca had heard, Mendoza
was careful to give the enterprise an evangelical camouflage. The Ternaux-
Campans translation (French) of a copy of Mendoza's instructions carries this
introductory sentence: "Fray Marcos de Niza, this is what you have to do in
the expedition which you are undertaking *for the honor and glory of the Holy Trin-
ity and for the propagation of our holy Catholic faith*" (italics mine). The instructions
themselves are charged with piety. The Indians Marcos was taking along as
porters and personal attendants were to be used, Mendoza directed, "as you
see is suitable to the service of Our Lord," and so on. Instructed to keep his
eye out for, and report in detail upon, any situation suitable for the establish-
ment of a monastery (i.e., a mission center), Marcos spotted and reported on
only a good situation for a military outpost, and in fact one was established
the next year in the district he recommended. On his journey, he had eyes
only for material wealth; and he envisioned Cíbola, not as a city of pagan
souls to be shepherded into the fold of the Church, but as a rich and belligerent
city ripe for looting.

That all this was inspired by Mendoza is contrary to his character as revealed
on other occasions. But if he desired a peaceful penetration of the country,
then why the three hundred armed soldiers of Coronado's expedition? And
why were such inhuman butchers as Alcaraz and Cárdenas appointed captains
in that expedition? There were humane and experienced officers available, such
as Andrés Dorantes and Melchior Díaz. Díaz was appointed, but was shunted
off on a side trip.

According to Winship, "Mendoza appears to have arranged his plans as
carefully as if he had been about to engage in some intrigue at court" in preparing the Fray Marcos reconnaissance. But he knew that he had to act
promptly, for both Cortés and De Soto hung like menacing clouds over his
pet project.

The reader has perhaps noted how carefully Mendoza avoids any reference
to Cabeza de Vaca in his instructions to Marcos. He speaks of the "Indians
who came with Dorantes," but does not say whence they came; and in fact
they came with Cabeza de Vaca rather than with Dorantes: the former was

the leader of the party and the Indians recognized him as such. But De Soto was trying at the time to associate Cabeza de Vaca with himself in his projected search for the Seven Cities, and Cabeza de Vaca, as the leader of all that survived of Narvaez' expedition, in a sense fell heir to Narvaez' commission. In fact, he himself sought a commission to lead the expedition that De Soto organized, and had he been able to finance it himself, he doubtless would have been appointed instead of De Soto.

So Mendoza may have regarded Cabeza de Vaca as an additional threat, and for this reason have avoided any reference to him, even as he avoided any reference to Cortés and De Soto.

But to get back to our main subject: if we take the view that Marcos throughout was acting solely as an agent of the viceroy—in mining slang, as a hired "claim jumper"— and not as an explorer, then every falsehood and exaggeration, as well as every sin of omission and commission in his account, at once finds a logical and plausible explanation.

Mendoza *may* not have been accessory before the fact to the friar's deception. But the canny viceroy must have foreseen the possibility of Marcos' failing to reach his goal, and therefore probably enlightened him, privately, upon what the essential part of his mission was to be—to bring back a report that he had penetrated the country of the terraced-house culture ahead of any other explorer, and to shape up that report to attract recruits for a military *entrada*. Mendoza apparently reflects that doubt in one of his instructions: "And if, with the aid of God, Our Lord, and the grace of the Holy Spirit, you shall find a route to go farther on [than Culiacán] and to enter the country beyond," etc.

There is evidence both for and against the view that Marcos was given secret orders. The year before, as we have noted, Mendoza tried to arrange with Andrés Dorantes to reconnoiter the north country; and while he reported to the Crown that he knew not why the plan failed, he must have known why, and perhaps was the only person who did know. This arouses the suspicion that Dorantes was not sufficiently pliant. From what we know of the man, he was truthful but not averse to blowing his own horn. Had he conducted the reconnaissance, he would have told the truth, and would also have made it clear that as one of Narváez' captains he had covered the ground before. That probably would not have suited Mendoza at all.

Then it remains to be explained why the viceroy so completely ignored the friar's disregard of his written instructions. There was one violation that was especially flagrant: Marcos had been instructed to observe "all secrecy" in reporting upon any noteworthy city or country that he might discover. Yet from the moment of his return, according to his contemporaries, he went about blabbing to all who would listen—and listeners were never lacking—of the glories of Cíbola; and thus he stirred up the very "commotion" that Mendoza had cautioned him to avoid. This was a serious offense, and ordinarily would have drawn severe punishment upon the offender. But notwithstanding this and other disregard of specific instructions, Mendoza had Marcos promoted to the position of father provincial of his order in New Spain—a post that he filled very indifferently.

But if Marcos was acting solely to advance Mendoza's private schemes, there is one of those instructions that we would expect him to fulfil: the one requiring him to take possession, in the name of the viceroy, of any new lands he might reach. He did fulfil that one with a vengeance: he not only took possession of everything he saw, but of everything he heard of, even to lands hundreds of miles away; and each time he thus "took possession" he added the words *"conforme a la instrucción"* (conforming to the instructions). Otherwise, he made no reference to his instructions.

There are some things in his *Relación* that I, along with others, believe were amended or introduced entirely after Marcos had conferred with the viceroy. Possibly some others were deleted at that time. The *Relación* may have been in part a collaborative effort.

Interpolations and amendments could, however, have been introduced by Marcos on his own initiative; and it is suggestive that Mendoza, in the fall of 1539, sent Melchior Díaz, *Alcalde* of Culiacán, in advance of Coronado to test points in the friar's narrative. This seems to indicate that the viceroy did not know how much of the story to believe.

Diaz was an unimaginative sort of man. He got as far as the Gila River before winter turned him back, and he saw very few turquoises on the way. The Indians as far as he went must have told him the bald truth about the cities of Cíbola, for it was the truth that he brought back. But his report was withheld from Coronado's recruits, lest Coronado's enterprise even then collapse.

Day, taking the view that Mendoza was not privy to the friar's deception from the beginning, suggests[187] that Marcos, on the homeward trail, realized that the failure of his mission not only would disrupt Mendoza's plans, but would bring ridicule and charges of cowardice upon himself. Then, reflecting that since he was alone, hundreds of leagues from any other European, any tale he chose to tell could not be disproved in time to embarrass Mendoza, and possibly would never be disproved, he framed up a yarn of having reached Cíbola, and otherwise embellished his story with intriguing fiction calculated to arouse public interest. Even his story of bloody doings at Cíbola, in addition to furnishing him with a sufficient excuse for retreating, may have been designed to win recruits from among the foot-loose adventurers of New Spain who were aching for some rich city to loot. The looting of a belligerent city was always permissible under the rules of civilized warfare, and the bellicose attitude of Cíbola, as pictured by Marcos, offered these hotspurs their opportunity. Lummis even declares that one of Mendoza's objects in organizing Coronado's expedition was to rid New Spain of this gambling, dueling element that was keeping the domain in a ferment.

At any rate, the friar's report served its purposes as well as if he had reached Cíbola and brought back photographs of its gem-encrusted façades and ten-story edifices.

But connivance with Marcos in the perpetration of this fraud would not have been Mendoza's only shady act in his efforts to checkmate his rivals. There stand against him his own lie to the Crown, to the effect that Guzmán had done nothing in the way of exploration, and his unauthorized interference with the coastwise activities of Cortés. From the time of his assumption of his duties as viceroy, in 1535, he, along with the *Audiencia* (of which he was president) had been harassing Cortés. The record of the "good viceroy"— and he was one of the best viceroys New Spain ever had—shows that he was not above winking at or assisting in any underhand activity that would promote his own schemes. In the case with which we are dealing, he probably acted upon the precept that "the end justifies the means," and perhaps in no other way could he have suppressed the unscrupulous Marqués del Valle. But the fact that Mendoza's activities were always directed toward the orderly development of New Spain does not exculpate Marcos from the charge of having been a notorious liar, as some students seem to hold.

Finally, I may say that as an initially neutral party, or one even inclined somewhat toward the friar, I was as much impressed by the instability of his defense as by the soundness of the prosecution. His defense in itself is so evasive as to have the effect of a prosecution. It appears to rest upon the assumption that because Marcos was a friar he was incapable of deliberate falsehood—an untenable proposition in the case of any mortal—and that therefore all contrary evidence too obtrusive to be excused or blamed upon the Indians and the atmosphere must be explained away, regardless of the strain the explanation places upon the mathematics of probability or upon one's reason.

Throughout this study, however, I confess that I have been harassed by the suspicion that the friar's more recent defenders have espoused his cause with their tongues in their cheeks, as a "comedy relief" from their staid work as professional historians. The writers with whom I have had the impudence to take issue are historians of top rank, as habituated to the impartial examination of evidence as are the friar's critics, and it is puzzling to find them defending a sequence of demonstrable falsehoods. It is difficult for me to believe that any careful student of the twentieth century would *seriously* defend Marcos.

The earlier historians—Bandelier, Bancroft, Winship, Shea, etc.—were handicapped by lack of data. The region involved was then, to Anglos, largely a *terra incógnita*. One has but to examine the maps of those days to realize this. No topographic maps of the region were available until 1916, and even the contour map issued by the U. S. Geological Survey in that year was erroneous as regards the drainage of Sonora. In addition, transportation in the Southwest, in the 1880's, was still rather primitive and accommodations were uncertain. Bandelier was the only one of these historians who had traveled in Arizona and Sonora. He was interested mainly in archeology, and everybody knows how oblivious one may be of things outside one's immediate interests. It is probable that no one else, under the conditions existing in those days, could have done much better than did those pioneer students who had to depend almost altogether upon the documentary material for their evidence.

Bancroft says no other man in history has been so persistently slandered as has Marcos, although he offers no evidence to show that the "slander" was not the unvarnished truth. I myself know of no other character in all history who, so obviously unworthy, has been so zealously defended. So let us pigeonhole "The Lying Monk" with the other Munchausens of history; but we cannot then forget him, as one writer has recommended, for his fictionized narrative resulted in the greatest exploring enterprise ever undertaken in the New World.

NOTES

Historical Background

1. The tradition of lands or islands beyond the Atlantic dates clear back to the time of ancient Greece. Even the name "Antilia" was not invented by these refugees: it had been applied to some legendary island or group of islands several centuries earlier.

2. Cortés also rebuilt Mexico City, superbly. The building that our school histories refer to as "the palace of the Montezumas" is the viceregal palace begun by Cortés and finished by Mendoza.

3. The *Audiencia* at the start was a council set up to regulate the affairs of New Spain; later it became also an advisory board for the viceroy.

4. The exact number of transmontane Piro pueblos is not known, but it was about seven. They were the towns that one coming up from eastern Mexico would first encounter, and were about forty days' journey, for Indians, from Pánuco.

5. It has been claimed that Guzmán transferred his activities to the west through fear of Cortés whom he, as president of the *Audiencia*, had harassed, and who, now returning from Spain with honors and a new commission, had his knife whetted for Guzmán. But since Cortés was interested in the west coast himself, it may be that Guzmán's aim was to forestall him in working northward.

6. Estévan was a slave belonging to Dorantes.

7. As was determined later, they were stranded at different points between Galveston and Matagorda bays. Two barges, carrying the four ultimate survivors, were wrecked on Galveston Island. Cabeza de Vaca was on one; the other three were on the other.

8. These men were pressed into service as medicine men at the start, the Indians maintaining that since their own *shamans* could effect cures, the white men, who were much wiser, should be correspondingly more efficient as healers. They claimed to have effected many cures, but took no credit to themselves for their success. Bandelier, a freethinker, states that "empirical hypnotism plays a part in the performance of their [the Indians'] medicine men. Cabeza de Vaca, unconsciously and by distinct methods, imitated the Indian *shamans*, and probably succeeded, in at least many cases, since the procedure was new and striking."

9. Two accounts were written, one a joint report, and the other and more extensive one Cabeza de Vaca's personal narrative, which was published under the title *Los Naufragios* (The Shipwrecked Men). Both have recently been republished, and the latter is available in English translation.

10. Don Antonio de Mendoza was appointed viceroy in 1535 and served until 1550. His appointment greatly curtailed the authority of Cortés, who, however, remained captain general.

11. The Council for the Indies was a body of men appointed by the Crown to exercise general supervision of public affairs in the Spanish overseas colonies. Its acts were subject to the approval of the Crown. It bore about the same relation to the king as the *Audiencia* bore to the viceroy of New Spain.

12. Marcos de Niza (Mark of Nice) was a native of Savoy, and was regarded as a Frenchman by his contemporaries. He saw service in Perú and Guatemala before coming to New Spain. At the time he made his journey he was a man of advanced years and not in very good health. He lived until 1558, but during the last fifteen years of his life he was an invalid.

13. Mendoza and Coronado were close friends. Mendoza had picked Coronado up at the court of Spain, in 1535, and brought him to New Spain. Here Coronado made a brilliant marriage, his wife being a cousin of the great Charles V. At the time of our story, Coronado was twenty-eight years old.

Instructions of Viceroy Mendoza

14. This is a reference to the seizure of Indians by Guzmán's henchmen, for enslavement. Cabeza de Vaca's bitter denunciation of that traffic led to its suppression by Mendoza.

15. Coronado had not been appointed by His Majesty. Mendoza had appointed him, and royal approval of the appointment had not yet been received. Coronado was occupying Guzmán's former post as governor of Nueva Galicia.

16. This refers to the Indians who accompanied Cabeza de Vaca southward in 1536 and who remained at Culiacán.

17. "The people who are there" means the Indians of any new country he entered. "There" (*allí*) in Spanish *always* means "in that place" or "in that region."

18. I translate the word *templaza* as "temperature," but it sometimes was used to mean climate in general, and I note that Baldwin so renders it.

19. The Atlantic then was known as the "North Sea" and the Pacific as the "South Sea."

20. That is, on the capes and headlands, the idea being to place signs where they could be seen from ships sailing coastwise.

21. By "monastery" really is meant a mission center.

Certification of Fr. Marcos de Niza

22. The Spanish is *esta instrucción*—"this instruction." I change it to the plural throughout.

23. "From word to word," or, in English idiom, "word by word."

24. This translation is made from the copy of the Marcos *Relación* found in *Documentos Inéditos del Archivo de Indias*, Vol. III, pp. 325 *et seq.* Words in parentheses are either alternative translations or the Spanish terms; those in brackets are my own explanatory interpolations. Otherwise my own comments are relegated to the footnotes. There is an occasional Spanish word that has no convenient equivalent in English: these I copy untranslated and define them in notes.

Narrative of Fray Marcos

25. *Seráfico*, usually rendered as "seraphic," is here used as a noun to designate the founder of the Franciscan order, Saint Francis, which also is known as the "Seraphic Order." Its official name is Order of Friars Minor.

26. Marcos attached to his narrative a copy of the viceroy's instructions.

27. The *villa* of San Miguel later became known as Culiacán, and I use that name in my discussion of the friar's journey. It then was on the Río San Lorenzo, about thirty miles south of the present town of Culiacán.

28. The Julian calendar was still in use at that time. March 7 on that calendar would be March 17 on ours.

29. Most writers refer to Estévan as a Negro because Marcos speaks of him as a *negro*, which is Spanish for "a black." The Spanish called all the Hamitic races, as well as the Negroes, "blacks." Cabeza de Vaca, who was associated with Estévan for nine years, says he was an Arab from Azamor, Africa. ("Arab" and "Moor" were synonymous.) Castañeda, who also knew him, says he was a *moreno*—a brown man.

30. Cuchillo and Petatlán were Indian villages, the latter about 65 miles and the former 150 miles above Culiacán.

31. The official Spanish linear league at that time was equal to 3.1 miles, but distances were all estimated: no surveys had as yet been made anywhere in New Spain.

32. Charles V had ordered that Indians be treated in all respects as subjects of the Crown of Spain. Pope Paul III shortly before this time issued a decree that any person found guilty of enslaving Indians would be excommunicated.

33. That is, in districts having no fixed populations. The "huts" Marcos speaks of were mere brush shelters.

34. This is another reference to the slave raids made by men operating under license from Nuño de Guzmán.

35. This would be the district between Petatlán and the Compostela River. For probable site of Petatlán, see map preceding page 1.

36. The Marques del Valle (Marquis of the Valley) was Cortés, the title having been conferred upon him in 1529. The island referred to was Guayaval.

37. The Indians probably spoke truly, for pearl fisheries were later established in the Gulf of California.

38. The word *despoblado* is often translated as "desert," implying that every time Marcos crossed a *despoblado* he crossed a desert. That is incorrect. The word means a region containing no fixed population; i.e., a region not suited to agriculture. Most *despoblados* received greater rainfall than did adjacent occupied valleys, but were too broken, or too lacking in streams large enough for irrigation, to be occupied. On the other hand, some tribes (e.g. the Moqui and the Papago) occupied deserts, but not *despoblados*. The *despoblado* that figures most prominently in the friar's narrative contains the finest and largest pine forest, as well as the most varied flora and fauna, to be found anywhere in the Southwest.

39. The end of this *despoblado* probably was at the Petatlán-Sinaloa River.

40. That is, Europeans.

41. During his journey Marcos was able to converse with the natives only through his interpreters, and we do not know how conversant they were with other languages. All were adept, however, in the sign language that was common to all southwestern tribes.

42. A *jornada* was a day's journey, but it is to be kept in mind that the Indians along the way stated distances in terms of day's journeys *for them*.

43. *Una abra llana y de mucha tierra.* Baldwin renders this as "an extensive and level open tract." "*Abra*" connotes narrowness, as a gorge or canyon, so I have compromised with "extensive and level valley." Marcos here really gives us an extensive plain in a mountain gorge! See also note 94.

44. These were the Cahitas.

45. Vacapa appears to have been beside or a little distance north of the Rio Fuerte and well upstream.

46. Estévan could not read or write; hence this arrangement for transmitting information.

47. This is the first time this name, Cíbola, later to become known throughout the civilized world, appears in historical literature.

48. This other document has never been found and no copies of it are known to exist, nor is there any other reference to it. Perhaps it was never written.

49. *Pintado* means "a painted man." These Indians were probably tattooed, as no southwestern Indians wore paint except in war and in religious ceremonials.

50. This is to be interpreted, I think, as meaning that there was one other tribe between these people and the Cíbola district, and not, as some students hold, that the *Pintados* themselves bordered on the cities of Cíbola.

51. That is, the Monday after Easter Sunday.

52. All other writers have taken it for granted that these "cowhides" were buffalo hides. But they were deerskins. Buffalo skins are so thick and stiff that no tribe ever used them for clothing if deer or antelope skins were to be had. Cabeza de Vaca remarked the great number of deerskins possessed by these same people, and each of the chroniclers of Coronado's expedition—Castañeda, Jaramillo, and the unidentified author of *Relación del Suceso*—says they were deerskins. Marcos' later praise of the way these skins were processed is merited, for as prepared by Indians they were as soft and flexible as cotton flannel, and thrice as durable.

53. Marcos' recollections are tangled here. He had left Vacapa three days before.

54. When Cabeza de Vaca and his companions passed this way, their reputation as healers ran far ahead of them, and Indians flocked to them to be cured, believing that beneficial results would accrue from merely touching them. Here the Indians were assuming that Marcos was one of the same breed of white magicians.

55. Marcos was mistaken here. The traffic in these skins was in the opposite direction. There were plenty of deer in the mountains of Sonora and Sinaloa—witness the more than six hundred dried deer-hearts given to Cabeza de Vaca at one village —while the Zuñi district had no deer. But the blankets may have come from Cíbola.

56. Marcos was traveling along the little Cedros and Chico valleys, between the Rio Mayo and Rio Yaqui, and in the valley of the Yaqui, among the Nebomes (Southern Pimas).

57. *Cargándome la mano* is a bit of apt Spanish idiom meaning, here, that Estévan taxed the friar's credulity to the limit.

Estévan evidently understood something of Indian character, for he used as messengers Indians he had picked up at their villages and had taken long distances with him. These, sent back with messages for Marcos, would be heading toward home and so would lose no time on the road. In this town, messengers had reached home before reaching Marcos, and, of course, stopped there.

58. Probably Matape; but it may have been Tepupa, on the Moctezuma River, at or near its juncture with the Yaqui.

59. This word was coined by Marcos from the Indian word *cacona.* It meant some sort of turquoise ornament.

60. *Conejos,* doubtless meaning ordinary rabbits.

61. No wool was used by any southwestern tribe prior to the introduction of sheep into New Mexico in 1598.

62. This *despoblado* was the hill and mesa country between the Yaqui and Sonora rivers.

63. This was the first Ópata village in the Sonora Valley, about twelve miles below modern Baviacora. Since the last village below the *despoblado* (Matape or Tepupa) also was Ópata, the natives probably led Marcos direct to their kin in the Sonora Valley, so missing the Piman village of Corazones. Thus, between the Yaqui and Sonora valleys, Marcos did not follow the Cabeza de Vaca route, but regained it in the latter valley.

64. Others than Marcos have commented upon the clean and becoming attire of the Ópata women, and Cabeza de Vaca almost exclaimed over the fact that they wore shoes. They were the first shod women he had seen for eight years.

65. The Indians must have told Marcos more of the structural details than he recorded; otherwise he could not have known that the lowermost story contained no doors. Marcos' word, *escalera,* is usually translated as "ladder," but it more frequently

means "staircase," *escala* being the usual term for "ladder."

66. That is, more than three hundred mounted soldiers (as a permanent military post).

67. Marcos uses the term *barrios*, which means "*compact* villages." He applies that word only to the villages of this valley.

68. Possibly Marcos here had the "land league" in mind. The land league was a square area measuring 2.6 miles on the side, or the equivalent of that area. There could not have been villages every half or quarter of a *linear* league (1.5 to 0.8 mile), but there may have been a village for every half or quarter of a *land* league of arable land.

69. Marcos leaves us ignorant of what offense this man had committed. It must have been serious if he had to flee to the Ópatas for sanctuary.

70. Here is an error of either Marcos or the copyist. Other students translate this as "the others of the seven," but Marcos plainly has it "the other seven."

71. Marcos has his directions tangled here. The Ternaux-Campans French translation puts Totonteac to the west instead of to the southeast. But there was no pueblo district either to the west or southeast. I am convinced that Marata was the group of Moqui pueblos and that Totonteac embraced the pueblo district of the Rio Grande. Indians certainly would not have spoken of the impoverished Moqui pueblos, in their absolutely desert setting, as "the greatest and richest kingdom in the world," but the pueblo district of the Rio Grande drainage did comprise the largest settled area in the entire Southwest, and was prosperous by comparison with the Moqui and Zuñi districts. It is often assumed that Marata was a group of pueblos southeast of Zuñi, but there is no evidence that any of the ruins in that region were occupied as late as 1539.

72. The second "Ahacus" must be a misprint for "Ácus." Ácus was the large but isolated pueblo of Ácoma.

73. Marcos seems to be referring to the same valley wherein he previously had said he traveled five days. But I agree with Bancroft (*History of Arizona and New Mexico*, p. 31) that he here meant three *more* days "in that or some other nearby valley." The Spaniards often divided what we would call a single valley into two or more, with different names, especially where it was naturally divided into separate basins. Thus, the valley of the Sonora River was called the *Valle Ures* below

the Ures gorge, the *Valle Sonora* from the upper end of that gorge to the Sinoquipe gorge, and the *Valle Arispe* above the Sinoquipe gorge. Marcos did not enter the Ures Valley, but reached the river just above the gorge, traveling five days in the Sonora Valley and three days in the Arispe Valley, but along the same river. For convenience, I shall call those two structural basins the Sonora Valley.

74. See note 52.

75. This was probably the only buffalo hide Marcos saw. But he failed completely to understand the shape of the horns, although the Indians, good at picture writing, probably drew it on the ground for him. It may be they drew only one horn, and he supposed that the animal possessed but one.

76. Just where he was when this last message from Estévan reached him is not clear, but from what the natives told him of the distance to the next *despoblado*, he was probably at the end of the *Valle Sonora*, or possibly at the beginning of the *Valle Arispe*.

77. This *despoblado* was the wild and diversified region between the Gila River and the Zuñi pueblos.

78. This town was on or very near the site of modern Bacoachi. Marcos made a slip in calling it a *villa*. A *villa* was a Spanish town or city possessing special chartered privileges.

79. The words "for my *jornadas*" (*por mis jornadas*) appear to be entirely superfluous and irrelevant, and are omitted by other translators.

80. *Liebres* (hares) probably was applied to the jack rabbits with which the Cananea plains abounded. But the "partridges" must have been a species of quail, for partridges are not native to North America.

81. That is, at the end of the twelve days of travel.

82. Estévan did not sit down and await the return of his messengers, as some seem to believe. He kept going, but the messengers went ahead at a faster pace.

83. These decorated calabashes were symbols of religious authority, but I have been unable to identify the tribe using the type carried by Estévan. It was not an Ópata symbol. Estévan had learned the peculiar significance of such gourds while crossing the Southwest with Cabeza de Vaca. He first became acquainted with them in western Texas. While in the Sacramento Mountains of New Mexico Cabeza de Vaca and one other mem-

ber of his party were given ceremonial gourds by the *shamans* of the tribe, in recognition of their efficiency as beneficial magicians, and the two Spaniards thus became full-fledged *shamans* themselves. Estévan may have copied his gourd from one of those, or he may have designed it himself. The "cascabels" were rattlesnake rattles.

84. The Spanish copy of the *Relación* carries this explanatory note, probably added by the copyist: "That is to say, the sun was on the horizon at the altitude of one lance, a little after having risen." That well-meant explanation leaves us exactly where we were before. The height of the sun would depend upon the length of the lance and its distance from the observer. We can conclude only that it was early in the morning.

85. That is, one of his permanent attendants ohw had accompanied him from Culiacán. These are not to be confused with the local Indians who traveled with the party from time to time.

86. The friar's words, *tiene muy hermoso parescer de pueblo*, have been translated in half a dozen different ways. Often they are incorrectly rendered as "it is a very beautiful city." Baldwin does better with "it appears to be a very beautiful city," but Winship gives us "it has a fine appearance for a village" (note the introduced derogatory implication). "It has the appearance of a very beautiful town" is as nearly exact as is possible in English. Here is the only instance where Marcos calls Cíbola a town, and he next refers to it as a *población*. Thereafter he always speaks of it as a city.

87. The friar's word, *población*, that I here render as "city," is an indefinite term, applicable to the smallest village as well as the largest city: in other words, a community of *any* size. Its meaning in any particular case often is determinable from the context. Since Marcos repeatedly refers to Cíbola as a city, it is proper so to translate the word here.

88. By "the discoveries" Marcos refers to all that had till then been discovered in the New World. He therefore rates the country of Cíbola above that of the Incas and the Aztecs, both of which he had seen.

89. "Where" has reference to the northernmost village of the Sonora Valley, whence these disgruntled Ópatas came.

90. That is, on the occasion of his three days' stay at that village when he was en route toward Cíbola.

91. The Sonora Valley.

92. Past the second *despoblado*, he would have been in the Yaqui Valley and out of reach of the Ópatas.

93. This refers to the well-populated valley of which Marcos says the Indians told him, on his outbound trip.

94. This suggests that the "mountain gorge of much land" was a broad valley, pinched into a gorge at its lower end by the convergence of flanking mountain ranges. See note 43.

95. The Assembly (*Capitulo*) was formed of the prelates of the Franciscan order in New Spain.

Certification of the Minister Provincial

96. The "governing deputies" were the same as the "Assembly" mentioned by Marcos.

Legalization of de Niza's Report

97. Temixtitán was the Aztec name for Mexico City and was still in use, it appears, by the Spaniards.

98. The names "Atlantic" and "Pacific" were not then in use, and by "Ocean Sea" was meant the two combined.

99. That is, the *Relación* and all attached documents filled nine leaves, or sheets, of paper.

Analysis of the Narrative

100. An *entrada* was an expedition into new country.

101. Castañeda recorded that notwithstanding this secrecy, some rumors of what Diaz had learned leaked out, but that Marcos soothed the misgivings of the soldiers by assuring them that all was as he had reported, and that when they saw Cíbola they would be satisfied. Castañeda himself was one of those soldiers.

102. Carl O. Sauer, *The Road to Cíbola*, "The Discovery of New Mexico Reconsidered" (*New Mexico Historical Review*, XII, 270-87), and "The Credibility of The Marcos Account" (*N. Mex. Hist. Rev.*, XVI, 233-43). Lansing B. Bloom, "Who Discovered New Mexico?" (*N. Mex. Hist. Rev.*, XV, 101-32) and "Was Fray Marcos A Liar?" (*N. Mex. Hist. Rev.*, XVI, 244-46).

103. *Legends of the Spanish Southwest*, pp. 20, 317,

104. "Fray Marcos de Niza and His Discovery of the Seven Cities of Cíbola," *N. Mex. Hist. Rev.*, I, 193. Baldwin has one "city" too many.

105. *The Road to Cíbola*, pp. 14-16.

106. *The Journey and Route of Álvar Nuñez Cabeza de Vaca*, pp. 188-90. Winship, Bancroft, Bandelier, and latterly Bloom contend that because Cabeza de Vaca saw none of the pueblos, he was not the

first white man to enter the state of New Mexico. I fail to follow this reasoning. Cabeza de Vaca crossed at least seven of the counties in the state, spent several months within its boundaries, and saw a greater portion of the state than was comprised within the entire pueblo region.

107. Thus, Coronado's route from the Pecos pueblo into Texas, as usually charted, is utterly impossible, as I know from personal acquaintance with the ground. A perfectly feasible route, farther north, has been overlooked, although later Spaniards are known to have used it for two centuries.

108. By "trail route" I mean a course along which a trail was feasible through being negotiable and sufficiently supplied with watering places. Such routes were so few and far between in the Southwest that it is pretty safe to conclude that each one was used to some extent. In my own excursions over the upper Gila watershed, whenever I laid out a practicable course, on contour maps, to some objective, I *always* found a trail following the very route I had traced. These were deer trails.

109. *Op. cit.*, p. 17.

110. The trail from Mogollon, New Mexico, down the west fork of the Gila to the Gila Cliff Dwellings.

111. The trail, long ago abandoned, through the foothills of the west slope of the Sacramento Mountains in New Mexico.

112. Summer heat saps more of a pedestrian's energy than does the walking. Winter is the ideal season for foot work.

113. In mountainous or broken country, the trails are ill-adapted to horse travel, the horse being by nature fitted to the plains. I may mention here that the flock of sheep taken with the Coronado expedition, over the trail that Marcos followed, though moving but two leagues a day had their hooves worn down to the quick before they were one-third the way to Cíbola.

114. An extreme case is found in the early annals of Texas. An Indian, sent with a letter to a point about sixty miles away, very conscientiously delivered the letter, intact, *a year later*. At the other extreme, I knew a Moqui Indian to cover about 290 miles in five and one-fourth days.

115. A *Camino Real* (Royal Road, or King's Highway) was a recognized thoroughfare protected and maintained at the Crown's expense.

116. Some trails in our Southwest have been widened and measured by the U. S. Forest Service, and I find that the ratio between their length and the air-line distance is fairly uniform, the former being about 18 per cent the greater in mountains and hills, and some 12 per cent the greater in fairly flat country. I have utilized this fact in checking my calculated trail distances as shown in the table.

117. *Contributions to the History of the Southwestern Portion of the United States*, pp. 106-78.

118. Coan, for example, places Vacapa "about halfway between Hermosillo and Nogales," in a region absolutely desert.

119. Introduction to Fanny Bandelier, *The Journey of Álvar Nuñez Cabeza de Vaca*, p. xix.

120. G. P. Winship, "The Coronado Expedition," *Fourteenth Annual Report*, U. S. Bureau of American Ethnology, p. 515. This source will hereafter be referred to as "Winship."

121. Winship, p. 584.

122. *N. Mex. Hist. Rev.*, XVI, 244.

123. Day, *Coronado's Quest*, p. 35. Marcos, in his report of this trip, stated that the Indians of Topira wore gold and jewels, used silver armor "fashioned in the shapes of divers beasts," and stored "great quantities" of gold in stone buildings. He reported this as a personal observation, not as hearsay.

124. *N. Mex. Hist. Rev.*, XII, 282.

125. Though Marcos makes no mention of having traversed any other valley, he traveled three or four days in the Yaqui Valley, through villages of the Southern Pimas.

126. Marcos employed four terms in speaking of the Indian communities he saw or heard of: *ciudad* (city), *población* (settlement), *pueblo* (town) and *barrio* (compact village). *Barrio* he applied only to the villages he found in this valley.

127. See note 73.

128. Baldwin, in rendering *largos quince dias de camino* (fifteen long days of travel), omits "long." This is an important error, inasmuch as the distance to Cíbola is involved.

129. Mescalero Apaches, asked how long it would take them to make that trip at a normal pace, after grave deliberation and consultation gave me the brief but sufficient answer, "Maybeso a week." It would be an even shorter journey if we placed the beginning of the *despoblado* at San Carlos, as some students do. According to Frank Russell (*Twenty-sixth Annual Report*, U. S. Bureau of American Ethnology, p. 93) the Pima Indians at Sacaton, Arizona, call it a week's journey, on foot, from that point to Zuñi—a distance about forty miles

greater than that from the mouth of the San Pedro to Zuñi. So for them the latter would be a journey of but six days.

130. Except for the cut-off detour mentioned in note 63.

131. *The Road to Cíbola*, p. 28.

132. This idea is not original with me: Castañeda first brought it out, and many others since have suggested that Estévan's haste was due to his determination to get there first, and not to any intriguing tales told him by the Indians.

133. *N. Mex. Hist. Rev.*, XV, 128. On the next page, however, Bloom states that Marcos "says repeatedly that he hurried on." Only *once* does the friar say he hurried, and that was for only four days, when he believed that Estévan was awaiting him; and for those four days he did not travel much if any over fifteen miles a day, for it is no more than sixty miles across the *despoblado* between the Yaqui and Sonora rivers.

134. During the first few days after they left Vacapa we can gain some idea of their rates of travel, and that of the Indians. Four days (really three and one-half days) after Estévan was sent on ahead, Marcos received a message from him. Later, Marcos traveled three days to reach the village whence that message was dispatched. Hence it is reasonable to assume that Estévan reached that village in two days and that his messengers used the remaining day and a half in returning to Vacapa, for they doubtless traveled faster than Estévan. So if the friar's normal pace was fifteen miles a day—and it was very close to that—then Estévan's rate of travel was some twenty-two miles a day and that of the Indians thirty miles a day.

Marcos could not have traveled the same stages as did Estévan, as he claimed to have done, for if Estévan took three days to reach that village, his messengers would have had but half a day for their trip to Vacapa.

135. This village was above the Rio Mayo.

136. In the copy of the *Relación* that I have used, the word *leguas* (leagues) had been substituted for *jornadas*. According to Sauer, it is *jornadas* that Marcos wrote.

137. If we concede that nothing was impossible for Marcos, then according to his own story he reached Cíbola before dark on the same day that Estévan met his death, assuming that Estévan was killed in the morning, as reported.

138. Mrs. Juanita H. Hallenbeck, who as self-appointed counsel for the defense subjected my

arguments to critical scrutiny, suggests that Estévan, and after him Marcos, followed the Cabeza de Vaca route clear up to the Gila instead of leaving it in the Sonora Valley, and, if so, several discrepancies in the friar's account would disappear: (1) the *despoblado* then confronting him (the unpeopled region between the San Bernardino Valley and Cíbola) would have been the one Estévan was crossing, (2) he would have been among the Ópatas from his first contact with them to the beginning of the *despoblado* and so would not have reached the Sobaipuris at all, (3) that *despoblado* would have been about fifteen *jornadas* in extent, (4) the trail leaving the San Bernardino Valley could have been a wide and well-traveled one, and (5) where that route crosses the Gila, the stream is easily fordable.

There was a practicable trail route from the Sonora River to Zuñi by way of the San Bernardino Valley. Estévan was acquainted with it as far as the Gila, and from there to Zuñi Creek I am acquainted with it myself. The trail used by the Ópatas of the Sonora Valley, however, went by way of the San Pedro River, and all students concede that Estévan took that road.

139. U. S. Weather Bureau: *Daily River Stages* (an annual publication).

140. Daily maximum temperatures are normally 105 to 115 Fahrenheit degrees below the Sonora Valley in June. It is the hottest district in all Mexico during June and July (Napier Shaw: *Manual of Meteorology*, Vol. II, pp. 68-73). Even in May, temperatures in that region range higher than in our midwestern states during July.

141. *Loc. cit.* Others than Bloom have also assumed that Marcos, at the time he learned of the Moor's death, was three *jornadas* from Hawikuh, inasmuch as he recorded that he had then traveled twelve days of what the Indians called a long fifteen-day march for them. He of course could not have covered fifteen Indian *jornadas* in less than a month— just previously he had consumed a month in covering about 45 per cent of a distance that the Indians called fifteen *jornadas*—but there can be no argument as to what he wrote. After the brief stop occasioned by the arrival of the first courier, he says, "Upon resuming our journey, one *jornada* from Cíbola, we met two other Indians," etc. It is clear from his account that he always got his information on distances from local Indians and not from those in his escort, and how could the former have known how far he could or would travel in a day? They stated distances in terms of days of travel for *themselves*.

142. *N. Mex. Hist. Rev.,* XVI, 246. The year before, however, he was able to conceive of it, for he wrote (*N. Mex. Hist. Rev.,* XV, 130): "He [Marcos] awaited in Compostela the reply of the latter [the provincial of his order] and then himself proceeded to Mexico."

I think we must accept one or the other of the alternatives: either Marcos accompanied Coronado to Mexico, arriving there by July 15, or he awaited the return of his messenger and reached the capital not later than August 5.

143. Winship, p. 476.

144. Winship says (p. 362) that Marcos was still in Compostela on September 2. But on that very date he came before witnesses in Mexico City to certify to the accuracy of his account.

145. *N. Mex. Hist. Rev.,* XV, 130.

146. *Ibid.,* p. 131.

147. Bancroft (*History of Arizona and New Mexico,* p. 35) says that preliminary reports sent back by Marcos reached Mexico City before July. But he fails to cite the source of this statement, and to date no one else has found it.

148. This illustrates my contention that nothing can take the place of personal observation. Too many things that ought to be obvious are likely to be overlooked.

149. *Op. cit.,* p. 130.

150. Shaw. p. 192. The district in which Marcos reported the Indians as saying that it had not rained for three years is far north of the rainy belt, but even there a single year without rain is a physical impossibility: the average is about six inches for the three summer months.

151. The word that Castañeda used, *estancias,* usually is translated by the friar's partisans as "mansions." That is one of its meanings, but as used in New Spain the word meant a country house, and the country houses were all cattle ranches. A cattle ranch in New Spain was made up of a one-story, patioed building of adobe or stone for the owner, a few cabins for the Indian herders, and a corral for livestock. It was less attractive than is the average western cattle ranch of today.

152. Morfi, in his description of New Mexico in 1779, gives the population of a few towns in both individuals and families; the average was 6.4 to the family. It may have been a little higher two centuries earlier. No information on the population of Mexico City prior to 1556 is available.

153. Gallegos, in 1581, reported first that Hawikuh had 125 houses (meaning family quarters, since there were no more than seven buildings): he later corrected this to 118 houses. He also recorded that both Ácoma and Taos had 500 houses, and since it is generally conceded that neither of these ever had a population in excess of 2,000, Hawikuh proportionately would have had between 450 and 500. At the time of Coronado, Matsaki was the largest of the group; forty years later Hawikuh was the largest. The latter, therefore, must have grown during the interval and was even smaller at the time of Marcos than its ruins would indicate. Gallegos found that the "cities of Cíbola," combined, totaled only 437 family quarters. Castañeda placed the combined populations of the Zuñi and Moqui pueblos at between 3,000 and 4,000. The Moquis were the more numerous.

154. The Indians of the Sonora Valley may have attempted to reproduce the terrain about Hawikuh, in miniature, on the ground for Marcos. Indians were good at that, and could trace a fairly accurate map of any region with which they were well acquainted.

155. *New Mexico in 1602,* p. 16.

156. *Op. cit.,* p. 197.

157. Winship, p. 366. Winship appears to be guilty of a few very free translations. The friar's sentence, *La población es mayor que la ciudad de Mexico,* is a positive assertion and cannot properly be rendered as other than "The place is larger than the city of Mexico," but Winship translates it thus: "Judging by what I could see from the height where I placed myself to observe it, the settlement appears larger than the city of Mexico."

158. W. J. Humphreys, *Physics of the Air,* pp. 448-55. Dr. Humphreys fully explains every type of atmospheric refraction and reflection ever recorded, and some that are possible but that have never been recorded.

159. In Winsor: *Critical and Narrative History,* Vol. II, p. 499.

160. *The Catholic Church in Colonial Days,* p. 117.

161. *N. Mex. Hist. Rev.,* IX, 224-25, 227.

162. *Op. cit.,* p. 197.

163. Winship, p. 475. Castañeda also states that Marcos was in a *despoblado* sixty leagues short of Cíbola when he turned back. Such a specific datum must have come from the friar himself, I think. Since he made the false claim of having traveled from the Sonora Valley to Cíbola in thirteen days, he must have assumed that the distance was about sixty-five leagues, for his normal daily mileage was

about five leagues. If, therefore, he did confess that he was still sixty leagues from Cíbola when he turned back, he must have traveled one day beyond the Sonora Valley. He does in fact tell us something of what he saw on that first day's travel, but nothing thereafter. His error, or misrepresentation, in the location of Cíbola appears to have led cartographers of the time into placing Cíbola much too far to the southwest. It also led Mendoza into sending supplies for Coronado to the head of the Gulf of California, four hundred air-line miles from Cíbola.

164. *Op. cit.*, p. 195. Baldwin attacks Castañeda's veracity solely on the ground that he spoke of three friars who started on the journey and of two when they turned back. But Castañeda was at that point recording his recollection of hearsay evidence. A report of three friars, instead of two, starting on the journey was widely current then; and several modern students, including Bandelier, have believed that three friars made a northward reconnaissance just ahead of Marcos. Castañeda probably saw Marcos for the first time when the latter got back to Compostela, and there Castañeda mentions no other friar as being with him.

165. *Op. cit.*, p. 195.

166. *Ibid.*, p. 194.

167. Winship, p. 554.

168. *Op. cit.*, p. 127.

169. *Op. cit.*, p. 196.

170. Tribal pride and loyalty were strong in the Indian. Witness that Cíbolan found by Marcos: driven from home and afraid to go back, he nevertheless spoke highly of his people. Most of the names that different tribes called themselves meant, in effect, "WE are the whole thing!"

171. This characterization of the Zuñi Indians is in accord with their record during the following three centuries.

172. Castañeda credited Hawikuh with about two hundred warriors, but part of those he saw were reinforcements from the other pueblos. The warrior body of a pueblo seldom equaled one-fourth its total population.

173. I find no statistics on the number of Ópatas, but judging from their numerous villages I would estimate them as between ten and twelve thousand. They occupied not only the Sonora Valley, but the area eastward to and including the Moctezuma and Bavispe valleys, and southward to Sahuaripa and Matape, embracing the choicest regions in all northwestern Mexico, which they held against all pressure from other tribes.

174. Winship, pp. 475, 563.

175. Cabeza de Vaca, after he and another of his party received ceremonial gourds in recognition of their skill as magicians, says that "thence onward we carried the gourds, which added greatly to our authority, since they hold these ceremonial objects very highly." So it appears that each of the tribes he thereafter encountered—Sumas, Jumanos, Mansos, Ópatas, Pimas and Cahitas—respected even alien religious symbols.

176. Thus, Coronado's men twice learned of Cabeza de Vaca, in Texas; and forty-five years afterward, Indians of the middle Rio Grande told Chamuscado (and, the next year, Espejo) of the passage of "three white men and a black one." In Arizona, eighty-five years after Oñate's journey from New Mexico to the head of the Gulf of California, the Indians of the Colorado River told the next white visitor, Kino, of it. Similar instances could be cited ad infinitum.

177. Day says two hundred miles, which it easily could have been if the trail to the coast led along the Sonora River. Bandelier has Marcos about three hundred miles from the coast, by trail, at this point, yet believed he made the trip! Winship suggests that the days Marcos does not account for would have sufficed for the round trip. But if Marcos rested on Sundays, only two days are not accounted for, while the round trip to the coast, even from the lower end of the Valle Sonora, would have consumed over two weeks, and from the San Pedro, where Bandelier and Winship place him, Marcos hardly could have made the round trip in five weeks. Winship concedes the distance, but suggests that Marcos might have viewed the coast from some mountain near the San Pedro. Even granting the friar such telescopic power of vision, he would have had to be about eighteen miles above sea level to see over the coastal ranges, and four miles on top of that to see over the intervening curvature of the earth.

178. *Op. cit.*, p. 211, note 5.

179. *Loc. cit.*

180. That "instruction," I think, was really intended for a warning to Marcos that Ulloa would be watching for such signs.

181. *Op. cit.*, p. 196.

182. *N. Mex. Hist. Rev.*, I, 478-88.

183. *The Journey of Álvar Nuñez Cabeza de Vaca*, note p. 124.

184. Baldwin alters this in his translation of the Marcos *Relación*. Thus, he renders *desde el primer día que yo tuve noticia de la ciudad de Cíbola, los indios me*

dixeron todo lo que hasta hoy he visto as "From the first day I had news of the city of Cíbola, the Indians had told me of everything that *till then* I had seen." A correct translation is "From the first day that I had information of the city of Cíbola, the Indians have told me of all that *until today* I have seen." Similarly, in the next sentence, he gives *haber andado, desde la primera nueva que tuve de la tierra, hasta hoy, ciento y doce leguas* as "I had then marched, from the first place where I had news of the country, one hundred and twelve leagues," but it should read "having traveled, from [where I received] the first information that I had of the land, *until today*, one hundred and twelve leagues." (Italics mine throughout.)

185. *The Road to Cíbola*, pp. 29-31, and *N. Mex. Hist. Rev.*, XII, 287.

186. De Soto was a more formidable and imminent threat than our historians generally recognize. He had the start of Coronado by one year; one of his avowed objects was to find the Seven Cities, and the pueblo district was no farther from Florida than it was from Compostela. He was heading right for it when his expedition collapsed. Had he been as competent a leader as was Coronado, the latter would have found him in possession when he arrived.

187. *Coronado's Quest*, p. 60.

BIBLIOGRAPHY

BALDWIN, PERCY M. "Fray Marcos de Niza and His Discovery of the Seven Cities of Cíbola," *New Mexico Historical Review*, I (1926), 193-223.

BANCROFT, H. H. *History of Arizona and New Mexico*. San Francisco, 1889.

BANDELIER, ADOLF F. *Contributions to the History of the Southwestern Portion of the United States*. Cambridge, 1890.

———. Introduction to Fanny Bandelier, *The Journey of Álvar Nuñez Cabeza de Vaca*. New York, 1905.

BLOOM, LANSING B. "Who Discovered New Mexico?" *New Mexico Historical Review*, XV (1940), 101-32.

———. "Was Fray Marcos a Liar?" *ibid.*, XVI (1941), 244-46.

CHAPMAN, CHARLES E. *History of California: Spanish Period*. New York, 1920.

DAY, A. GROVE. *Coronado's Quest*. Berkeley, 1940.

HALLENBECK, CLEVE. *The Journey and Route of Álvar Nuñez Cabeza de Vaca*. Glendale, 1940.

———, and JUANITA H. WILLIAMS. *Legends of the Spanish Southwest*. Glendale, 1938.

HAMMOND, G. P., and AGAPITO REY. *New Mexico in 1602*. Albuquerque, 1928.

HAYNES, HENRY W. "Early Explorations of New Mexico," in *Narrative and Critical History of America*, Justin Winsor, ed., II, 473-504. Boston and New York, 1889.

HODGE, F. W. "The Six Cities of Cíbola, 1581-1680," *New Mexico Historical Review*, I (1926), 478-88.

HUMPHREYS, W. J. *Physics of the Air*. Philadelphia, 1920.

RUSSELL, FRANK. "The Pima Indians," *Twenty-sixth Annual Report*, U. S. Bureau of American Ethnology, pp. 3-390. Washington, 1908.

SAUER, CARL O. *The Road to Cíbola*. "Ibero-Americana," No. 3. Berkeley, 1932.

———. "The Discovery of New Mexico Reconsidered," *New Mexico Historical Review*, XII (1937), 270-87.

———. "The Credibility of the Fray Marcos Account," *ibid.*, XVI (1940), 233-43.

SHEA, JOHN GILMARY. *The Catholic Church in Colonial Days*. New York, 1886.

SHAW, NAPIER. *Manual of Meteorology*, Volume II. Cambridge, 1928.

U. S. Weather Bureau. *Climate of Mexico*. Washington, 1920.

WAGNER, HENRY R. "Fr. Marcos de Niza," *New Mexico Historical Review*, IX (1934), 184-227.

WINSHIP, GEORGE P. "The Coronado Expedition," *Fourteenth Annual Report*, U. S. Bureau of American Ethnology, Part I, pp. 339-613. (Contains Castañeda's and Jaramillo's *Relaciónes*, *Relación del Suceso*, *Relación Postrera de Cíbola*, *Translado de las Nuevas*, Coronado's letter to Mendoza, and Mendoza's letter to the Crown.) Washington, 1896.

WINSOR, JUSTIN, ed. *Narrative and Critical History of America*, Volume II. Boston and New York, 1889.

BIOGRAPHICAL NOTE

Cleve Hallenbeck was born in Xenia, Illinois, February 4, 1885. The early years of his adult life were spent in teaching and school administration. At the same time he worked in the field of his principal interest, physical science, in which his college training was obtained.

In 1908 he was appointed to the scientific personnel of the U. S. Weather Bureau. In 1915 he was placed in charge of the bureau's work in southeastern New Mexico, with headquarters at Roswell, which became his permanent home. During the following decade he published in the *Monthly Weather Review* many contributions to the sciences of meteorology and climatology. In recognition of his work in these fields he was elected in 1920 a Fellow of the American Meteorological Society—the youngest Fellow of the Society at the time. He continued to write scientific articles, which were published widely in both technical and general journals: "The Weather Forecast," for example, appeared in the Spring 1949 issue of *The American Scholar*.

Soon after he settled in New Mexico Mr. Hallenbeck became interested in the Spanish period of the history of the Southwest, an interest which he was never to abandon. He acquired a thorough knowledge of Spanish in order to examine the original documents in that language and prepare his own translations. His desire to know at first hand the physical characteristics of the areas in which specific events took place led him to cover most of western Texas, New Mexico, Arizona, and parts of northern Mexico, by auto, motorcycle, horse, mule, and afoot.

In 1941 a prolonged illness brought about Mr. Hallenbeck's retirement from the federal service. At this time he had already written three books on the history of the Spanish Southwest. The first, *Spanish Missions of the Old Southwest*, was published in 1926. *Legends of the Spanish Southwest*, written in collaboration with Juanita H. Williams, appeared in 1938, and *The Journey and Route of Alvar Nuñez Cabeza de Vaca* in 1940.

Mr. Hallenbeck also illustrated many of his own historical and scientific writings. The drawing of Hawikuh by José Cisneros which appears at the front of the present volume is after the author's sketch of a miniature reconstruction of the pueblo which he built to scale, basing his work partly upon Victor Mindeleff's ground plan (*Eighth Annual Report*, U. S. Bureau of American Ethnology) and partly upon his own examination of the site. The map of Fray Marcos' route is also based on a drawing by the author.

The manuscript of *The Journey of Fray Marcos de Niza* was in completed form at the time of Mr. Hallenbeck's death on February, 20, 1949.

INDEX

Sinoquipe gorge: 100
Skirts: 24
Sobaipuri (Indians): 52, 53, 59, 103
Sobaipuri Pima (Indians): 52
Sonora: 4, 48, 59, 60, 61, 72, 83, 85, 87, 95, 99
Sonora River: 43, 50, 51, 100, 103
Sonora Valley: 4, 45, 47, 50, 51, 52, 55, 58, 59, 61, 63, 69, 74, 76, 82, 83, 99, 100, 101
South Sea: 10, 43, 98
Southern Pima (Indians): 87, 99, 102
Spain: 1, 2, 6, 29
Stones, Marcos' pretended heap of: 34, 76, 81, 84
Stream, near Hawikuh: 30, 81
Sumas (Indians): 105

— T —

Taos: 40, 104
Temixtitán: 37, 101
Temperature, high summer: 61, 67, 69, 102, 103; effect on travel, 61, 67, 68, 69, 102
Tepupa: 99
Texas: 4, 100, 102, 105
Tonalá: 7, 11
Topia: 12, 50
Topira, Marcos' trip to: 12, 50, 75; report on, 50, 75, 102
Totonteac: 21, 23, 24, 25, 26, 27, 34, 40, 74, 87; identification of, 100
Towering: 71
Trail route: defined, 102
Trails, character of: 43, 102
Travel, rate of: of Europeans, 44; of Indians, 44, 48, 55, 56, 60, 100, 103; Estévan's, 55, 56, 60, 61, 103; Marcos' outbound, 48, 50-51, 52, 53, 55, 56, 61, 88, 103, homeward, 34, 61, 62, 63, 64, 67, 69
Tucson, Arizona: 60
Turcios, Antonio de: 37

Turquoises: 4, 19, 21, 22, 23, 24, 26, 27, 30, 72, 75, 93, 99; where obtained, 21, 87, 88

— U —

Ulloa: 69, 83, 105
Ures gorge: 43, 100
Ures Valley: 100

— V —

Vaca: 50
Vacapa: 47, 48, 49, 50, 53, 54, 65, 73, 74, 82, 99, 102, 103; when reached, 18, 48; when left, 20, 55, 56, 58
Valley, the gold-bearing: 35
Valley, the well-settled: 17, 24, 25, 47, 51, 52, 76, 86, 101
Venison: 57

— W —

Wagner, Henry R.: cited, 58, 67, 82; quoted, 72-73, 75
West Indies: 1
Winship, George P.: 41, 71, 95; cited, 102, 104, 105; quoted, 70, 91; mistranslations of, 101, 104
Wool: 99; of Totonteac, 24, 25, 26

— Y —

Yaqui River: 4, 45, 47, 48, 58, 63, 88, 99, 103
Yaqui Valley: 45, 55, 82, 99, 101, 102

— Z —

Zacatula: 1
Zumárraga, Bishop: 7
Zuñi: 102, 103
Zuñi Creek: 81, 103
Zuñi pueblos: 5, 39, 46, 54, 73, 87, 99, 100; number, 5, 86; size, 5, 104; character, 40; visited by Coronado, 40, 77; ruins of, 41
Zuñians: 70, 87; pacific nature of, 77, 79, 88, 105; a suspicious people, 77, 78, 79, 80

C11498663

WITHDRAWN

WITHDRAWN

WITHDRAWN